Garth Clark

The Artful Teapot

Special photography by Tony Cunha

Pages 2-3: Marek Cecula
3-piece Divided Teapot
1990. Glazed ceramic
(see page 211)

Pages 4-5: Richard Notkin's
studio

First published in the United Kingdom in 2001 by
Thames & Hudson Ltd, 181A High Holborn,
London WC1V 7QX

British Library Cataloguing-in-Publication Data
A catalogue record for this book is available
from the British Library

ISBN 0-500-51045-8

Printed and bound in Singapore by C.S. Graphics

Published to accompany
a major travelling exhibition:

May 16 - Sept. 2, 2002
COPIA: The American Center for Wine,
Food and the Arts,
Napa, California

Nov. 2, 2002 - Jan. 5, 2003
Montgomery Museum of Fine Arts,
Montgomery, Alabama

Feb. 6 - May 25, 2003
The George R. Gardiner Museum of Ceramic Art,
Toronto, Ontario

June 20 - Sept. 14, 2003
Long Beach Museum of Art,
Long Beach, California

Feb. 1 - June 1, 2004
Mint Museum of Craft + Design,
Charlotte, North Carolina

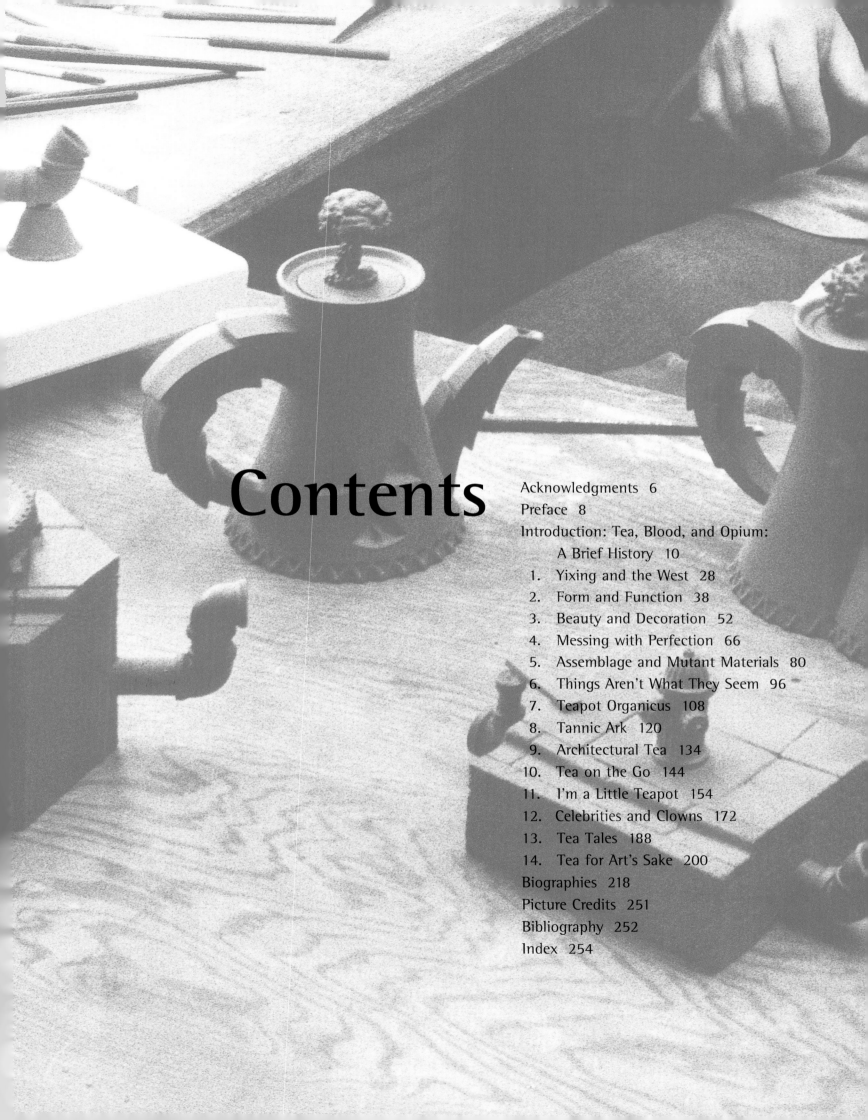

Contents

Acknowledgments

Michael and Maureen Banner
Melon
1997. Sterling silver
9.75 x 10 x 5 in.
(24.8 x 25.4 x 12.7 cm)

My thanks go first and foremost to Sonny and Gloria Kamm for being so considerate, helpful, and flexible in putting together this book and the accompanying exhibition. My thanks also go to Joan Blair for being such a conscientious and cheerful go-between in my often daily contact with Sonny. The artists featured on these pages have all been responsive and helpful, as have their galleries, in particular Mobilia, Leslie Ferrin, and del Mano. Tony Cunha has, as always, brought his photographic genius to bear on this project: thanks also to Noel Allum for additional photography. My gallery staff – Gretchen Adkins, Osvaldo Da Silva, Timothy Lomas, and Jennifer Green – have been invaluable. I am grateful, too, to Mark Del Vecchio and John Pagliaro for their work on the biographies. Mark also helped in countless other ways, including the brave and thankless task of commenting on the book's first drafts. Finally, my thanks go to Beverly Sanders for alerting me to the history of the "Teapot Song," to Pearl Dexter of *Tea: A Magazine*, who kindly gave me access to many of her photographic sources, and to David Hanks and his staff at Exhibitions International, who will be touring the teapot exhibition, and who have been unfailingly helpful and good-natured throughout a complex process.

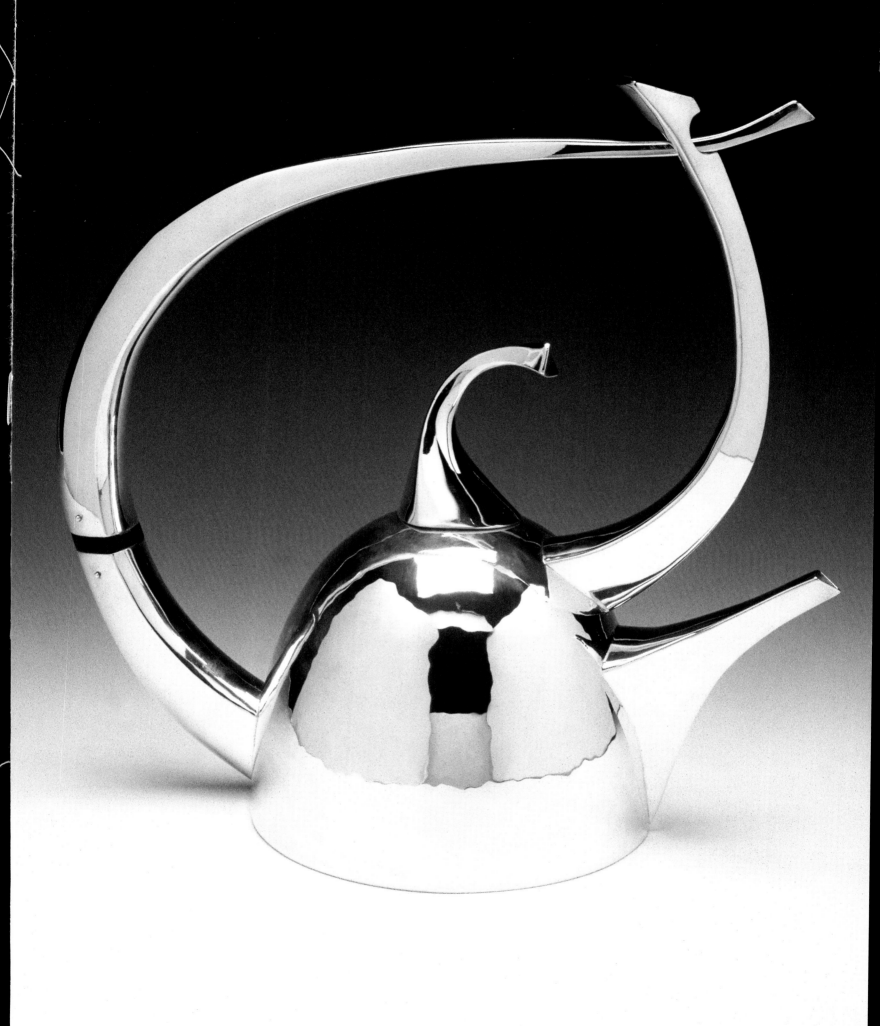

Preface

This book contains some of the masterpieces from an extraordinary collection of teapots assembled
by Sonny and Gloria Kamm. Through my much valued friendship with the Kamms I have been fortunate
to have been a witness to, and an occasional participant in, the growth of this cultural treasure since
its early informal beginnings more than a decade ago. I began working on this book as a prematurely
anointed "teapot expert," having authored *The Eccentric Teapot*, the most popular teapot book to date.
However, I was quickly demoted to student by the scope of this remarkable collection. Gently the Kamms
encouraged me to accompany them on their journey, to explore areas hitherto untouched, to rethink
premises, and to experience with them the discovery of new masterworks.

The passionate sense of mission with which this collection has been pursued can be gleaned from
the legend on the license plate surround on Sonny's car. It reads: "He who has the Most Teapots Wins!"
That Sonny is the victor is uncontested, yet, when he arrives at his home in Southern California
and climbs out of his car, he is met at the garage door by another sign. This has been placed there
by Gloria, and is a drawing of a teapot within a red circle with a diagonal line across it. The message
is telegraphically clear: "No More Teapots." The two signs demarcate the boundaries of a warm and playful
relationship between the two. Sonny's foot is on the accelerator and Gloria's is ever so lightly on the
brake. "The only times I have ever 'cheated on' Gloria have been over the purchase of teapots," Sonny
admits. So Gloria does not have to look out for lipstick marks on the collar. It's tea stains that are the
giveaway in this case.

As much as Gloria tries to moderate the flow of teapots, she also brings her refined and informed
taste to the process of selection. This has been honed by years of collecting in her own right (antique
silver serving pieces are one area of fascination), owning a glass gallery with Sonny, and nearly a quarter-
century of duty as a volunteer museum docent. Sonny, himself a successful corporate attorney who
lectures throughout the United States on tax law, makes the call on buying the cheaper "collectible"
teapots that he finds on internet auction sites and at the myriad flea markets that he so assiduously
scours over weekends. However, the purchase of a major work by an artist is always the result of mutual
agreement, a process of debate and critical analysis that sharpens the quality of the collection and is
a lively primary source of the pleasure the couple and their close-knit family derive from the collection.

The collection is now the largest of its kind in America and arguably in the world. Certainly,
there is no other that I know of, either in private or public hands, that approaches its depth and
breadth. At its core is the unique, one-of-a-kind teapot, made by an artist. Many of these have been
specially commissioned by the Kamms from both the crafts and fine arts worlds. Finding rare treasures
from the past is certainly a big thrill, particularly for Sonny, but working with living artists was the
original impetus for the collection and remains the Kamms' greatest satisfaction. These freely-explored
sculptural forms – the focus of this book – are given context by thousands of 20th-century factory-
made teapots, and a growing collection of earlier rarities – ceramic and silver masterpieces from
the 18th and 19th centuries.

What makes this collection so significant is the magic of the teapot. A similar collection of, say,
thousands of vases would not have the same sense of social complexity, tumultuous cultural history,

creative diversity, nor that cosy, nurturing intimacy that the teapot engenders. The teapot is simply one of the most potent of domestic icons. Arman calls it one of society's fetish objects, suggesting that its place in our lives is even more complex and subconscious than we realize. It holds clues to social station, to manners and protocols, to matters of gender, to fashion and stylization in popular art. It meshes issues of visual art with culinary history. It intersects both fine and decorative art. It is stained with the tea and blood of the West's insatiable thirst for this fragrant leaf. It is graced by civilized, charming social rituals. All of this meaning, metaphor, and memory is miraculously compacted into a small pot, a handle, and spout.

Along with an extensive collection of contemporary paintings, sculptural glass, and ceramics, the Kamms live with a rotating selection of several hundred teapots. The rest are stored elsewhere in boxes labeled to indicate their subject matter (dogs, houses, royalty, etc), the artist or factory. The scope of their collection is staggering. To give an example, a few years ago, when a relative was married, they decided to use teapots as the centerpiece for the wedding shower and scoured the collection for pieces dealing with marriage. They came up with over thirty matrimonial teapots, and no doubt a fuller search would have produced even more.

Their net has been cast wide, from unknown folk and outsider artists to many of the 20th century's most important designers, architects, painters, sculptors, ceramists, and craftsmen. The Kamms have also been non-traditional in their approach to media, with teapots made from tin cans, plastic wrapping materials, ivory, lapis, coconuts, salmon skin, and ostrich eggs. Neither Sonny nor Gloria are thrilled by ownership per se, rather they are excited by the fun of sharing that acquisition allows. Each has a passion for education and a compulsive generosity that has driven the destiny of "Teapot Central," as the collection is now reverentially termed in the art and crafts worlds.

However, what finally places this collection in its own realm is not just the expansive artfulness that it communicates, nor the high quality of its masterpieces. Quantity is its key. Sonny's license plate surround actually touches on a crucial element in a populist collection – critical mass. Once that mass is achieved, even the humblest objects take on a collective importance and grandeur that is often denied the individual components. In the process the Kamms have become the contemporary equivalents of the 18th-century antiquarians. These were gifted, amateur researchers and collectors whose independent pursuit of their personal fascinations left behind great collections and a wealth of cultural knowledge.

The Kamms have chosen to delve deep into the meaning of a potent single form and have traced its role over five hundred years in both the social functions of daily life and the most rarefied expressions of artistic imagination and craft facility. Aware that their teapot collection is too diverse and extensive for any one museum to embrace, Sonny's creative solution is to form a non-profit foundation which he visualizes will be a prototype for other large specialty collections. Over time the Kamms' spouted icons will have their home in the Collection Foundation, a kind of lending library of objects that will house, protect, catalogue, and make these collections widely available for exhibition and study. This act will bring to completion (but not closure) the cycle of creation that this assembly of teapots has always been intended to be – a public gift from two visionaries that will delight generations to come.

Introduction

Tea, Blood, and Opium: A Brief History

Tea

"Tea" is, apart from "sex," arguably the most evocative three-letter word in the English language (and there is enough of the latter to be found in the history of tea as well). The same is true of French (*Thé*), Japanese (*Cha*), German (*Tee*), Portuguese (*Cha*), and several other languages. In China, Vietnam, India, Afghanistan, and many other countries, tea is known as *Chai*, corrupted from the original three-letter Chinese, *Ch'a*.

Tea is universal. After plain water, it is mankind's most frequently consumed beverage. Over two billion cups are served each day. Its fragrant leaves evoke a flood of tea-stained associations: a companion to meditation and religious ceremony; medicinal powers (real and imagined); memories of mother pouring steaming cups of tea at the hearth on a wet, blustery afternoon; the art of fortune telling; gambling on the clipper ships that raced from China to bring spring's first pick or "blush" of tea; colonialism, war, tea taxes, and the Boston Tea Party.

Tea elicits images beyond the small scale of the tea cup, from the beautifully groomed tea estates undulating over verdant terraced hillsides of "green snow" in Japan, India, Sri Lanka, and China to its many architectural connections – Charles Rennie Mackintosh's Willow Tea Room, the serenely minimal tea houses of Japan, and even absurd vernacular buildings in the shape of teapots. Tea has produced its own culinary traditions in a score of countries, launching an endless array of scones, tea cakes, fruit cakes, finger sandwiches, and sweet and savory treats of every kind. Tea has inspired ritual, both formal and casual, religious and secular, and even had its own attendant line of fashion – the diaphanous tea gown that was worn in the afternoon by 19th-century ladies.

For millennia it has inspired the making of exquisite *objets d'art*, the impedimenta of tea: urns, kettles, caddies, caddy scoops, tea poys, tea bowls, tea bag holders, tea socks, strainers, infusers or tea eggs, cups, sugar bowls, sugar tongs, spoon holders, teaspoons, caddy spoons, mote spoons, creamers, trays, cake plates, tea trays and tables, and of course, the *grande dame* of this paraphernalia – that spouted, steaming engine of hospitality, the teapot. The teapot is almost as ubiquitous as tea itself, widely collected, made for use as well as for art's sake, and continuously subjected to attempts at reinvention. Yet, for all our efforts to sophisticate its simple mechanics, it remains unaltered, much the same spouted vessel today as it was when it first poured tea five hundred years ago.

As the chapters of this book all deal with the teapot, I will use this introduction to look at tea itself, the tea trade, and the rituals both Eastern and Western, that this fragrant leaf has inspired. Understanding tea helps us to understand the teapot. The history of tea extends back for at least 4,000 years, and maybe longer. Tea connoisseurship is every bit as complex and passionate a field as wine. The primary divisions of tea

Contour lines of a highland tea plantation, Sri Lanka

come from the way that the leaf is processed, producing green, oolong, and black teas – a process the Chinese kept secret – and not as 18th-century botanists once thought, from different species of tea bushes. Green tea is unfermented, oolong tea is semi-fermented, and black tea is fully fermented. Fermentation is achieved by roasting the tea.

From there on it gets a little more complicated. All tea derives from *Camellia Sinensus*, one of the four-hundred-plus members of the *Camellia* genus and named after Kamel, a German Jesuit priest who was in Japan in 1600 as a missionary. Herbal teas are therefore not real teas but are described in the trade as "tisanes." The three main tea producers are, in order, India, China, and Sri Lanka (for branding reasons, tea from the latter country retains the old name, Ceylon). There are over three thousand varieties of tea. Most are named, like wines, after the region in which they are grown. Beware of names that suggest regions but are not from those countries. Russian-style black tea, for instance, was not grown in Russia but until 1900 came from China by way of camel trains, hence the name Russian Caravan tea. It was brewed in samovars imparting a slightly acrid smell that was suspiciously like camel sweat.

While some teas are described only by their country of origin, others are more precisely designated and are named after provinces and even the estates in which they are grown. Assam, a province in northeastern India, gives its name to the largest production of black tea in the world. Darjeeling is named after its home in northeastern Bengal, 6,500 feet above sea level. Yunnan is named after the misty mountainous province in China that borders Vietnam. Some teas have names that make them sound exotic. Orange Pekoe, for instance, suggests a sunny citric exoticism, but in fact has nothing to do with taste or aroma but is the name given to one of the lowest qualities of mass-marketed tea.

Scented and spiced teas take their names from their additive, either a scent (jasmine, rose), a fruit tea that offers both bouquet and flavor (lychee, mango, ginger, peach) or a spice (cinnamon, mint, nutmeg), usually combined with a black or an oolong tea. Smoked tea – Lapsang Suchong (which happens to be my favorite;

a taste I apparently share with Queen Elizabeth II), and in particular the dense, tarry Hu-Kwa tea from Taiwan – is amongst the best. (Hu-Kwa is the corruption of the name of one of China's greatest merchant princes, Houwa, who was born a peasant in 1769 and rose to become one of China's richest men. He was the trading partner of the Astors, Peabodys, and Girards in America and it was his excellent silks, teas and porcelains that helped make America's earliest personal fortunes.)

Blended teas are often more complex and named after their inventor or the tea patron for whom they were originally concocted: Earl Grey, Lady Londonderry, Prince of Wales, and even J. P. Morgan. Charles, Earl Grey, was the scion of a wealthy Whig family and the British prime minister under King William IV from 1830 to 1837. Grey, who served as an envoy in China, claims to have been given the recipe for this tea by a Chinese mandarin. This claim is unlikely for many cultural reasons and the tea was most likely created by the venerable London firm of tea merchants, Jacksons. The best Earl Grey gets its body from large-leafed Darjeeling tea and its special bouquet and flavor from the oil of the Mediterranean citrus fruit, bergamot.

The flavor in tea comes from oils and the feeling of well-being from caffeine. To preserve the taste and not have it overwhelmed by the bitter tannic acid, the leaves need to be removed once the tea is fully brewed. Tea usually has more caffeine per pound than coffee but then one can make many more cups of tea per pound than is the case with coffee so the caffeine per cup is less. Also tea drinkers, this one included, will swear that tea's caffeine delivery system takes a gentle and soothing arc compared to the roller-coaster of soaring highs and plunging lows that comes with coffee. Black teas tend to have more caffeine because the process of fermentation makes the caffeine more soluble. However, it is unwise to generalize about this as some green teas produce more caffeine than black, and a few teas even produce more caffeine per cup than coffee.

Names of teas do not necessarily help one locate or avoid the most intense caffeine high. Gunpowder tea sounds like a safe bet for those seeking a wake-up punch, but this tea is in fact a shy, understated green tea that takes its name from being rolled into small pellets that resemble buckshot. Claims of tea's medicinal values are mostly bogus, although it does lift the spirit and that must have some healing value. Green tea works well as a digestive, and tea contains anti-oxidants which, in theory, slow down the ageing process. Science is inconclusive on this subject so the belief in tea's regenerative qualities today remains, as it was four thousand years ago, a matter of faith.

China

Tea leaves should curl like the dewlaps of a bull, crease like the leather boots of a Tartar horseman, unfold like the mist over a ravine, gleam like a lake touched by a zephyr, and soften as gently as fine earth swept by rain.

Lu Yu (733-804), *Ch'a Ching,* 780

There are two stories about the arrival of tea. One is mythical, the other more prosaic. According to Japanese lore, tea came from saintly Bodhidharma, the missionary monk who brought Buddhism from India to China. Arriving in Nanking he took a vow to sit facing a wall for nine years of sleepless meditation. Not surprisingly, after five years he began to nod off. In anger he cut off his eyelids and threw them, bloodied, to the ground. Where they landed, a tea bush sprouted and the beverage made from the leaves kept him awake for the next four years. Interestingly, the Japanese tell exactly the same story about the arrival of the poppy flower. Later, in fact, tea and opium were to be conjoined in a cruel embrace, one of the great scandals and tragedies of the tea trade.

The second explanation is that in the year 2737 BC Emperor Shen Neng, who advocated drinking boiled water to avoid illness, was traveling on the road when some leaves from a tea bush fell into his pot of boiling water. The emperor enjoyed the flavor of this brew and the rest is history. Whether Shen Neng was indeed the first to discover tea as a beverage is unlikely but the tale nonetheless suggests the likely course by which this leaf came into our lives. Shen Neng was a firm proponent of

the virtues of this drink, arguing that, "Tea is better than wine for it does not lead to intoxication, neither does it cause man to say foolish things and repent thereof in his sober moments. It is better than water for it does not carry disease; neither does it act like poison as water does when it contains foul and rotten matter."

Early tea preparation required the leaves to be boiled into a pungent brew with the addition of salt and, sometimes, spices. The addition of salt was probably to overcome the flat, iron taste of water boiled in a metal kettle. This was still much the same way of brewing tea during the Tang dynasty (618–917) when Lu Yu wrote his classic masterpiece on tea, *Ch'a Ching,* although by now the purists had turned against the adulteration of tea with additives. This is the so-called "Classic" tea, the first of three "periods" of tea that Kakuzo Okakura defines in his slender but magisterial *Book of Tea.* The second period is "Romantic," the third is "Naturalistic" and the fourth, added by this author, is 20th-century "Pop" tea.

Classic tea produced a dark-colored brew and the bowls in which it was served were glazed blue because this changed the color of the tea into that of green jade. The Sung dynasty (960–1280) marks the beginning of the Romantic period. Tea was still made from tea cakes or bricks (compressed blocks of tea leaves) but it was ground into a fine powder and then vigorously whisked in a tea bowl of boiling hot water and served pure, unadulterated by salt or any other additives. This "grinding the fragrant dust and brewing the fresh, milky froth," produced a lighter colored tea and so the tea bowl's glazes changed color to compliment this shift. Brown, black, blue-black, purple, and other dark colors were now considered the most complimentary. Sung tea purists followed tea as religiously as Lu Yu, and a Sung scholar of the time lists the three most deplorable activities "the spoiling of fine youths with false education, the degradation of fine paintings through vulgar admiration and the utter waste of fine tea through incompetent manipulation."

Tea's third period – Naturalistic – emerges in the latter part of the Ming dynasty (1368–1644). Until then the practice of making tea from the tea brick had endured for the very practical reason that tea bricks were a form of currency known as "tea money," and were paid to the

Myth, as recorded by Chou Kao-ch'I (Wan-Li period 1573–1619), has it that a strange monk turned up in Yixing, and walked through the streets crying out, "Riches and honors for sale!" When the villagers merely laughed at him he countered, "If you do not want to buy honors, how about riches?" He then took the village elders to a cave in the hills where they started digging and found clay of five different colors as brilliant as brocade. Certainly the clay deposits are no myth and these fine velvety materials – the "purple earth" after which Yixing is named – have made the town a pottery center since Neolithic times, long before the arrival of Buddhist monks. Its wares have influenced the aesthetics and design of ceramics worldwide. More to the point, Yixing is considered to be the birthplace of the teapot.

Yixing was, and remains, well situated for its role as a pottery-producing center. It is 150 kilometers west of Shanghai and 125 kilometers south of Nanking. Its site, on the Yangtze River delta, and proximity to a network of water transport, lakes, rivers, and canals made the profitable distribution of Yixing's wares feasible. Just as Jingdezhen became known as the porcelain capital of China, providing wares to the Imperial family, so Yixing took on the mantle as the pottery capital. The fine-grained clays were so satiny and beautiful that it was not necessary to glaze the wares, rather they celebrated the richness and earthiness of Yixing's famous clays.

The production of teapots began in the Cheng-te period of the Ming dynasty (1506–1521), with the first teapots reputedly made by a monk in his spare time, originating the technique of hand-building each teapot from a lump of clay. Teapots were now needed because the Ming emperor's abolition of the tea tax discouraged the production of tea bricks and encouraged the brewing of tea from loose leaves. From this inauspicious beginning in the hands of a hobbyist, the Yixing teapot began to emerge. These modestly-scaled objects were to have a greater impact on ceramic design than any other single ceramic style, imitated in Japan, Korea, Thailand, and throughout Europe. Moreover, alongside Japanese tea bowls, Yixing was the first pottery in the world to be made by individual artist-potters, thus breaking the tradition of anonymous production of ceramics in China.

emperor as a tax. The dimensions of the brick were standardized and in some outer provinces tea bricks were used as actual money, scored so that a brick could be broken into precise segments to pay for services or goods. When the tea brick tax was abolished around 1500 the Chinese found it easier and more delectable to brew tea from the leaf. This posed a dilemma: there was no vessel in which to brew the leaves, and so the teapot was invented, with the pottery town of Yixing leading the way.

The Wan-Li period saw the emergence of the artist-potter movement which produced several masters who were widely imitated, not out of commercial gain, but in sincere homage to their skills. What changed the stature of Yixing teapot makers from nameless artisans to creative stars was the link between these potters and the Chinese intelligentsia – poets, writers, painters, philosophers, and art connoisseurs.

From their studio retreats, these scholars examined the teapot, debated its design and proportions, designed teapots themselves, and composed poetry and sayings to be incised on the vessels. Many of the standards they set four hundred years ago are still upheld by some contemporary Yixing teapot makers: the exact arc that tea should take from spout to cup when being poured, the idea that the pouring tea should not create any bubbling as it enters the cup, and that the top of the spout, the handle, and the mouth of the teapot should all climax on the same horizontal line.

This was a perfect synthesis: an informed, intelligent debate about the aesthetics of the teapot, a long tradition of craftsmanship, a reverence for utility, a love of tea, and a respect for maker, materials, and process. It is no wonder, given these strong foundations, that the Yixing teapot was to have, and continues to have, such an important role in material culture. The teapots fell into two broad groups, the one a reductive classical aesthetic and the other a playful organic mimicking of cloth, leather, wood, nuts, rocks, gourds, vegetables, and fruit. To this could be added another sub-category and that is teapots, usually from the classical forms, bearing poems and messages that had been incised into the surface.

Yixing teapots began to arrive in Europe with the first teas. Teapots were often shipped in the tea chests themselves, tea making a perfect packing material. They were the first teapots any European had ever seen and their influence was both pervasive and indelible. From the late 17th and early 18th centuries, they were the standard for teapot design. Yixing was the basis for the work of Johann Friedrich Bottger in stoneware ceramics (he is the alchemist who discovered the porcelain formula for Europe) and for the Elers brothers, who founded stoneware production in Staffordshire, setting this British county on its course to becoming the ceramic powerhouse of Europe. Josiah Wedgwood's one great innovation (his skill was improvement not invention) was Jasperware, which, while begun as an imitation of carved cameos, also owed a great deal to Yixing influence.

European taste was able to embrace both the stylized naturalism, expanding it with colored glazes, as well as the more minimalist forms that easily morphed into a Western neo-classical mode. This influence continued into the 19th century as can be seen in the work of influential designers and artists such as Christopher Dresser. Throughout this period teapot making in Yixing continued uninterrupted. There were periods of creativity and periods of dull imitation but the umbilical cord linking the first teapot to the most contemporary production today is unbroken. In the 1970s, having become somewhat forgotten and ignored by both scholars and collectors, Yixing started to make a comeback, spurred on mainly by wealthy collectors in Taiwan and Hong Kong, and led by the perceptive K. S. Lo. By the mid-1980s the market for works by acknowledged masters had become white hot. Even recent teapots by grand masters were fetching over $100,000 at auction, while older works fetched even more.

Collecting Ming period teapots is a challenge. It attracts devotees such as the architect I. M. Pei. But it is a perilous activity. One of the ways in which a student learned to make a teapot was to copy those of the early masters, all the way down to their chop marks. Again, the purpose was homage not forgery but it makes dating work difficult. This has been further complicated by the fact that in the 20th century it became profitable to make copies of Ming period teapots and to sell them as period works. Early pieces need to come armed with impenetrable provenances.

Therese Tse Bartholomew, one of the best known scholars of Yixing, spoke at the 2nd Yixing Teapot Conference in New York in 1993 and recounted the tale of going to Yixing with her carefully researched catalog from the China Institute in America. She showed her catalog to one of Yixing's leading and oldest potters and as he went through the illustrations he would point to "antique" teapots, ostensibly hundreds of years old, and comment again and again, "I made that one, I made that one." It turned out that the potter had been approached by a European dealer in the late 1930s, armed with photographs of teapots in museum collections that had impeccable provenances, and this dealer had asked him to make replicas which, in turn, were sold to other museums and to private collectors.

However, Yixing potters did not produce the most beautiful tea bowls of this new era. These came from the Imperial kilns of Jingdezhen and other regions where glazing was more of an art form. The new style of tea brewing required a change in the color of the tea bowl. The new tea from unfettered leaves, often almost clear in color with just a hint of gold or green, looked best with bowls that had white interiors so this became the vogue. In turn the white glazes provided an ideal canvas for the exterior of the bowl to be decorated with blue underglaze and other techniques.

During this period tea estates grew in size and efficiency. Poorly run, small farms were now replaced by large, carefully managed plantations using progressive agricultural techniques. Tea production was now a modern industry and ready for the profitable tea trade that would engulf Europe.

Japan

Tea represents the true spirit of Eastern Democracy by making all its votaries aristocrats in taste.

Kakuzo Okakura, *The Book of Tea*, 1906

Japan was as addicted to tea as China. Initially, Japan obtained its tea and tea implements through trade with China. In 805 the Japanese Buddhist priest, Dengyo Daishi, returned from China with seeds and successfully started the first tea garden in Japan. Tea drinking started as what James Norwood Pratt, author of *The Tea Lover's Treasury*, terms "a medico-religious stage ... a sort of divinely mixed snake oil and holy water." The abbot Yeisei wrote the first Japanese tea book, *The Book of Tea Sanitation*, devoting much of the text to the spurious

claim that tea was the cure for almost every affliction known to man. Early in the Muromachi period (1338–1568) tea moved to its second stage – hedonism. No longer quiet Buddhist ceremonies, the new tea "tournaments" were orgies of eating and drinking and pretentious displays of wealth, mimicking similar tea parties in China.

The tournaments took place in a tea pavilion with guests sprawled out on brocaded silk cushions placed on the skins of wild animals. Their host's finest possessions, rare silks, vessels in precious metals, porcelains, weapons, inlaid armor, and other treasures, mostly from China, were laid out to exhibit his wealth and discernment. The size and importance of a tournament was indicated by the number of tea bowls, from as few as ten to over one hundred. These indicated how many teas would be tasted. The gatherings were similar to a wine tasting today. Participants were invited to enjoy the tea and to compete for prizes in guessing the type and region of different teas.

The apex of decadence was reached when, in 1473, Yoshimasa resigned his shogunate so that he could devote his life to art collecting and tea parties; thereafter the pendulum began to swing back to aestheticism. One of Yoshimasa's fellow imbibers, a lapsed Buddhist abbot, Shuko, tired of this excess and, in search of the enlightened state of *satori*, realized that the simple act of filling an ordinary tea bowl with hot water could, in itself, become a sacrament. At this point taking tea began to be simplified into a ritual, part religion and part minimalist performance art.

Shuko preferred the cruder Japanese tea utensils to the imported wares from China. "More than a full moon shining brightly on a clear night," he is quoted as saying, "I prefer to see a moon that is partially shaded by cloud." He began to attract followers, largely from the merchant class, and developed a secular ceremony known as Chado, or "the Way of Tea." A second master, Takeno Jo-o (1502–55), took this further with *cha-no-yu*, literally "hot water for tea," a celebration of the humble and the ordinary.

Sen Rikyu, a disciple of Jo-o, added the final refinements to the tea ceremony, establishing a form

Japanese tea being whisked
during the tea ceremony in
"Romantic" style

that is still followed closely today in Japan. He based the ceremony on four principles – harmony, respect, purity, and tranquility (*wa, kae, sae, jubuo*). "In Zen," Rikyu wrote, "truth is pursued through the discipline of meditation in order to realize enlightenment, while in Tea we use training in the actual procedures of making tea to achieve the same end." Rikyu required that *cha-no-yu* be performed in a separate tea house built with common materials to represent humility. The small private tea houses were built with such obsessive attention to humility that they were, paradoxically, exceedingly expensive to erect.

The ceremony produced one of Japan's greatest artistic achievements – tea wares and, in particular, the tea bowl. These seemingly coarse objects are the most original aesthetic achievements of the Japanese potters. Apparently crude, yet in fact stunningly sophisticated and subtle, they are one of the few aspects of Japanese art of the period not derived directly from Chinese or Korean influence. The tea bowls, particularly the early

raku bowls, are the perfect embodiment of the core character of the tea ceremony, a quality known as *wabi*. Directly translated *wabi* means rusticity but it is a much more complex and elusive concept, suggesting a tranquil and frugal state of mind that is at one with both nature and man.

Rikyu's teachings have had enormous influence on the direction of Japanese art, and not just limited to the tea ceremony. He is cited as one of the most significant catalysts in that extraordinary flowering of the humanities in Momoyama-period Japan. His considerable aesthetic influence came to an end when his powerful and brutal protector, the mercurial shogun Taiko Hideyoshi, heard rumors that Rikyu was planning to assassinate him by poisoning his tea. Hideyoshi "invited" Rikyu to commit *sepaku*, ritual suicide, resulting in the most famous tea ceremony of all time. "The Last Tea of Rikyu," wrote Okakura, "will stand forth forever as the acme of tragic grandeur."

Europe and Britain

Thank God for tea! What would the world do without tea? How did it exist? I am glad I was not born before tea.

Sidney Smith (1771-1845), British Evangelist

The tea ceremony has endured to this day in Japan where it is still widely celebrated but it did not transplant to the West. In the late 19th century, Basil Hall Chamberlain wrote a blunt assessment of the British view of *cha-no-yu*: "To the European, the ceremony is lengthy and meaningless. When witnessed more than once it becomes intolerably monotonous. Not being born with an Oriental fund of patience, [the European] longs for something new, something lively, something with at least the semblance of logic and utility." Chamberlain at least concedes that, while "some may deem [the tea ceremonies] pointless, none can stigmatize them as vulgar."

The monastic approach of the Japanese held little appeal and the European tea ceremony, particularly that of the British, would emerge as a charming afternoon interlude for gossip, fine china, delicate table linens, diaphanous gowns, and tea tables groaning with cakes and savories. But the English tea that marks the belle époque of Western tea drinking would still take a couple of hundred years to evolve after this magic elixir first reached the shores of Europe.

Tea is first mentioned in Europe in 1559. Giambattista Ramusio, secretary to Venice's governing body, the Council of Ten, quotes a Persian traveler, Jaijji Mahomed in *Navigatione e Viaggi*, who explains that "one or two cups of this decoction removed fever, headache, stomach-ache, pain in the side or joints and it should be taken as hot as you can bear it." The next mention was a year later in a letter from the Portuguese Jesuit priest, Gaspar Da Cruz, the first European Christian missionary in China. Da Cruz obviously never saw tea being made. He describes it inaccurately and moralistically as "a herb from which they press a delicate juice [which] frees them from all the evils that the immoderate use of wine doth breed in us."

Portugal brought the first tea to Europe at the end of the 16th century, establishing an early taste for the beverage amongst their nobility but the Portuguese never became tea traders. This role went to the enterprising Dutch who distributed the tea the Portuguese brought to Lisbon. Then from 1610 the Dutch East India Company began to trade with China directly, importing the tea themselves and distributing it throughout Europe. The story of the tea trade is one of the great tales of mercantile greed, filled with pirates, smugglers, gamblers, political unrest and, of course, opium, which later became the key currency for the leaf in China.

The Dutch monopolized the tea trade for over one hundred years and their trading policies, high prices, and wars with France are part of the reason why Europe, after a century of enjoying the tea leaf, ended up preferring the coffee bean. But for a while the Europeans, and particularly the Dutch, were as crazy about tea. Jean Louis Guez de Balzac (1594–1654), the early master of French prose style, was one of its first adherents and he managed to acquire a small cache of the precious leaves (tea then cost the equivalent of about $2,500 a pound and was sold by apothecaries and even jewelry stores and upmarket millinery shops).

As Goslan, Balzac's friend, recounts, "He never gave any [tea] to the profane and we did not drink every day ourselves. Only on feast days he would take it from the kamchatcka box in which, like a precious relic, it was enclosed. The sun, he would say, ripened it only for the emperor of China; mandarins of the first rank were charged, as a privilege of birth, with watering and tending it on the stem. It was picked before sunrise by young virgins who carried it singing to the emperor's feet. If you took this golden tea three times, Balzac claimed, you became *borgne*, dumb; six times, you became blind." Balzac further claimed that the leaves were sprinkled with flecks of human blood from the murderous combat the caravan that brought the tea to Russia had endured, explaining that "it was a sort of Argonaut tea."

Mandarins and virgins had nothing to do with the manual labor of tea growing. This was now a vast agricultural enterprise, employing an army of coolies and producing not the "few pounds of tea" per year that Balzac imagined but hundreds of tons. The Chinese welcomed Europe's gold in exchange for tea but sought to inoculate themselves against the influence of the Western world by restricting trade to a few treaty ports, first the Portuguese in Macao, then the Dutch and later the English. The nations set up what were known as "factories," not industrial manufacturing plants, as the name suggests, but offices and warehouses to receive and export a variety of products – silk, china for ballast, and tea. The men who ran these franchises were known as factors and handled the complex web of bribery and corruption that accompanied the trade.

The puritans resisted importation of tea to Britain, fearing that it would cause social ills. The tea trade did in fact have this effect and the consequences were severe but visited on the Chinese and not the British. By 1769, the annual imports from China were approaching five million tons with no end in sight to this growth! This caused a monetary crisis. The British had nothing to trade. The Chinese had no need of that British export staple, broadloom cloth. They wanted payment in gold and silver and this placed a strain on the Crown's currency reserves.

The ugly solution to Britain's dilemma was opium, one addiction funding another, pipes filled with drugs in exchange for teapots filled with tea. From about 1800 opium was produced in huge quantities in India, sold in China through the British for silver, which was then kept in Canton to pay the tea bills. Although the Chinese and opium were old friends, usage was not widespread and it was enjoyed mainly around Sichuan where it was grown. However, with importation of large quantities of opium or "foreign mud" as the Chinese derisively named the substance, addiction spread rapidly. In the decade after the end of the second Opium War alone (1857–1860), addiction soared tenfold. Even the two Opium Wars, in which Britain forced China to legalize the drug, did not slow trade in the slightest. Smugglers took over during hostilities and the supply continued with the connivance of corrupt Chinese officials. It was not until 1908 that opium ceased being a mainstay of British trade in China, leaving a society raddled by addiction for generations thereafter.

Although there are English references to tea as early as 1615, the launch date for this British institution is generally considered to be Tuesday, September 2, 1658,

"the very month that Oliver Cromwell died and presumably went to hell," as the historian James Pratt so forcefully describes it. *The Gazette* of that day carried both Britain's first advertisement for tea (at the Sultaness Head Cophee House in Sweetings Rent) and the notice of Cromwell's death. The confluence of the two events is not without relevance. No tea could enter Britain during Cromwell's control of the British Commonwealth. He even banned the popular currant-filled Eccles cake as a pagan food because it gave too much pleasure.

The name "cophee house" is due to the fact that coffee arrived on these shores before tea but by the early 1700s the sale of tea at these all-male establishments far outstripped that of coffee. Coffee originally came from Yemen and, with its conquest by the Ottoman empire, coffee drinking began to spread rapidly through North Africa and, in 1624, via Venice, into Europe. Ian Bersten, in his book *Coffee Floats, Tea Sinks*, describes the journey of the coffee bean from Yemen to London as a transfer from "the sugar countries to the milk countries." Coffee was taken black with sugar, as in most Middle Eastern and some Mediterranean countries, because these peoples were part of the seventy per cent of the world's population that is lactose-intolerant. Central Europeans and the British had no difficulty digesting milk products so they changed the way that coffee was consumed.

The Europeans enjoyed coffee with milk and this soon became the preferred way of drinking the beverage. By the mid-17th century *café au lait* was being discussed as a health cure by Europe's physicians, much as they had once invested tea with the same virtues. Bersten claims that one of the reasons that drove the Europeans to coffee and the British to tea, was the quality of their milk supplies. Europe's milk was more sanitary than Britain's. As late as 1771 Britain had not yet resolved this problem, as the English writer Tobias Smollett explains in this description of milk delivery in London: it was "carried through the streets in open pails, exposed to foul rinsings, discharged from doors, spittle, snot and tobacco squids, from foot passengers; overflowings from mud carts, spatterings from coach wheels, dirt and trash chucked into it by roguish boys ... the spewing of infants, who have slabbered in the tin measure, which is thrown back

Above: the Vauxhall
Public Gardens

Opposite above:
Staffordshire, England
Cauliflower Teapot
c. 1760. Creamware
4 x 6.5 x 3.75 in.
(10.2 x 16.5 x 9.5 cm)
Pineapple Teapot
c. 1765. Creamware
4.5 x 7.4 x 4.25 in.
(11.4 x 18.8 x 10.8 cm)

Opposite centre:
Staffordshire, England
Teapot
mid-18th century.
Redware
4.5 x 7.75 x 3.75 in.
(11.4 x 19.7 x 9.5 cm)

Opposite below: Sowter
and Co., Yorkshire, England
Swan Teapot
c. 1805. Black basalt
6.5 x 10 x 5 in.
(16.5 x 25.4 x 12.7 cm)

in that condition among the milk, for the benefit
of the next customer; and finally the vermin that drop
from the rags of the nasty drab that vends this precious
mixture under the respectable denomination of milkmaid."

Other factors turned the British to tea instead
of coffee. They had cheap sugar compared with Europe
and tea and sugar, even without milk, made an appealing
drink. However, some braved the dismal dairies and took
tea with small quantities of milk or cream, both heated
and unheated. This way of drinking tea is usually credited
to the British but was actually begun in France. Moreover,
the Anglo-Dutch War with France from 1689 to 1697
restricted coffee supplies to Britain for nearly a decade,
by which time tea had taken over. The reverse applied in
Europe where the war halted tea supplies from the Dutch.
Smuggling of tea in Britain was so widespread that it
forced the East India Company to reduce prices until,
with the development of tea estates in India in the mid-
19th century, tea was widely affordable even by the
poorer classes.

Fashion played its role as well. The "Merry
Monarch," Charles II, and his queen, Catherine of
Braganza, were both tea drinkers. The Restoration ruler
acquired his habit while an exile in The Hague, Holland,
and Catherine acquired hers from the Portuguese court.

Her morning habit of tea and light breakfast stood
in stark contrast to Queen Elizabeth I, who began her day,
as did many in her court, with bread, meat, and a gallon
of ale. Charles's example was followed by Britain's
aristocracy and the rest of the country that could afford
the then still costly tea.

Tea, or what poet William Cowper described as "the
cups that cheer but not inebriate," transformed the daily
life of the Briton despite the fact that the guardians of
the Englishman's morality fulminated against it as though
it were something akin to opium addiction (which later
paid for Britain's tea). In 1678, not mincing words, Henry
Sayville denounced tea as "a filthy custom." Even in 1822
the writer William Cobbett warned that it encouraged
"a softness, an effeminacy, a seeking for the fire-side,
a lurking in bed, and in short, all the characteristics
of idleness."

In fact, the salutary effects of tea drinking on
Britain were immense. The most popular daily beverages
before tea's arrival were mostly alcoholic. The poor drank
a rotgut gin that was just a few levels below rat poison in
toxicity. As Shen Neng had realized a few thousand years
before, the boiling of water for tea had a remarkably
beneficial effect on public health. Also, partly due to the
popularity of tea, the potteries could effectively and
profitably mass-produce hygienic tableware, which also
improved public health standards. Alcoholism, water-
borne disease, and a medley of other social ills were
drastically reduced by the arrival of tea.

The coffee houses, which played an important role
in tea's growing popularity, also produced a host of other
changes in British society that are still with us today. They
attracted sales rooms and both Sotheby's and Christie's
began their lives as adjuncts to coffee houses. The august
houses of Lloyd's Registry of Shipping and Lloyd's Insurance
began life in a coffee house frequented mainly by sea
captains. To ensure that one received good service, habitués
would drop a few coins into the T.I.P. box (To Ensure
Promptness). The staid private men's clubs of London were
an offshoot of these rowdy, rank, smoke-filled establishments,
designed to have all the facilities of the coffee shop minus
the noise and the annoying riff-raff. The shops were also
the first public libraries, or "penny universities" as they were

known, providing current magazines and newspapers for their customers to read, at least until evening, "when the light from oil lamps and candles fought a losing battle with the thickening atmosphere."

Women were not allowed in the coffee shops and given their pungent, rowdy ambience, it is unlikely that they felt slighted. Men and women first drank tea together in public in the late 18th century with the arrival of the so-called pleasure gardens or tea gardens in Vauxhall, Marylebone, and Ranelagh, where the fashionable set could parade in public, listen to music, and partake of tea. The entrance fee included as many "dishes" of tea (the handled cup did not become the standard until later) and slices of buttered bread as one could consume. Tea was prepared and served by women known as "blenders" who had the reputation of being as loose as the tea leaves they brewed. Admiral Lord Nelson met his mistress, Emma Hamilton, later Lady Hamilton, at a pleasure garden. She was also a "blender" for King George III, a devoted tea drinker whose son, the Prince Regent and later George IV, was one of the first teapot collectors.

The pleasure gardens were a passing fad, unsuited to Britain's soggy climate. What women claimed as their own domain was the afternoon tea introduced by Anna, the 7th Duchess of Bedford, in 1840. Dinner in the better homes was served late, between eight-thirty and nine, and so by four or five the Duchess found her energies flagging and ordered tea, cake, and buttered bread to be sent to her bedroom. When she invited friends to enjoy this repast, the afternoon tea ceremony was born. What began simply as a light pick-me-up in the Duchess's bedroom soon expanded into an increasingly elaborate ceremony with complex protocols, dress codes, and etiquette. As Okakura wrote, "In the delicate clatter of trays and saucers, in the soft rustle of feminine hospitality, in the common catechism about sugar and cream, we know that the worship of tea is established beyond question."

By the late 19th century, the menu for a tea could include, aside from tea, coffee (for heretics), the ubiquitous bread and butter, at least five kinds of sandwich, oyster *vol-au-vents,* chicken cutlets, two creams, four jellies, several cakes and small pastries (both sweet and savory), and a claret cup or port. To present this feast required a large array of tea equipage. Tea was partly responsible for the success of the British ceramic industry which dominated European production for several centuries. By the end of the 18th century, the five towns of Stoke-on-Trent in Staffordshire had become the largest production center for ceramics in the world, and the teapot and tea service were an important part of their growth and profits. The potteries were clever in marketing tea services as fashion items and while there were the classic designs that endured for generations, many hostesses replaced their tea services frequently to keep up with new styles.

Below left: J. J. Kandler
(modeler)
Monkey Teapot
c. 1740. Porcelain
7.5 x 6.75 x 3.25 in.
(19.1 x 17.1 x 8.3 cm)
Meissen Porcelain Factory

Right: Chelsea Porcelain,
England
Chinaman Teapot
c. 1745-59. Porcelain
6.75 x 7.4 x 4.6 in.
(17.1 x 18.8 x 11.7 cm)

Below right: Jacob Petit
(attributed), France
Veilleuse-Personages
c. 1830-50. Porcelain night
light in the form of a lady
of the court.
Assembled (three parts):
13.25 x 7.5 x 7 in.
(33.7 x 19.1 x 17.8 cm)
Veilleuse-Personages
c. 1830-50. Porcelain night
light in the form of a beast
10 x 4.6 x 5.9 in.
(25.4 x 11.7 x 15 cm)

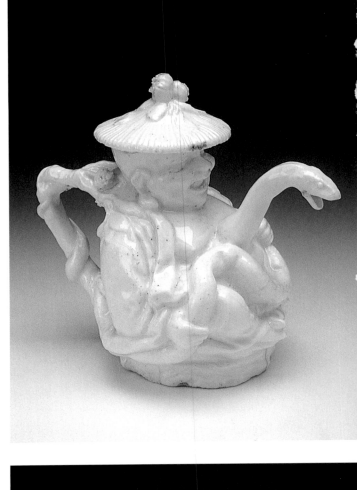

Silversmiths were kept just as busy producing silver services and tea canisters for the wealthier homes while furniture makers turned out mountains of tea tables, tea caddies, and tea poys (three-footed cabinets, in which caddies were stored, that could be locked to prevent servants from stealing the valuable tea). Then there were all the other items needed for a formal tea: mote spoons to scoop any floating leaves from the cup, caddy scoops to take tea from the caddy to the teapot, strainers to prevent tea leaves from falling into the cup, and a whole host of infusers that could be filled with tea, placed in the pot, and withdrawn when the tea was perfectly brewed.

Teas were developed for everyone, not just the upper crust. High tea, mistaken by many to mean "high" society, was just the opposite and was also known by the more blunt name of "meat tea." High tea was essentially a farmer's supper served around six o'clock with pork pies, scotch eggs, and other substantial foods. There were also simple worker's teas with a tea biscuit and a chipped mug of the beverage served strong enough "to trot a mouse on." The men's clubs had teas accompanied by potted shrimp, devilled ham, anchovy paste on toast, and scotch woodcock (anchovies, cream, and egg on toast). Students at boarding schools and universities held afternoon teas, toasting bread in the coal-fired fireplaces in their rooms. Tea was everywhere and every group managed to create a variant of the afternoon repast to suit their taste, pocket, and leisure.

Tea shops democratized the elaborate afternoon tea in the late 19th century. The first tea shop was opened by the Aerated Baking Company (ABC) in 1864 and proved to be immensely popular, serving "cream" teas that were widely affordable and enabled working class women to occasionally treat themselves and play Duchess. Lyons followed soon afterwards. However, the most famous tea shop today is the Mackintosh-designed Willow Tea Room in Glasgow. The tea shop spread throughout Britain and other parts of its empire. I still treasure my own childhood memories of highly anticipated visits with an aunt to the tea shop in the small town of East London in South Africa, where I grew up, and being awed by the tempting array of iced buns, cream cakes, and dainty petits fours.

A key development in the broadening of the British tea market was the discovery in 1815 that the Assam tea bush grew wild in India. Britain began the process of setting up estates and in 1839 they tasted the first crop of Indian tea, ending the three-hundred-year monopoly that China had enjoyed in the tea trade. Each year thereafter the quantity of tea from India increased and the prices dropped. In India the industry was new and began with the most modern farming methods and ingenious mechanical means of preparing and packing the tea. In 1872 the cost of production in India was eleven pence a pound. By 1913 this had dropped to three pence a pound.

A natural catastrophe brought the Island of Serendip (renamed Ceylon and then Sri Lanka) into the tea market. Disease struck its coffee plantations and wiped them out completely. The island turned to tea and 305,000 acres were under cultivation by 1835, bringing the cost of tea down even further. Today Sri Lanka remains the number three producer of tea in the world.

Miss Cranston's Willow Tea Room, Sauchiehall Street, Glasgow: the Dining Room ('Ladies Luncheon Room'), designed by Charles Rennie Mackintosh, 1904

America

The Waters in the rebel bay
Have kept the tea-leaf savor;
Our old North-Enders in their spray
Still taste a Hyson flavor;
(And freedom's teacup still o'erflows
With ever fresh libations
To cheat of slumber all her foes
And cheer the wakening nations!)

Oliver Wendell Holmes (1809-94)

"Ballad of the Boston Tea Party"

America was as eager a customer for tea as any of
the British colonies. It was avidly consumed by everyone
from East Coast bankers sipping it from delicate imported
porcelain cups to cowboys on the range who brewed
and drank it from tin mugs. Tea drinking in New York City
was so popular that by the mid-1700s special "Tea Water
Pumps" had to be installed around the city to provide
safe clean water for tea drinking. Tea's days in America,
however, were numbered when the British passed the
infamous act of 1767, placing duties on tea and other
commodities imported by the colonies. The furor was so

great that the act was repealed three years later, lifting all
duties except for a modest three pence per pound on tea.

The cost of this was not onerous – two pennies
on the English pound – but the symbolism of taxation
without representation caused great anger. To make
matters worse, the East India Company was facing trading
problems. Its warehouses were packed to overflowing
with seventeen million pounds of unsold tea and
smugglers still kept forcing the price down. Sales in
Britain were further hampered by the hated tea tax –
one shilling a pound on tea imported by the East India
Company and two shillings for other importers.

The solution for this problem of oversupply was
the misguided Tea Act of 1773, which gave the Company
a monopoly on the sale and direct distribution of tea in
the colonies. This meant that it would ruin the commerce
of the middlemen and merchants in the colonies who
imported and distributed tea. American colonists
considered this a usurpation of their right to regulate
their own commerce and their outrage had a galvanizing
impact. In the words of Sir Winston Churchill, "The Act
succeeded where [Samuel] Adams had failed; it united
colonial opinion against the British."

On 16 December 1773, a party of settlers, dressed
as Mohawk Indians, boarded the three ships loaded with
tea that had just arrived from Britain, and the Boston Tea
Party took place. The settlers dumped tons of tea, worth
about ten thousand pounds, into the harbor, creating
a briny brew of floating tea, and 342 tea chests covered
the water all the way south to Dorchester Neck. A series
of similar events, known collectively as "the tea disorders,"
followed throughout the country, launching not only the
American Revolution but also swaying the country from
tea to coffee consumption. As James Pratt puts it, "Amidst
the roar of cannon and musketry, therefore, this great
republic was born – with a prenatal disinclination for
tea." It was considered unpatriotic to drink tea thereafter,
even if the source was other than Britain.

Only a fraction of the pre-Revolutionary market
survived. However, tea was not totally abandoned and,
as Beulah Munshower Sommer and Pearl Dexter record
in *Tea with Presidential Families* (Scotland, Conn.: Olde
English Tea Company, 1999), many presidents and first

ladies were tea lovers. Thomas Jefferson was more than just a tea drinker: he was an addict and had an octagonal tea room that adjoined his parlor at Monticello. It was in this temple to the leaf that he wrote and edited the *Declaration of Independence*. Eleanor Roosevelt and her husband had grown up with the custom of afternoon tea and took this indulgence with them to the White House. Madame Chiang Kai-shek, French premier Edouard Herriot, and Britain's prime minister, Winston Churchill, were amongst many who were invited to lavish afternoon teas at the White House. But this did not impact on the rest of America, which was resolutely committed to coffee.

Ironically, given America's resistance to tea, no other country had a greater impact on modern tea drinking. It has recovered from its abhorrence of the leaf and is today the second largest importer of tea in the world. Its first innovation was the clipper ship. America's first great family fortunes were made in trade with China. It is estimated that in 1850 one-fifth of all the goods in a home in New England came from China. Seeking to speed up the shipping time to the East the first "extreme" clipper ship, the *Rainbow*, was launched in New York in 1845. With its sleek, streamlined hull and vast acreage of sail, it made the trip in 102 days, nearly half the time it took for the conventional, ponderous cargo ships. Moreover, the *Rainbow* repaid its cost of $45,000 and an equal amount in profit after its first run. In 1850 the *Oriental* was the first American clipper to bring tea to England, making the trip from Hong Kong to London in a record 97 days.

The clippers became the greyhounds of the sea and set many records. *Lightning* still holds the speed record for a cargo ship under sail – 436 nautical miles in 24 hours. They were the subject of intense public interest and speculation. Each year there was a contest to see which would be the first to arrive with the new tea, their progress being eagerly followed in London on Mincing Lane, the tea trade's epicenter. Fortunes were made and lost gambling on which ship would dock first, and that cargo of tea always carried a special premium and a hefty bonus for the crew. The most famous of these races took place in 1866 with forty or so ships, all British, taking part. But in 1871, with the first early awkward steamships traveling the tea route, the last of the clipper tea races took place, ending an era of sail.

America further advanced tea drinking with three of the most revolutionary advances in tea consumption: iced tea, instant tea, and tea bags. While denounced by tea connoisseurs for their apostasy, America's innovations saved tea from being further marginalized by coffee by simplifying brewing. Iced tea gave tea a new lease of life as a refreshing summer treat. It was introduced by Richard Blechynden, who, unable to sell hot tea in the humid climate at the St. Louis Exposition of 1904, simply poured it over ice and had an immediate winner on his hands.

Thomas Sullivan, a New York food merchant, invented the tea bag when he sent his tea samples to his clients in small silk bags instead of small tin cans as was the usual custom. They could be brewed and tasted by tea buyers without fuss or muss while still in their bags. Finally in the 1940s instant tea arrived on the scene. In the efficiency-conscious society of the United States tea would simply never have survived had the tea bag, and to a lesser extent, instant tea, not simplified the brewing process, also allowing tea to be made a cup at a time – another convenience.

America has succeeded in demystifying tea and moved the Western ceremony into the sunlight, from the parlors to the summer porch. In the tradition of Kakuzo Okakura, this could be named the fourth period in tea – the "Pop" period.

The Pop Period

The modern period is fascinating, more for its cultural manifestations than its culinary ones. Throughout the 20th century, both high and low culture have exploited tea's deeply evocative character. Even for non-tea-drinkers it has served to evince emotions of warmth and comfort. Aside from a cup of tea itself, nothing symbolized this romantic association more potently than the sturdy, steam-powered engine of hospitality, the teapot. In the 1940s tens of thousands of young girls and boys at dance schools performed the dance rage, the "Teapot Tip". It reminds

Above: Phoenix Arts
Commission, Phoenix, Arizona
Giant Teapot Gazebo
1992. Mixed media
Squaw Peak Parkway
Mitigation Project

Opposite above:
David Hockney
**Untitled
(Geldzahler's Teapot)**
1971. Pen and black ink
on paper
19.5 x 21.5 in.
(49.5 x 56.6 cm)

Opposite below:
Jean Carries
Teapot
c. 1888. Stoneware
6.5 x 10 x 6.75 in.
(16.5 x 25.4 x 17.1 cm)

older generations of the *thé dansant*, the tea dance, that was so popular in the 1930s and through the War years. The name has remained with us today but contemporary tea dances have only retained the timing: they are late afternoon dance parties with half-price bar drinks and nary a cup of tea to be seen.

As we have less and less time to make an event of afternoon tea, so its symbolic meaning has increased. A teapot placed strategically in scenes in movies, in set-ups for advertisements or in illustrations of magazine articles, acts as an icon for home and hearth. Teapots outlined in neon tubing are a universal sign for the tea shop or café. In case the point is missed, some roadside establishments have even been built in the shape of a teapot.

Modern writers from James Joyce to Anthony Burgess have written paeans in praise of its social charms. Animated teapots have even taken to the silver screen, notably Disney's chubby mother-figure, Mrs. Potts. Furthermore, it is the single most collectible item in the pantheon of domestic ceramic products, although it is also collected in silver, glass, and metal and, as the teapots in the section on mutant materials demonstrate, a host of unlikely materials besides. Collecting teapots is a growing obsession. Nowhere is this exhibited with greater vision and spirit of adventure than in this book where almost all the teapots are culled from Sonny and Gloria Kamm's

extraordinary collection, less than one-half of one per cent of their overwhelming assembly of over five thousand teapots. It is difficult to go through a single day without several encounters with the teapot, whether as an image in print or on television or in its full three-dimensional splendor at home or even in art museums. Teapots define the word "ubiquitous."

Their semiotic power has not been lost on the fine arts world. Some of the 20th century's most famous artists have succumbed to the charm of the teapot, from the Russian founder of Suprematism, Kasimir Malevich, and his sculpturally fascinating "idea of a teapot" for the Leningrad State Porcelain Factory in 1920, to Pop masters Roy Lichtenstein and Claes Oldenburg. Those artists who arrived through the contemporary crafts movement have had a particular stake in exploring the teapot's potential. Indeed some, such as Richard Notkin and Leopold Foulem, have specialized in the teapot, at least for periods of their career. As the following chapters demonstrate, they have explored every imaginable subject matter, and a few that are unimaginable. Politics, religion, dreams, sex, history, architecture, flora and fauna both real and imaginary, celebrities and angst-laden relationships are all fair game as subjects for the new teapot makers.

The usually misused term "new" is important to understanding the significance of this immense wave of creativity that has sprung from the teapot. Unusual teapots are not new. They have been with us since the first potter or silversmith began to play with the form hundreds of years ago and realized that the teapot provided an opportunity for pantomime and masquerade. What is new is that these makers have been free for the first time to ignore utility and approach the teapot without any functional limits, bounded only by their imagination and the sense of adventure of their collectors.

Many of the teapots here, like those of Ron Baron, John McQueen and Arman, make an aesthetic virtue of the fact that they are "useless" and cannot contain much more than air and a concept. Instead they turn that denial of function on itself and give it meaning as a visual tease, a dislocation of purpose. When one is no longer expected to lift the pot, scale can be ignored, as attested by the huge teapot gazebo that is part of the Art Project in Phoenix, Arizona, allowing the teapot to take on sculptural or architectural monumentality. Yet what they all have in common is that their cultural potency as art objects is dependent in part upon the rich and complex history of tea trade and consumption.

This can be sensed in *Untitled (Henry Geldzahler's Teapot)* by David Hockney, in which the teapot becomes an imaginary personal diary. It carries the history of its owner and the teas, real and imagined, that have been poured from its spout. The drawing is part of the two-dimensional aspect of Sonny and Gloria Kamm's great collection but is also accompanied by the original teapot, itself by one of France's best fin-de-siècle artist-potters, Jean Carries.

In essence the pen and ink drawing is a symbolic portrait of Geldzahler, one of the most influential figures in New York's fine arts world, advisor to some of the most successful artists of our time and the city's peripatetic commissioner for culture. Even though it is unlikely that Geldzahler actually brewed tea in this pot, it takes on a mythic quality, symbolizing his serving tea to some of the great artists and contemporary culture czars who populated his life, from Hockney himself to Andy Warhol, Jasper Johns, the legendary dealer Leo Castelli, and the Metropolitan Museum's ex-director Thomas Hoving;

moments both sacred and profane that helped shape the direction of American art. The teapot – the neutral mediator at these gatherings – is, as a result, more than a simple device to dispense golden liquid, but an object of great conceptual potency, containing not just the imagined history of intimate tête-à-tête's with a great impresario but also the collective nostalgia that we hold in our hearts for the nurturing, restorative spirit of tea itself.

Chapter 1
Yixing and the West

Collecting contemporary or 20th-century Yixing teapots from China is an exciting activity because it requires an acute aesthetic judgment. Yixing is the birthplace of the teapot and these elegant ceramics have been made in the region's traditional clays and styles without interruption for five hundred years. The factories, as the potteries are known, are all now a short drive outside Yixing in Dingshu (also, just to confuse matters, known as Jingshan, Dingshuzhen or Dingshan).

One can buy Yixing teapots that cost $5 or less while the work of the masters – often a similar form – can cost $50,000 or more. At first this causes novices to the field some anxiety. However, when one places a cheaply made teapot next to the work of one of the master potters, the difference is clear and dramatic. The finesse of the maker can transform the banal into the magical. The pricing structure has to do with artisanal experience and skill. A strictly controlled hierarchy exists whereby Yixing potters are promoted through the ranks from apprentice, through various levels of accomplishment, to ultimate grand master status, the latter producing signature works for the highest prices.

The top masters tend to be very traditional in their approach and are particularly revered in Asian markets such as Hong Kong and Taipei. In the Western market, particularly the United States, which has recently developed a passion for these objects, the focus tends to be less on pedigree than on creativity. Thus two of the most popular potters in the United States are young women, Zhou Ding Fang and Lu Wen Xia, whose works are the most playful and experimental even though the artists have not reached grand master stature as yet. In turn the warmth of their reception in the United States and Britain has led to an increase in their celebrity in China, and their work has even been immortalized on postage stamp designs.

Lu Wen Xia is known for a wide range of forms but in particular for her exquisite and poetic renderings of faux bamboo as in *Bamboo Bridge*, a charming and elegant construction. A contemporary of Xia, Fang has also drawn on the bamboo plant to create a teapot that manages to convey the ferocious, invasive fecundity of the bamboo root. Much larger than the conventional Yixing teapot it has an eerie presence reminiscent of the man-eating plant in *Little Shop of Horrors*. Fang is also famous for her trompe l'oeil renditions of soft surfaces and fabrics, from leather to burlap.

Not only have the makers in Yixing experienced a renaissance in the last quarter of the 20th century, but the West has also enjoyed a second wave of influence. Led by Richard Notkin, an American ceramist living in Helena, Montana, potters all over America and Europe have begun delving into this rich trove of tradition with the same enthusiasm and sense of discovery first witnessed in the 17th and 18th centuries. Dominique Morin in France, Jeroen Bechtold in the Netherlands, and Geo Lastomirsky in Seattle are just a few of the Western artists who are working in this format today.

Lastomirsky brings the traditional Chinese love of organic found objects, driftwood, and scholars rocks into his abstracted teapots. One has to search for the handle and spout in his subtle vessels, which are quiet and meditative responses to nature.

Detail: Richard Notkin
Curbside Teapot
Yixing Series
1983. Stoneware
3.5 x 7.25 x 3.875 in.
(8.9 x 18.4 x 9.8 cm)

Yixing Zisha Ware
Arts Factory,
Teapot Studio # 2,
Dingshu, Yixing, China;
January 1992

Gerald Gulotta was one of the first Western designers to be invited to Yixing to design for their factories. But, as Louise Anderson, a dealer in Yixing wares, pointed out at the first Yixing Symposium in New York in 1992, the makers of Gulotta's tiny, exquisitely designed teapots did not sign off with their chop marks as is the usual custom because, despite being stunning tours de force of hand-building, the teapots do not pour well, or at least, not in conformance with Yixing rules. Functionality is still a golden standard for the top Yixing makers, no matter how creative the form may be, and the craftsmen are embarrassed by teapots that do not function perfectly. While this may seem conservative, it is also a defense against arbitrariness.

Notkin is the doyen of the Western Yixing revival. His signature form, the *Double Cooling Tower Teapot*, derives its shape from two teapots, one a four-hundred-year-old, conical-shaped form superficially similar to the cooling tower, the other in the Yixing tradition of double-volumed pots. The handle in Notkin's work comes from film of early nuclear bomb tests in which telephone poles become plastic, undulating, almost cartoon-like shapes in the face of the bomb's blast. This teapot is a chilling reminder of the ecological danger imposed by technology. Moreover, the notion of pouring tea from one of these vessels gives the anti-nuclear message an added sense of horror.

Notkin's "Heart" teapots are table-top memorials to the most evil of man's recent deeds. They use the heart as the symbolic seat of the human conscience ("heart felt", "have a heart") and allude to some of modern man's worst moments: the hostage-taking in Iran, the Sharpeville riots in South Africa, and the tragic mistake of the Vietnam conflict. Notkin's *Hostage Teapot* is wrapped in chains and clad in armor, and a metaphor can be easily understood by all. His *Curbside Teapot*, though gentler and more sentimental, concerns homelessness and desertion.

The use of symbolic language has, from the outset, been a part of Yixing tradition. Notkin decided to use a system of universal but contemporary symbols. His choices are not esoteric but rather contentious and literally politically explosive: mushroom clouds, army camouflage, armor plating, radiation signs, crude-oil barrels. Notkin's works aspire to the most radical edge of one of the two traditional aesthetics guiding Yixing potters, "qi" – shock or unbalance. (The other principle is "qu," literally "the heart of the child" – an idea that conveys natural tastefulness and simplicity.)

The work of the Dutch potter and computer whizz, Jeroen Bechtold, also brings together the old world and the new. In his teapot *Blue Twist*, the five-hundred-year-old Yixing teapot comes face to face with the information age. The teapot is made by Guh Wei Fen, a top Yixing craftsman, from designs created digitally by Bechtold on the computer. The limitations of clay and fire produced a few adjustments between the artist's virtual reality and the potter's more concrete ceramic reality. This marriage of Eastern pre-Industrial craft traditions and Western exploratory vistas of the information age points to the merging of the home and the digital as the collaborative source for teapot designs of the future.

Richard Notkin
with Zhou Ding Fang
in Fang's studio,
Arts Factory #2,
Yixing, China;
January 1992

Opposite: Zhou Ding Fang
Bamboo Root
1993. Stoneware
8 x 14 x 7 in.
(20.3 x 35.6 x 17.8 cm)

Lu Wen Xia
Bamboo Bridge
1998. Stoneware
4.4 x 11.9 x 4.25 in.
(11.2 x 30.2 x 10.8 cm)

Opposite:

Above: Gerald Gulotta
Five Teapots
1990. Stoneware
From 6.7 x 5 x 3.5 to
3.25 x 4.5 x 3.75 in.
(from 17 x 12.7 x 8.9 to
8.3 x 11.4 x 9.5 cm)

Below: Geo Lastomirsky
Teapot
1998. Terracotta
5 x 8.75 x 4.25 in.
(12.7 x 22.2 x 10.8 cm)

Jeroen Bechtold
Blue Twist
1999. Stoneware
4.4 x 5.75 x 3.25 in.
(11.2 x 14.6 x 8.3 cm)
Executed by Guh Wei Fen,
Yixing, China

Opposite:

Above: Richard Notkin
Curbside Teapot
Yixing Series
1983. Stoneware
3.5 x 7.25 x 3.875 in.
(8.9 x 18.4 x 9.8 cm)

Below: Richard Notkin
**Double Cooling
Tower Teapot**
Yixing Series
1983. Stoneware
6.25 x 8.5 x 3.75 in.
(15.9 x 21.6 x 9.5 cm)

Richard Notkin
Hostage Teapot
Yixing Series
1987. Stoneware
6.25 x 11.25 x 5.5 in.
(15.9 x 28.6 x 14 cm)

Chapter 2
Form and Function

Those who have not tried to make an everyday functional object often believe that the process is simple and proscribed, something along the lines of the Bauhausian tenet "form follows function." However, the extraordinary objects featured in this book quickly prove that, while utility sets up some boundaries, it does not inhibit the imagination.

One of the distinguishing qualities of a functional teapot is its heft and balance. When this is conceived effectively there is a contrapuntal rhythm between weight and movement that is sensually pleasurable. Britain's first successful industrial designer, Christopher Dresser, gave considerable thought to the pleasure of use. His designs for metal teapots are amongst the most progressive design concepts of the late 19th century and they would have seemed perfectly at home almost fifty years later in a Bauhaus metal workshop.

In the period between the two World Wars, functionalism was considered by many to be the most unsullied source of beauty. Certainly this was the view of Bauhaus followers who stripped dinnerware of all ornament and color. White was the modernist uniform for ceramics. The superb tea service by Otto Lindig, one of the leaders of the Bauhaus Pottery Workshop, with

its severity, clean lines, and absence of decoration or ornament, clearly defines the aesthetic of the movement. The end result was indeed functionally efficient but what did it do for the human spirit? At least for the working class proletariat for whom these works were designed, it seemed to do very little and manufacturers often had to embellish these works with singularly inappropriate decoration – even pink roses – to get the wares to sell.

The American, George E. Ohr, the so-called "Mad Potter of Biloxi," was the country's first true studio potter. His approach to functionalism was quixotic, to say the least. He made "art" teapots between 1895 and 1905 that were usable but challenging. The example shown here is more classical and conventional than most and reveals the elegant sensuality of Ohr's approach to form. The walls of the pot are thrown to paper-thinness, calling for extreme caution in use. Other teapots from this maverick artist were more complex, offering a small forest of handles or spouts (the user had to decide which one worked) and, in one monumental work in the collection of the Smithsonian Institution in Washington, he created a combined teapot/coffeepot with separate interior volumes and long, assertively drawn spouts. To Ohr, function was a game to be played with plastic ingenuity.

Functionalism was also the core belief of the British studio ceramists who rallied around the influential potter Bernard Leach from 1921 onwards; they included Katherine Pleydell Bouverie and Michael Cardew, one of the most proficient exponents of feathering, trailing, sgraffito, marbling, and other techniques in traditional English slipware decoration. However, although they shared the same starting point as the modernists – a belief in functionalism – their approach was radically different from that point on: the romance of the materials was played up to the hilt, decoration from certain approved historical sources (early Chinese decoration and British medieval slipwares) was

Detail: Michael Graves
Tea and Coffee Set
1983. Silver, aluminum, bakelite, and mock ivory
Teapot: 10.5 x 4.7 x 8 in (26.7 x 11.9 x 20.3 cm)
Designed for Officina Alessi, Italy; edition of 99 plus three artist's proofs in different metals

encouraged, and the individuality of the maker was stressed. At the end of the day the teapots of both camps poured with equal élan, leaving the question, which gave the greatest pleasure to its user?

The Scandinavian designers between the wars tried to bring together utility and a sensual approach to materials, notably the luscious stoneware surfaces of Nathalie Krebs at Saxbo Pottery in Denmark and others. Art Deco designers like Jean-Emile Puiforcat also produced a stylish modernist look but without the social agenda.

Ah Leon, the master of trompe l'oeil ceramics, learnt to make teapots according to the strict regimen of Yixing, whereby the object must not only look beautiful but must also pour tea in a perfect smooth arc so the liquid flows into the cup or bowl without bubbling or splashing. More than most, Ah Leon knows that the making of a teapot is an act of technical and aesthetic complexity. He lists fourteen principles in a good teapot, which are briefly stated here with occasional paraphrasing for brevity's sake.

The first nine points all deal with objective issues of craft: "1. Begin with good clay. 2. The main form must be thin-walled. 3. The lid must fit tightly and still look graceful. 4. The rim must be level. 5. The tea must flow smoothly. 6. The spout must control the tea. 7. The handle must be appropriate, as it is the first thing we touch and it establishes the pot's disposition. 8. The pot must be steady when lifted, balanced, and easy to use. 9. The base must be round and gentle, as it is where the teapot touches the table and if it does not sit well, the whole teapot looks wrong."

The next five points are more subjective but herein lies the difference between the magical and the banal: "10. The body should be elegant and unique and if its shape is unnatural or awkward it will appear vulgar and untrue. 11. The firing must be appropriate. 12. The teapot must look sound, all the parts must coexist happily and achieve unity; exaggeration may destroy the feeling of quality. 13. The spirit must be enduring. Spirit is to the pot what life is to a human being. It is the bone, the structure of the work, and so must express something universal in the maker's disposition. 14. The tone must be profound." Tone is what Ah Leon admires above all, a visual pitch that summarizes the entire presence of an object.

Most of the studio potters follow these rules, as can be seen in the sturdy work of Anne Hirondelle, Mark Pharis and Wally Keeler. James Makins's porcelain teapots make the most of the thin walls with their throwing rings elegantly displayed. In this group only Michael Sherrill ignores the rules, creating a mammoth, statuesque teapot that by its scale alone defies function or any intimation of function.

In 1967 Walter Gropius, the architect and founder of the Bauhaus school, signed a contract with Rosenthal Porcelain (he was then designing its new factory complex) to design the *TAC1* Teapot. The teapot, first produced in 1969, the year of Gropius's death, has become a classic of the genre. The shape and position of the handle come close to Christopher Dresser's ideal, but Gropius and his collaborator on the project, Katherine De Sousa, added another touch of functional bliss.

As all tea pourers know, serving tends to be a two-handed event. One hand holds the handle and the other keeps the lid in place. Even the so-called "safety-lids"

cannot be relied upon. Gropius introduced what he called the "lid arrestor." This was a tab on the lid that merged with the line of the handle so that with a single hand one could pour the tea while one's thumb placed on the arrestor prevented the lid from fleeing the pot – particularly crucial when one gets down to that all-important last cup of tea and the angle of the teapot is most acute.

More architects were enlisted in the search for the beautiful, functional teapot by the Italian firm of Alessi. In 1979 the company set up one of the most exciting postmodern design experiments, known as the "Tea and Coffee Piazza Project." Architects and designers were invited to create solid silver services in limited editions that Alessi hoped would be "in the thick of the current debate on neo- and postmodernism." Arata Izosaki, Stanley Tigerman, Richard Meier, Aldo Rossi, Alessandro Mendini, Paolo Portoghesi, Robert Venturi, Kazumasa Yamashita, and even Charles Jencks, the American-born, London-based architect whose writings have defined postmodern culture, took part.

Matheo Thun, one of the Memphis artists, and Michael Graves both deal well with function and form in two different but equally successful designs. Thun's elegant, clean-lined teapot incorporates a light, linear but subtly decorative stand that serves either to present this powerful object or acts as a tea warmer. Michael Graves's whimsical, ingenious *Nanna Warming Teapot*, made from blown glass by Miko in Italy, feels almost space-age in its freshness and visionary edge, while the tea mechanism, by contrast, is curiously anachronistic, low-tech, and almost medieval in feeling. Surprisingly it works quite well, all the way down to the glass warmer on which the teapot rests.

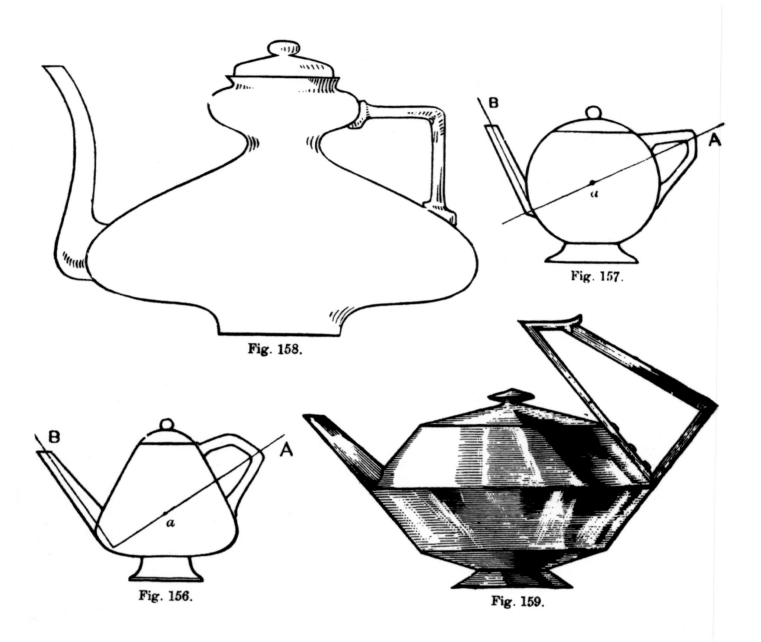

Fig. 158.

Fig. 157.

Fig. 156.

Fig. 159.

Opposite above: illustration by Christopher Dresser from the *Technical Educator*, 1873. "In nineteen cases out of twenty, handles are so placed on teapots that they [can be] lifted only by a force capable of raising two or three such vessels." Dresser's Law for the Teapot Handle then follows: "Find the center of gravity... draw a line through the center of the handle, and continue it through the center of gravity of the vessel. The spout must now be at right angles to this line... this law, if obeyed, will enable liquid to be poured from a vessel without [the teapot] appearing heavier than it actually is."

Opposite below:
Jean-Emile Puiforcat
Teapot
c. 1937. French silver, vermeil, rock crystal
5.25 x 8.9 x 4.5 in.
(13.3 x 22.6 x 11.4 cm)

Christopher Dresser
Triangular Teapot
designed 1880
Silver and ebony
8.5 x 2.5 x 6.5 in.
(21.6 x 6.4 x 16.5 cm)
Reissued in limited edition
by Officina Alessi, Italy

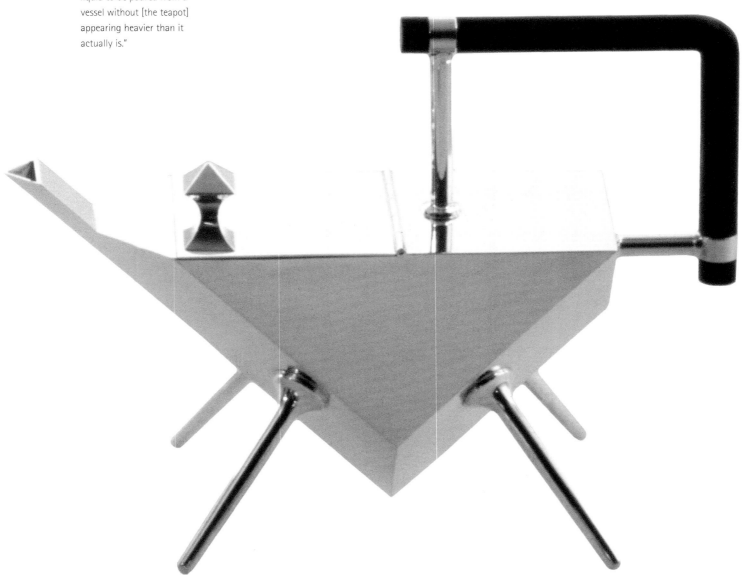

Opposite:

Otto Lindig
Tea Service
1929. Earthenware
Teapot: 5.25 x 9 x 6 in.
(13.3 x 22.9 x 15.2 cm)
Designed for Karlsruhe
Majolika, Germany, and
produced on special order
from 1929 to 1933 and from
1946 to 1962; only 22 sets
were made after 1946

Above: Walter Gropius
TAC1 Teapot
1969. Porcelain
5 x 9.25 x 6.75 in.
(12.7 x 23.5 x 17.1 cm)
Designed for Rosenthal Studio
Line, Rosenthal, Selb,
Germany, and produced
throughout the 1980s, with
decoration commissioned
from artists and architects

Below: Nathalie Krebs
Teapot
c. 1940. Stoneware
6.5 x 7 x 5.25 in.
(16.5 x 17.8 x 13.3 cm)
Designed for Saxbo Pottery,
Denmark

Opposite: Mark Pharis
Teapot
1984. Stoneware
10.25 x 10.5 x 3.5 in.
(26 x 26.7 x 8.9 cm)
One of a series of ten for
Garth Clark Gallery Editions

Above: Anne Hirondelle
Cadent Teapot Diptych
1997. Stoneware; wood (stand)
8.4 x 21 x 9 in.
(21.3 x 53.3 x 22.9 cm)

Below: Wally Keeler
Double Spout Teapot
1990. Thrown salt-glazed
stoneware
7.75 x 7.5 x 4.25 in.
(19.7 x 19.1 x 10.8 cm)

Right: James Makins
Teapot
1992. Porcelain
5.75 x 10 x 6.6 in.
(14.6 x 25.4 x 16.8 cm)

Below: Michael Sherrill
Red Lacquer Teapot
1997. Ceramic
16.5 x 26.5 x 13 in.
(41.9 x 67.3 x 33 cm)

Opposite: Ah Leon
Hanging Heart Teapot
1991. Stoneware
8 x 4 x 3 in.
(20.3 x 10.2 x 7.6 cm)

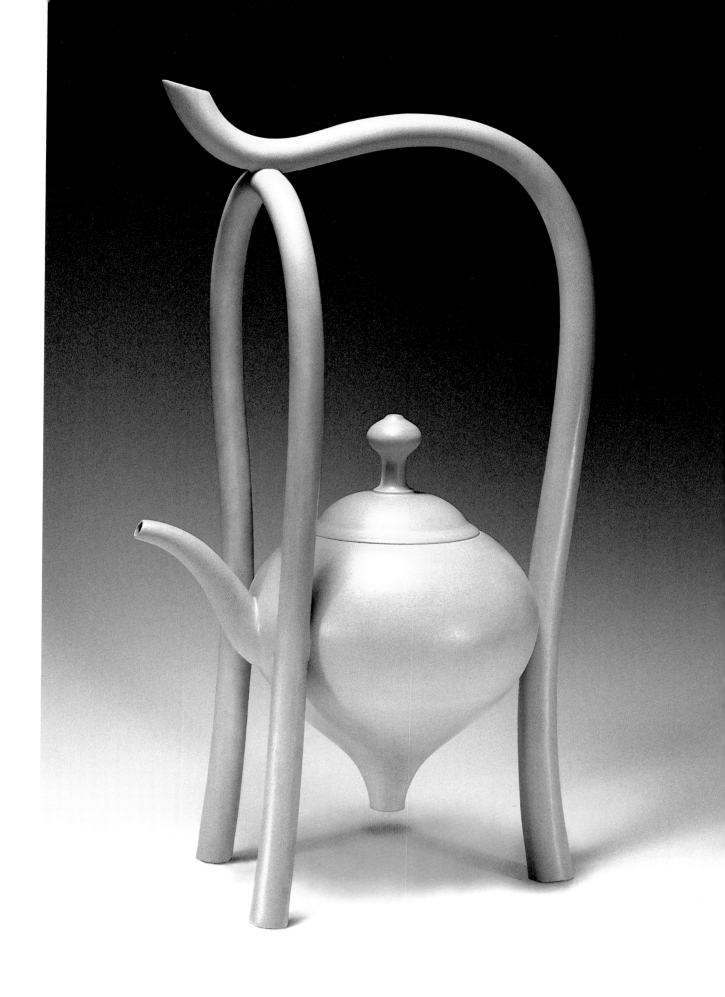

Right: Matheo Thun
Teapot
King Series
1989. Stainless steel
11.75 x 8.1 x 8.1 in.
(29.8 x 20.6 x 20.6 cm)
Designed for WMF, Germany

Below: Michael Graves
Tea and Coffee Set
1983. Silver, aluminum,
bakelite, and mock ivory
Teapot 10.5 x 4.7 x 8 in.
(26.7 x 11.9 x 20.3 cm)
Designed for Officina Alessi,
Italy; edition of 99 plus
three artist's proofs in
different metals

Opposite: Michael Graves
Nanna Warming Teapot
1997. Glass
11 x 9.4 x 7.25 in.
(30 x 23.8 x 18.4 cm)

Chapter 3
Beauty and Decoration

While most potters agreed with the general tenets of the modernists when it came to functionality, they drew the line at two points. One was using industrial means to produce their wares (they preferred to keep to the slower, time-honored potter's wheel). The other was modernism's prohibition of decoration. According to the stricter modernist edicts, decoration was inherently decadent and bourgeois. It was, in retrospect, one of the sillier notions of the movement. If one believes that decoration is somehow morally wrong, then what does it say about those pockets of so-called primitive peoples who live isolated from the rest of the world and still pursue decoration whether on their homes, their bodies or their clothes, with an obsessive but human passion?

Modernism's war on decoration was, however, an effective device for sorting out the confusion over form and surface that had evolved during the Victorian and Edwardian eras. Fin-de-siècle design had been overtaken by what Roger Fry described as "an eczematous eruption." Excessive ornament, both flat and in relief – a dizzying flurry of floral stylizations, scrolls, and patterns – was applied as camouflage to disguise the fact that the form was poorly designed. As the potter Michael Cardew stated, "Pottery, whether decorated or not, is ninety-five per cent form."

Studio potters, rooted in form as they were, were ideal guardians to carry on the tradition of pottery decoration. Indeed the only way one could acquire a new teapot with color and decoration in Britain from 1939 until 1954 was to purchase it from a studio potter. To conserve resources for the war effort and later, the recovery, industrial potters were forbidden to use decoration or color. This also meant that in the 1960s when a taste began to emerge for more playful teapots that were patterned or had more richly textured glazes, studio potters were often the inspiration for industry.

Finally, it was that amorphous movement, postmodernism, difficult to define because it is so sprawling, capacious, and promiscuous in its means, that brought decoration out of the pottery closet. The thrust of postmodernism was not the rejection of modernism per se, but rather, as Charles Jencks states, it was both its "transcendence and its continuation." Decoration, historical referencing, figuration, narrative – all taboos in our modern past – were now heartily welcomed back into the fold.

As modernism lost power after the war, the studio potters had a field day. The decorative momentum kept building until the 1980s, a decade characterized by one of the most exuberant outbursts of pattern and decoration we have ever witnessed. In keeping with the Appropriationist character of postmodernism, much of this came from plundering the past – Ralph Bacerra's Imari-based decoration style, Gail Busch's playful remake of the 19th-century "Barge teapots" with their teapot-shaped finials, Betty Woodman's "egg and spinach" Tang-inspired wares, and James Lawton's revisionist approach to Japanese raku are just a few examples. These objects all revel in their rich surfaces, color, and pattern.

Writing of Bacerra's work in 1999, Ken Johnson, art critic for the *New York Times* applauded the artist's "visual hedonism" adding that it "does not try to express any important meaning, social, psychological,

Detail: Ralph Bacerra
Cloud Vessel
1997. Earthenware
21 x 18.75 x 4.75 in.
(53.3 x 47.6 x 12.1 cm)

Above: **James Lawton**
at work, 1999

Right: **Betty Woodman**
in studio, New York City,
c. 1985

philosophical or otherwise. His works are witty and sophisticated in their manipulation of influences ranging from Japanese to early modernist to Pop but mainly he wants to delight the eyes of his viewers. Sometimes one wishes avant-garde art could be so unashamedly sumptuous."

Amy Goldin, the art historian and voice of New York's Pattern and Decoration Movement in the late 1970s, said it differently: "Decoration can be intellectually empty but it need not be stupid." She championed the decorative in serious painting and sculpture, a movement to which ceramist Betty Woodman, muralist Joyce Kozloff, painters Robert Kushner, George Woodman, Robert Zakanich, and others belonged, bringing a new respectability to this once beleaguered field of visual exuberance.

No material is more responsive to the decorative impulse than glaze, with its beautiful colors enhanced by translucency and light. In this realm, teapot-making has an exceptional master, the glassmaker Richard Marquis. For many years he worked and taught in California but now lives on an idyllic island off Seattle. His output is varied but he is particularly revered in the glass world for his teapots. Modestly scaled but ambitious in terms of process, they are a virtual catalog of the ways in which glass can be manipulated to bring out its decorative élan. These works are every bit as intelligent in their play with decorative schematics and historical precedent as Goldin might have wished.

Marquis was the first contemporary American artist to take on the challenge of murrine. This is a technique that was known to the ancient Egyptians but reached its apotheosis in 16th-century Venice. Murrine is achieved by fusing thin rods of different colored glass which are then cut into wafers and joined like a patchwork quilt to form a glass vessel. In the 1940s the Italian architect Carlo Scarpa experimented with murrine for the Venini factory. This intrigued Marquis and he made his first trip to Venice in 1969. He worked at the Venini Fabbrica in nearby Murano. Anna Venini, daughter of the factory's owner Paola Venini, remembers his first visit, noting the "quiet way he came into the factory and was accepted by the workers. It was not

easy: the masters on the whole were quite surprised that somebody from such a far land wanted to do what was a very hard job and make such strange and unexpected shapes."

In the years that followed, Marquis's work has evolved, as he has continued to innovate and transform all the gifts that came to him out of the murrine tradition into a distinctive style that seems effortless yet demands the most exacting understanding and control of process. His interest in the teapot was due to several impulses. Firstly, he had already worked with ceramics in his early career and was friends with the bad boys in the Abstract Expressionist Ceramics group – Ken Price, Ron Nagle, and Peter Voulkos. They all avoided the teapot then because "it was anathema," too definitive and too domestic a ceramic archetype for these revolutionaries. This low-brow status did not bother Marquis and the teapot gave him a form his friends were not exploring and one which was not common in glass. The teapot also appealed formally because "it had more elements than any other form I could think of. It had a spout, a handle, a lid plus the body. Just being able to apply all of those parts, and it could still be recognizable even when you went to extremes."

The proto-postmodern mood can also be sensed in the Art Deco sensibility of Clarice Cliff's highly collectible, hand-painted wares for the British pottery, A. J. Wilkinson Ltd. The wares – inexpensive, colorful, and unconventional – were surprisingly popular and by the outbreak of World War II in 1939, which effectively brought the enterprise to an end, Cliff was employing almost three hundred men and women to paint tea and dinner services.

The teapots that are most specifically postmodernist in style are those made in the architectonic spirit of the Memphis Group, founded in 1981 by the masterful Ettore Sottsass. Italian artists, designers, and architects were in the majority (Matheo Thun, Marco Zanini, and others) but the program was international and included Californian ceramist Peter Shire, a perfect fit in terms of his irreverent approach to Constructivist art, as one can see in his amusing *Scorpion* teapot. Although Michael Duvall was not formally a member of this group, his work is one of the purest evocations of the postmodern architectural spirit.

In all of these pieces an ideal compromise is reached between modernist form and postmodern decorativeness. Their approach is less one of *decoration*

Above left: **Ralph Bacerra**
in Eagle Rock Studio,
Los Angeles, 2000

Above right: **Richard Marquis**
(on the left) in his studio

Right: **Judith Salomon**
in studio, Cleveland, 1985

Below left: **Michael Duvall**
in studio, 1985

Below right: **Peter Shire**
in studio, Echo Park,
Los Angeles, 2000

Opposite: Betty Woodman
Teapot and stand
1988. Glazed, thrown
and altered whiteware
12.75 x 16 x 10.75 in.
(32.4 x 40.6 x 27.3 cm)

as one sees in, say, Bacerra and Marquis, than one
of *decorative form* in which ornamental elements are
employed structurally. This is even more apparent in
Judith Salomon's use of bright color on her handbuilt
forms. Color has both a decorative and compositional
role, defining the flat planes of clay from which the
pot has been formed and directing the eye, making
parts of the surface recede and others advance.

So many of the teapots from this aesthetic
give the distinct impression that they have been
assembled from a child's building blocks – primary
in color, fundamental in geometry, and disarmingly
innocent in structure – because each element of color,
while seeming decorative, actually explains the interior
architecture of the form: what Mark Del Vecchio,
in his book *Postmodern Ceramics*, calls, "a romper
room for adults."

Right: Ralph Bacerra
Teapot
1989. Earthenware
16.25 x 10.75 x 7.75 in.
(41.3 x 27.3 x 19.7 cm)

Below: Ralph Bacerra
Cloud Vessel
1997. Earthenware
21 x 18.75 x 4.75 in.
(53.3 x 47.6 x 12.1 cm)

Right: Gail Busch
Teapot
1993. Ceramic
12.4 x 7.5 x 2.6 in.
(31.5 x 19.1 x 6.6 cm)

Below: James Lawton
Footed Teapot
1991. Raku fired earthenware
14.4 x 10.25 x 4.4 in.
(36.6 x 26 x 11.2 cm)

Left: Richard Marquis
Retro Stuff:
Stars and Stripes
1997. Glass
5.5 x 7.6 x 4.6 in.
(14 x 19.3 x 11.7 cm)

Below: Richard Marquis
Lumpyware Teapot
1998. Glass
4.5 x 6 x 3.75 in.
(11.4 x 15.2 x 9.5 cm)

Opposite: Richard Marquis
Teapot Sample Box # 3
1993. Blown-glass latticinio
teapots, murrini, paint,
metal car, and glass marble
in plate glass box
14.25 x 12.1 x 3.75 in.
(36.2 x 30.7 x 9.5 cm)

Peter Shire
Scorpion Float
1993. Earthenware
12.9 x 22.25 x 11.75 in.
(32.8 x 56.5 x 29.8 cm)

Opposite:

Above: Michael Duvall
Postmodern Teapot
1984. Glazed earthenware
11.4 x 8.6 x 3.625 in.
(29 x 21.8 x 9.2 cm)

Below: Judith Salomon
Tea Set
c. 1993. Glazed earthenware
Teapot: 10.5 x 6.1 x 3.3 in.
(26.7 x 15.5 x 8.4 cm)

Left: Marco Zanini
Colorado
1983. Ceramic
8.5 x 12 x 7 in.
(21.6 x 30.5 x 17.8 cm)
Designed for Memphis,
Milan

Below: Matheo Thun
Nefertiti
1981. Ceramic
Height 7.75 in.
(19.7 cm)

Opposite: Ettore Sottsass
Cherries
1972. Ceramic
11 x 8 x 4.75 in.
(27.9 x 20.3 x 12.1 cm)
Designed for Alessio Sarri,
Italy

Chapter 4
Messing with Perfection

There is a 19th-century saying that goes, "Build a better mousetrap and the world will beat a path to your door." This explains, in part, man's great propensity to meddle, rarely obeying that equally sane and measured truism, "If it isn't broken, don't fix it." We always feel that we can improve even the most sublime of inventions. The drive is twofold: the pure intellectual challenge of pitting one's imagination and logic to the task of improvement, and the lure of the vast profits that will be the reward for ingenuity. It has driven us to invent some of the most extraordinary creations and some of the most hapless follies.

Some inventions have changed our lives while others remain only as a source of hilarity and disbelief. In searching for "better mousetraps," the teapot became an obvious victim of the legions of improvers. Teapots were being used and sold in ever growing quantities from the 18th century onwards as tea became affordable to all. It seemed quite logical that if you could produce a better teapot and patent the result, a fortune was waiting.

Alas, the basic teapot has proven resistant to five centuries of reinvention. Despite onslaughts of designers intent on making it better, it remains basically unchanged from the Ming model established half

a millennium ago, except for one 19th-century addition – the built-in sieve to hold back tea leaves. As this proud vessel has sailed through time it has left in its wake piles of curious-looking teapot debris: hundreds of guaranteed drip-less spouts including the Camel, Stop-Drip, Nevva-Drip, and other patents (that nonetheless continued to remorselessly drip tea), teapots with multi-chambered interiors, elaborate mechanical self-pouring teapots, generations of electric teapots from 1930 onwards that now gather dust in science and design museums, safety-lid teapots, double walled teapots to prevent scalding, teapots that spuriously claimed to be "anti-tannic," teapots that simultaneously produced boiled eggs, teapots to brew in the car, teapots with multiple spouts to speed up pouring tea for groups.

Pouring is one of the functions that improvers tried to change. Double spouted teapots are organized for different kinds of efficiency. Those with spouts close together, like the British rustic teapot in marbled clay, aim to pour more than one cup of tea at the same time. Those with a spout on either side, such as the Worcester porcelain pot, are created to ease communal pouring from a teapot at a table. Neither proved to have much more than novelty value.

The safety-lid teapots are also indirectly about pouring. The "Cosy" teapot has a locking lid that prevents the lid from falling out of the pot when the last cup of tea is trickled out. The "cadogan" teapot is based on a Chinese wine pot and is filled from a hole in the base. Interior plumbing keeps the tea in place. Its disadvantage is that you cannot brew tea in the pot and it only serves as a decanter, which dooms it to being a mere curiosity piece. R. R. Royles's "self-pouring" teapot was produced in ceramic by Doulton and Co. and in silver by James Dixon. It is not actually "self-pouring" but pumps the tea out via a lever in the lid. It was reportedly inspired

Detail: R. R. Royles
Royles Self-Pouring Teapot, c. 1886. Ceramic and silver plate lid 8.25 x 8.85 x 5.5 in. (21 x 22.5 x 14 cm) Produced by Doulton and Co., England for R. R. Royles, England

Eric van Eimeren
in studio, Helena, Montana,
1992 (see **Oiler** and other
teapots on his shelves)

by a titled lady who had weak wrists and therefore found it difficult to lift a full pot.

One of the most effective teapots in solving the tea-brewing problem (removing the leaves once the tea has reached its ideal strength) is the *S.Y.P. (Simple Yet Perfect)* teapot of the 12th Earl of Dundonald. The tea is kept in an inner pocket at the top of the teapot. Lying on its back it brews. When the pot is stood upright, the water drains out of the leaves and the process is complete. This worked well and sold better than most but even so did not last more than a decade in production.

The most successful patented teapot ever was the Cube. It is one of the only teapots to have an entire book written about it (Anne Anderson, *The Cube Teapot*, 1999). It was invented in 1916 by Robert Johnson of Leicester and remained in use on the Cunard Steamship Line until the 1980s. It was the formation of the CUBE Teapots Co. Ltd in 1925, a marketing company to sell the concept, that set it off on its long and successful life. The company licensed various potteries (Foley China, Wedgwood, George Clews, Arthur Wood, Gibson and Sons) and A. J. Wilkinson Ltd of Birmingham to make the metal teapots.

They advertised its virtues extensively – it was compact and had no protruding spout or handle to break ("Mary [the maid] won't chip this one," proclaimed one advertisement) – and they also claimed that it did not drip. After ten years of aggressive marketing, the teapot was given great cachet when it was selected as the Cunard Line's official tea and coffee service. The Cube's stability, durability, and compactness were cited as perfect for Cunard's shipboard purposes. The CUBE company marketed the design in every variation including a 1925 version in a metal box with a burner for the outdoors called the "Compact Camp Outfit."

This idea of tea on the road was another popular area for invention. There were teapots, like the *Traveling Tea Maker* shown here, which could be plugged into a car's cigarette lighter; Christopher Dresser's elegantly compact picnic service where all the parts fit inside the teapot; the superb, gold wash over silver, traveling tea maker shown here, which is small and light and includes a stand and burner for heating water; and many others besides. This chapter deals more with the past than with contemporary expression. Artists and designers today have pretty much given up on trying to improve this form. One notable exception is Eric van Eimeren who lives and works in Montana, making sci-fi teapots with a "Blade Runner" sensibility; inventions that play with all of the issues raised so far. He has devised ways for assisting pouring and brewing, and even come up with earthquake-proof teapots.

This function is of more than passing interest to Sonny and Gloria Kamm. In 1994 their art collection was upended by an earthquake that ripped through Southern California. Although the teapot collection fared well enough (many were kept boxed), in a touch of irony, Van Eimeren's Quake-Proof model, while surviving nature's upheaval, swayed backwards and forwards on its spring as designed, but with such enthusiasm that it demolished objects on either side of it.

What these attempts at invention have in common, aside from delivering brewed tea, is that they all, ultimately, failed. In terms of functionality no teapot is superior to the common "brown Betty," that ubiquitous teapot, glazed a dark treacle-brown that can be found in more than half the households in Britain and beyond. It is worth noting that while the teapot has survived, the traditional coffeepot has not. The coffeepot endured an even more furious barrage of reinvention, with victory for the re-inventors. In developed countries today, the contest is largely over. Electric coffee-makers have won and ceramic coffeepots are now an endangered species. Contemporary coffee-makers for the home are now amazingly sophisticated. One can make coffee automatically by setting a clock, control the strength of the brew with a dial, grind the beans, steam milk, and produce espresso alongside servings of the more mundane drip coffee, which can be kept hot for hours, all from one surprisingly compact and reliable machine.

So while ceramic coffeepots are on their way to extinction, the old-fashioned teapot still rules. Some simple changes have survived. Combined cup and teapot sets still endure, as do stackable teapots for catering. The teapot's survival has to do with the different mechanics of brewing tea and coffee. While you can make a superb cup of coffee by running scalding water through ground coffee beans, tea needs to steep or soak for some time in the water to liberate the oils that give it its taste. But that does not explain the reason why the teapot is still with us in the 21st century, unchanged from when Ming scholars brewed the first blush of tea in the exquisite silky-brown Yixing teapots five hundred years ago.

In part it is the tea bag that rescued the teapot from the same fate as the coffeepot. Making tea from loose leaves is mainly for the connoisseur these days. Disposing of the tea leaves can be messy, although there are solutions to this but they only complicate the process for the average tea drinker, and would have doomed this kind of brewing in the long run. However, I am enough of a romantic to believe that even in this day and age, the teapot's resistance to improvement has to do with more than its efficiency alone. Mystique is part of its survival.

The emotional associations of the teapot are potent. It is friendly to use, warm to the touch, plump, and comforting. Surely by now, if we were prepared to surrender the teapot to brute efficiency, we would have found a way to brew tea automatically. The resistance

has not come from the impossibility of the task but from resolute affection for this little pot and its long history of dispensing cheer in our lives. The teapot has settled back into its position of security, free from the meddlers, and seemingly destined to be with us, still unchanged, for the foreseeable future. However, this makes our tour of some of the attempts of the past to improve and simplify tea-making all the more intriguing and hilarious.

Early Morning Waiter, 1930. Automatic tea-making machine invented and built by Ron Grumble

Unknown manufacturer,
Staffordshire, England
Cadogan Teapot
c. 1870. Glazed ceramic
6.25 x 8.25 x 4 in.
(15.9 x 21 x 10.2 cm)

Opposite:

Above: Worcester Porcelain
Company, England
Double Spouted Teapot
c. 1880. Porcelain
6 x 8.75 x 6.75 in.
(15.2 x 22.2 x 17.1 cm)

Below: Staffordshire, England
Double Spouted Teapot
c. 1901. Glazed agate clay
7.75 x 10 x 6 in.
(19.7 x 25.4 x 15.2 cm)

Right: Abram Allware Ltd.
(Burslem, England)
"Cosy" Safety-Lid Teapot
c. 1923. Ceramic
4.9 x 5.25 x 4.5 in.
(12.4 x 13.3 x 11.4 cm)

Opposite below:

Royles Self-Pouring Teapot
c. 1886. Silver plate
7 x 8.25 x 5.5 in.
(17.8 x 21 x 14 cm)
Produced by James Dixon
and Sons, Sheffield, England,
for R. R. Royles: inscribed
J. R. Sculey, Ironmonger,
Worthington

Royles Self-Pouring Teapot
c. 1886. Ceramic and
silver plate lid
8.25 x 8.85 x 5.5 in.
(21 x 22.5 x 14 cm)
Produced by Doulton
and Co., England, for
R. R. Royles, England

Below: Earl of Dundonald
Simple Yet Perfect
(2 teapots) c. 1908.
Blue and white earthenware
6 x 6.25 x 4.1 in.
(15.2 x 15.9 x 10.4 cm)
Invented in 1901 by the 12th
Earl of Dundonald with an
improved version in 1905

Left: Christopher Dresser
Picnic Tea Set assembled
for storage

Below: Christopher Dresser
Picnic Tea Set
1879. Silver plate
Teapot 3.5 x 7 x 4 in.
(8.9 x 17.8 x 10.2 cm)
Designed for Jonathan Hokin
and John Thomas Heath,
Birmingham, England

Opposite:

Above left: G. Kellum et Cie.
(Paris, France)
Traveling Tea Maker
c. 1925. Gold wash over
sterling silver
Assembled (six items in all):
5.75 x 6.5 x 4.25 in.
(14.6 x 16.5 x 10.8 cm)
Compacted for travel:
2.75 x 4.25 x 3.75 in.
(7 x 10.8 x 9.5 cm)

Above right: G. Kellum et Cie.
(Paris, France) **Traveling Tea
Maker** unassembled

Below: Unknown
manufacturer, Germany
Traveling Tea Maker
c.1950. Stainless steel, plastic
5.1 x 5.5 x 4.5 in.
(13 x 14 x 11.4 cm)

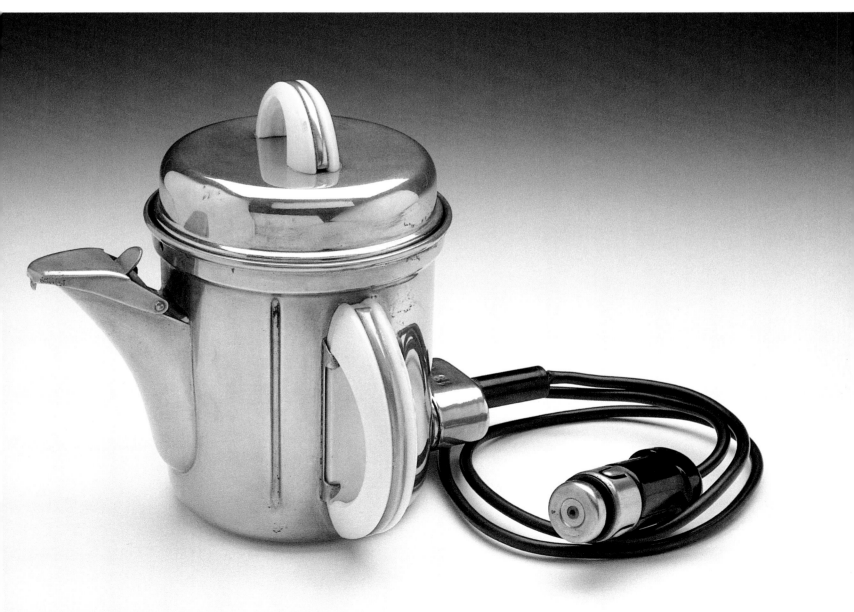

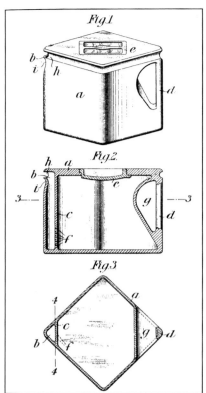

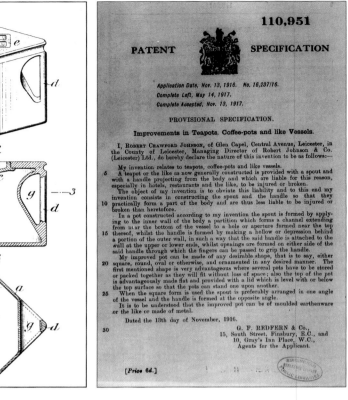

110,951

PATENT ![crest] SPECIFICATION

Application Date, Nov. 13, 1916. No. 16,237/16.
Complete Left, May 14, 1917.
Complete Accepted, Nov. 13, 1917.

PROVISIONAL SPECIFICATION.

Improvements in Teapots, Coffee-pots and like Vessels.

I, ROBERT CRAWFORD JOHNSON, of Glen Capel, Central Avenue, Leicester, in the County of Leicester, Managing Director of Robert Johnson & Co. (Leicester) Ltd., do hereby declare the nature of this invention to be as follows:—

My invention relates to teapots, coffee-pots and like vessels.
A teapot or the like as now generally constructed is provided with a spout and with a handle projecting from the body and which are liable for this reason, especially in hotels, restaurants and the like, to be injured or broken.
The object of my invention is to obviate this liability and to this end my invention consists in constructing the spout and the handle so that they practically form a part of the body and are thus less liable to be injured or broken than heretofore.
In a pot constructed according to my invention the spout is formed by applying to the inner wall of the body a partition which forms a channel extending from near the bottom of the vessel to a hole or aperture formed near the top thereof, whilst the handle is formed by making a hollow or depression behind a portion of the outer wall, in such a way that the said handle is attached to the wall at the upper or lower ends, whilst openings are formed on either side of the said handle through which the fingers can be passed to grip the handle.
My improved pot can be made of any desirable shape, that is to say, either square, round, oval or otherwise, and ornamented in any desired manner. The first mentioned shape is very advantageous where several pots have to be stored or packed together as they will fit without loss of space; also the top of the pot is advantageously made flat and provided with a lid which is level with or below the top surface so that the pots can stand one upon another.
When the square form is used the spout is preferably arranged in one angle of the vessel and the handle is formed at the opposite angle.
It is to be understood that the improved pot can be of moulded earthenware or the like or made of metal.

Dated the 13th day of November, 1916.

G. F. REDFERN & Co.,
15, South Street, Finsbury, E.C., and
10, Gray's Inn Place, W.C.,
Agents for the Applicant.

[Price 6d.]

Opposite:

Above: Robert Crawford
Johnson, patent drawing
for the Cube Teapot, 1917

Below: Cube Teapots Ltd.,
Leicester, England
The Cube (various teapots)
c. 1938. Glazed ceramic
From 4.6 x 4.6 x 4.6 in.
(from 11.7 x 11.7 x 11.7 cm)
Produced by Foley and other
potteries for The Cunard
Steam Ship Co. Ltd.

Cube Teapots Ltd., Leicester,
England
Cube Tea Set
c. 1925. Silver-plated and
hammered metal
Teapot: 3.4 x 3.25 x 3.25 in.
(8.6 x 8.3 x 8.3 cm)
Produced by A. J. Wilkinson
Ltd, Birmingham, England

Opposite: Eric van Eimeren
Quake-Proof Teapot
1992. Whiteware, steel
11 x 12 x 5.8 in.
(27.9 x 30.5 x 14.7 cm)

Eric van Eimeren
Oiler
1996. Vitreous redware, steel
6.5 x 13.6 x 7.75 in.
(16.5 x 34.5 x 19.7 cm)

Chapter 5

Assemblage and Mutant Materials

The title of this chapter is inspired partly by "Mutant Materials in Contemporary Design," the groundbreaking 1997 exhibition at the Museum of Modern Art, New York, by Paula Antonelli. The exhibition set off an inquiry into materials, their conventions, and appropriateness. However, the term "mutant" takes us here in a very different direction. All of the objects in the MOMA show were meant to function. Most of these do not. They are made up of the most unlikely materials: Native American jewelry, dollar bills, beads, ceramic shards, fluorite, rock crystal, granite, bathroom hardware, cups, bottle caps, olive oil cans, coconut shells, and ostrich eggs.

This collection of eccentric objects is by a mix of known artists with sophisticated intent and anonymous outsiders making "airport art" and personal curiosities. Except for a few of the works, such as the *Coconut Teapots*, they all represent exceptional craft skills combined with a restless and inventive imagination. We see this in the work of Peter Grieve, for instance, with his strange teapot creatures, a porcupine and an armadillo, created with household brushes and recycled

tin but put together with masterful ease. Ismael Gonzalez shows the same virtuosic craftsmanship, sculpting with olive oil cans, and Rick Ladd with bottle caps.

Our fascination with the form of the teapot can, however, blunt our inquiry into the artist's broader message. Harriete Estel Berman's *Caffeinated Arrangement Black or White* is part of the artist's assault on the kitchen and its appliances as well as on those who see tea as no more than a caffeine delivery device. No housewife's helper is safe from her satiric scrutiny. A crock pot opens to reveal a doll's-house. A cake mixer powered by a high-speed electric drill conceals a cosmetic case. Writer Charlotte Moser refers to Berman as "a woman artist who has looked into the face of domestic engineering and lived to tell the tale, unashamedly, from the perspective of woman. The teapots, blenders and bathroom scales, food processors and sewing machines that she fabricates exaggerate, in excruciating perfection, the utter banality of the 1950s existence experienced by mothers of middle-class Baby Boomers."

Unlikely as some of these material choices might seem, there is great beauty in some oddball media. David K. Chatt's *Karilyn's Tea Service* is an exquisite composition of teapot, tray, cup, saucer, spoon, and even sugar cubes in a vivid, bright palette of colors. Weaving and crochet is employed in three pieces, two of which are conventional enough – Kate Anderson's homage, *Lichtenstein Teapot*, and Irene C. Reed's *Tension Tamer Teapot Tote*. Zoe Morrow's *Five on The Line* is made up of strips of money – five-dollar bills, to be precise – woven with great skill into a pattern that optically distorts the image of the banknote.

Detail: Ron Baron
Dear Mother
2000. Teacups, plates, metal, sugar, polyurethane, sculpty clay
56 x 22 x 22 in.
(142.2 x 55.9 x 55.9 cm)

Assemblage of found objects is behind the
work of Lynn Mattson. Each teapot is created out of
a collection of shards and artifacts. In this case, *Western
Teapot* takes on cowboys and Indians with an arrow-
head finial. It also includes real silver and turquoise
Navaho jewelry, given to Mattson by a friend with whom
she later had a spat, and thus the gift was consigned
to the teapot. Conversely, Hap Sakwa, Keiko Fukazawa,
and Richard Milette all manufacture their own debris
with which to assemble teapots. The most complex

single piece in this grouping is unquestionably *Dear
Mother* by Brooklyn, New York, sculptor Ron Baron.
Baron is a scavenger when it comes to his material
choices. He has made sculpture from floating buoys,
from copper pennies, and from dinner plates. It was
the latter work that brought him to the attention of
the New York art world. In the 1980s he began to exhibit
vase "shapes" assembled from plates. He created them
by piling plates up, one on top of the other, drilling
a hole through the center of each plate, and securing
them all together. He stacked plates of various diameters
so that when viewed in silhouette, the compilation took
on a classical vase shape. But the plates had an added
dimension. Each work had a theme. One, for instance,
dealt with travel and every plate in this totem was
a souvenir plate from a different city. This creates
a teasing curiosity for the viewer because one knows
that this theme runs throughout the twenty to fifty
plates that make up a work and yet only the top plate
can be seen.

Dear Mother incorporates many of Baron's
approaches to sculpture. On the one hand it is a mixture
of objects: the pedestal for the work is made from
hundreds of teacups. The teapot is made from wire

and plates, and is coated with sugar that has been sealed with polyurethane to preserve the wonderfully fragile, crystalline formation of the surface. The plates are a collective homage to "mother," a reference to the teapot as one of the symbols of maternal authority. "Who shall be mother?" was the traditional way of framing the question of who would pour the tea. The sugar ("one lump or two") adds a certain sentimental sweetness to the title yet the odd, asymmetrical skin around the teapot is visually difficult and gives the piece a toughness that informs the viewer that this is not just another Hallmark Mother's Day moment.

Ostrich eggs, quail eggs, and coconut husks make for excellent teapot forms even if their functionality is questionable. This work from the 1950s was made by outsider artists and low-skill craftspeople turning out products for tourist shops. By contrast the late 19th-century Chinese teapots that are carved from various rock types are magnificent examples of technical skill by anonymous artists. Teapots carved in rock are very rare, particularly those in chalcedonic quartz or jasper. The rock illustrated here is known as "tea colored," giving the carver's choice of the teapot form particular meaning in this case.

Harriete Estel Berman
Caffeinated Arrangement Black or White
2000. Pre-printed recycled material, brass rivets, aluminum rivets, Penguin Caffeinated Mints
Teapot: 10.5 x 12.25 x 7.5 in. (26.7 x 31.1 x 19.1
Cups and saucers: 2.625 x 5.25 x 5.25 in. (6.7 x 13.3 x 13.3 cm)

Left: Ismael Gonzalez
Teapot
1997. Olive oil tins
and mixed media
8.5 x 7 x 4 in.
(21.6 x 17.8 x 10.2 cm)

Below: Rick Ladd
The Perfect Brew
1997. Bottle caps
and collage on wood
13.4 x 11 x 5.75 in.
(34 x 28 x 14.6 cm)

Right: Peter Grieve
Porcupine Teapot
1999. Wood, tin, bristle
8 x 18.75 x 6 in.
(20.3 x 47.6 x 15.2 cm)

Below: Peter Grieve
Armadillo Teapot
1997. Recycled tin
6.75 x 16.25 x 5 in.
(17.1 x 41.3 x 12.7 cm)

David K. Chatt
Karilyn's Tea Service
1997-98. Beading
Teapot: 7.125 x 8.75 x 5.5 in.
(18.1 x 22.2 x 14 cm)

Opposite above: Zoe Morrow
Five on the Line
1999. US paper currency
8.5 x 10.25 x 2.375 in.
(21.6 x 26 x 6 cm)

Opposite below left:
Irene C. Reed
Tension Tamer Teapot Tote
1997. Crocheted fiber
15 x 12 x 9 in.
(38.1 x 30.5 x 22.9 cm)

Opposite below right:
Kate Anderson
Lichtenstein Teapot
1999. Waxed linen
8.4 x 8.4 x 2.5 in.
(21.3 x 21.3 x 6.4 cm)

Hap Sakwa
Marilyn Monroe
1994. Ceramic and mosaic
8.9 x 7.75 x 5 in.
(22.6 x 19.7 x 12.7 cm)

Right: Lynn Mattson
Western Teapot
1993. Ceramic, mixed media,
Native American jewelry,
and found objects
9.375 x 8.25 x 7.5 in.
(23.8 x 21 x 19.1 cm)

Below: Richard Milette
Teapot
1992. Glazed earthenware,
decals
10.25 x 13.25 x 6.75 in.
(26 x 33.7 x 17.1 cm)

Keiko Fukazawa
Tea-Bag Teapot
1995. Whiteware
9.75 x 16 x 8 in.
(24.8 x 40.6 x 20.3 cm)

Opposite: Ron Baron
Dear Mother
2000. Teacups, plates,
metal, sugar, polyurethane,
sculpty clay
56 x 22 x 22 in.
(142.2 x 55.9 x 55.9 cm)

Opposite:

Above: Anonymous,
South Africa
Teapot
c. 1995. Ostrich egg,
wood, metal
8 x 6.6 x 5 in.
(20.3 x 16.8 x 12.7 cm)

Below: Anonymous, Hawaii
Two Coconut Teapots
c. 1990. Coconut, wood, horn
7.25 x 8.25 x 5 in.
(18.4 x 21 x 12.7 cm)
5.8 x 7.6 x 5.2 in.
(14.7 x 19.3 x 13.2 cm)

Anonymous
Quail Egg Tea Set
c. 1900. Quail eggs, metal
Teapot: 1.5 x 1.5 x 1.5 in.
(3.75 x 3.75 x 3.75 cm)

Left: Anonymous, China
Teapot
c. 1850. Rock crystal
3.5 x 7.5 x 4.5 in.
(8.9 x 19.1 x 11.4 cm)

Below: Anonymous, China
Teapot
c. 1875. Brown jasper
4.5 x 7.5 x 3.5 in.
(11.4 x 19.1 x 8.9 cm)

Anonymous, China
Teapot
c. 1850. Purple fluorite
5.75 x 8 x 4.75 in.
(14.6 x 20.3 x 12.1 cm)

Chapter 6

Things Aren't What They Seem

The tradition of potters playing with clay's chameleon-like character – in other words, the way in which it can take on the camouflage of another material – began long before the introduction of the teapot. Celadon glaze was created in China to mimic jade. Luster glazes were developed in 7th-century Mesopotamia to mimic precious metals. Even before this there were more rudimentary attempts at deceiving the eye. The birth of the teapot is tied to mimicry as the earliest of these potters made realistic nuts, fruit, and wood from their fine stoneware clays and incorporated them into the teapot form to give the objects symbolic meaning. Given the playful nature of the teapot and its readiness to be a container of whimsy and wit, this game between eye and mind seems to be a perfect match.

In the early 18th century when porcelain was first introduced to Europe, the potters had no formal tradition to apply to this clay body, which was chemically, temperamentally, and plastically so different from either stoneware or earthenware. The forms that looked good in earthenware and stoneware did not suit this "white gold" so the manufactories often took teapots from the best

silversmiths in Germany, France, and Britain, molded them and reproduced them in clay. The potters of Stoke-on-Trent, Staffordshire, took this a step further and developed a commercial luster that applied an even, metallic film to the surface. Soon they were producing what was known as "poor man's Sheffield," teapots molded from silver originals with over-glaze, silver-colored luster. This enabled more humble households to serve tea in what looked like the grand and expensive silver services from Sheffield that were used in wealthier homes.

Playing with metallic surfaces is something that glaze science does well, as can be seen in the work of Susan Beiner's *Screw Ecstasy*. Steven Montgomery's *Carburetor* and *V8* teapots display the fact that clay will even readily mimic iron and steel industrial forms, while Margaret Realica's teapot in the slightly disturbing shape of a detonator mimics metal to an extraordinary degree.

In the case of David Hutchinson's *Fill 'R Up, Teapots for Men*, the game with material reality is a little more complex. In this case, making an earthenware teapot look like a gasoline can removes the supposed effeteness of the teapot and makes it the kind of testosterone-charged object from which a mechanic could safely pour tea without injury to his manhood.

However, taking on this aesthetic has proven to be a dilemma for contemporary artists, particularly those working in craft-based media: potters, silversmiths, weavers, glassmakers. One of the golden rules of the Arts and Crafts movement, out of which the present day crafts movement has evolved, was the "truth to materials" dictum of the movement's pioneering philosophers, John Ruskin and William Morris. The belief was based on the idea that a material had a "natural" aesthetic which, through tradition and the physicality of the material,

Detail: Ah Leon
Acacia Trunk Teapot
1995. Hand-carved stoneware
18 x 19.5 x 4.5 in.
(45.7 x 49.5 x 11.4 cm)

Ah Leon working on a teapot, Taiwan

Opposite above:
Steven Montgomery
V8 Teapot
1995. Whiteware
7.75 x 14.1 x 6.25 in.
(19.7 x 35.8 x 15.9 cm)

Opposite below:
Steven Montgomery
Carburetor
1999. Painted whiteware
8.5 x 13 x 4 in.
(21.6 x 33 x 10.2 cm)

was the appropriate way to use that medium. Disguising this "naturalness" was considered a cardinal sin and an act of material dishonesty.

The impetus for this thinking was the war against "art manufacture" by industry, and the decay in craftsmanship and taste that it promoted. Now as we look back at this, we can recognize both the moral necessity at the time for this ideal and the restrictions that it placed on artists to draw from a material whatever they saw or felt, regardless of whether it ascribed to the "natural qualities" of the material – at best a subjective notion. Added to this, modernism took the same stance as Messrs Ruskin and Morris and so trompe l'oeil offended the pre-1950s art establishment as much as it did the crafts.

The changes came in the 1960s with the arrival of one of postmodernism's first commercially successful movements, variously referred to as Hyper-Realism, Super-Realism (or Superrealism), Photo-Realism, Sharp Focus Realism, Illusionistic Realism, and even by the misnomer, Magic Realism. This was promoted by an array of artists, painters Chuck Close and Mel Ramos, sculptors John De Andrea and Duane Hanson, and ceramists Marilyn Levine and Richard Shaw, finding its defining moment in Sidney Janis's legendary survey exhibition "Sharp Focus Realism" at his New York gallery in 1971.

Eight years later this movement in ceramics was given the title "Super-Object," a label that has produced controversy and debate ever since. The title was applied to those objects that used a particularly refined, high-process approach to imitate other materials in clay – at once a dazzling conceit and a baffling deceit. By the end of the 1970s the interest in this style had become all-pervading and Richard Shaw, one of the Super-Object's most persuasive practitioners, was arguably the most influential and imitated ceramist in America. His striding teapot figure, *A Sunny Cameo for Tea,* shows his mastery of this time-consuming, complex technique. Shaw is able to convey a real sense of poetry, molding everyday objects and converting them by means of painterly skill into a new reality. Paul Dresang, with his erotic "zippered leather" teapots, follows this stylistic lead.

Wood is one of clay's favorite disguises. Gail Ritchie's *Birch Bark* teapot set demonstrates this well, as does Gregory Roberts's compelling but optically odd rendition of a woodgrain surface. Michael Cohen plays with René Magritte's famous painting of a pipe, *Ceci n'est pas une pipe,* and adds a few more dimensions to the joke. The pipe is not a pipe but a teapot and its material is not wood, as it seems, but ceramic. However, it is Ah Leon who has taken this device into a new realm of scale and ambition. He produced two of the remarkable "wood" teapots shown in this book, using a needle to replicate the textural striations of the wear that wind, water, and age produce on wood surfaces. The work makes the convincing point that this style, once considered a debased technique suitable only for commercial novelties, has a wider horizon and greater power for the artist than was ever imagined.

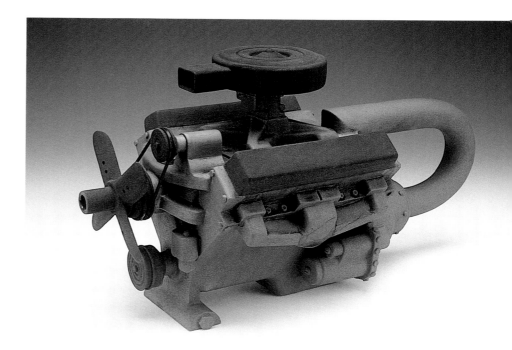

Susan Beiner
Screw Ecstasy II
1997. Glazed ceramic
10.25 x 12.25 x 6.25 in.
(26 x 31.1 x 15.9 cm)

Opposite: Margaret Realica
Detonator T
1997. Porcelain
9.25 x 9.25 x 3.75 in.
(23.5 x 23.5 x 9.5 cm)

David Hutchinson
Fill 'R Up, Teapots for Men
1995. Earthenware
Teapot: 15.25 x 13.25 x 6.25 in.
(38.7 x 33.7 x 15.9 cm)

Opposite: Richard Shaw
A Sunny Cameo for Tea
2000. Porcelain with decals
and overglaze
34.5 x 16 x 10.6 in.
(87.6 x 40.6 x 27 cm)

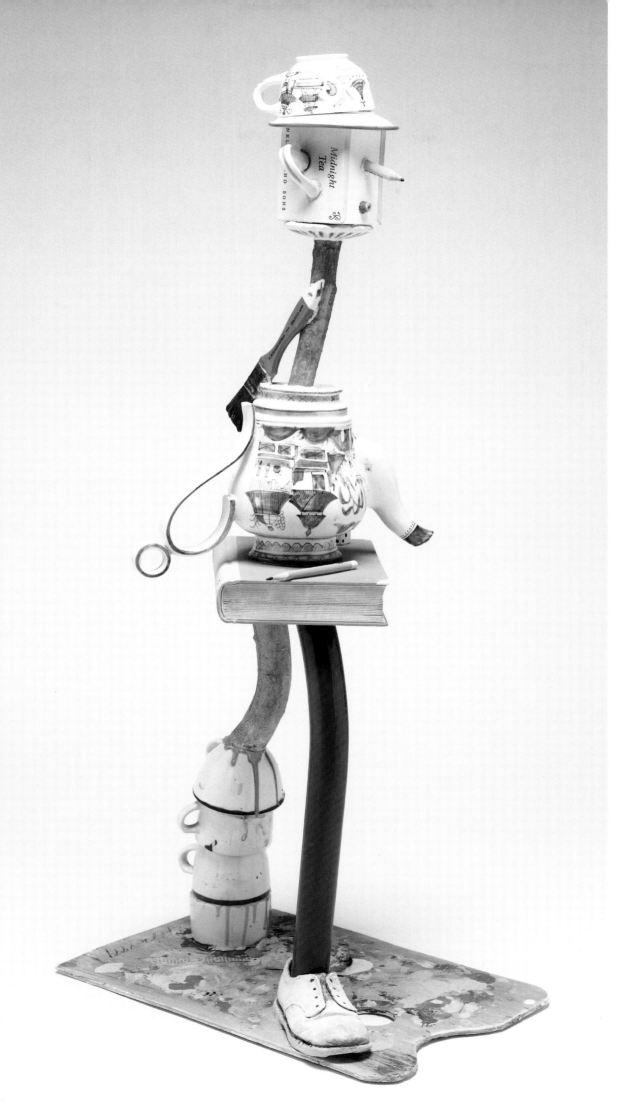

Right: Paul Dresang
Bag
1994. Porcelain
14.4 x 15.25 x 8.25 in.
(36.6 x 38.7 x 21 cm)

Below: Michael Cohen
Ceci n'est pas une pipe
1993. Ceramic
7.25 x 12.25 x 4.25 in.
(18.4 x 31.1 x 10.8 cm)

Right: Gregory Roberts
Yellow Teapot No. 1
2000. Carved, honeycombed
ceramic and low-fire glazes
12.75 x 8.25 x 7.5 in.
(32.4 x 21 x 19.1 cm)

Below: Gail Ritchie
**Birch Bark Teapot
with Cup and Saucer**
1983. Low-fire ceramic
Teapot: 8.25 x 6 x 2.75 in.
(21 x 15.2 x 7 cm)

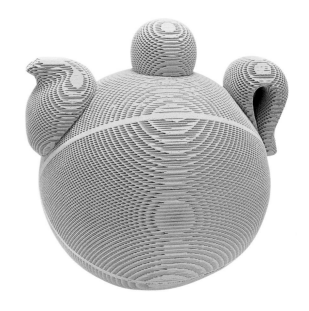

Ah Leon

Horizontal Log Teapot

1992. Stoneware and stains

12 x 25 in.

(30.5 x 63.5 cm)

Opposite: Ah Leon

Acacia Trunk Teapot

1995. Hand-carved stoneware

18 x 19.5 x 4.5 in.

(45.7 x 49.5 x 11.4 cm)

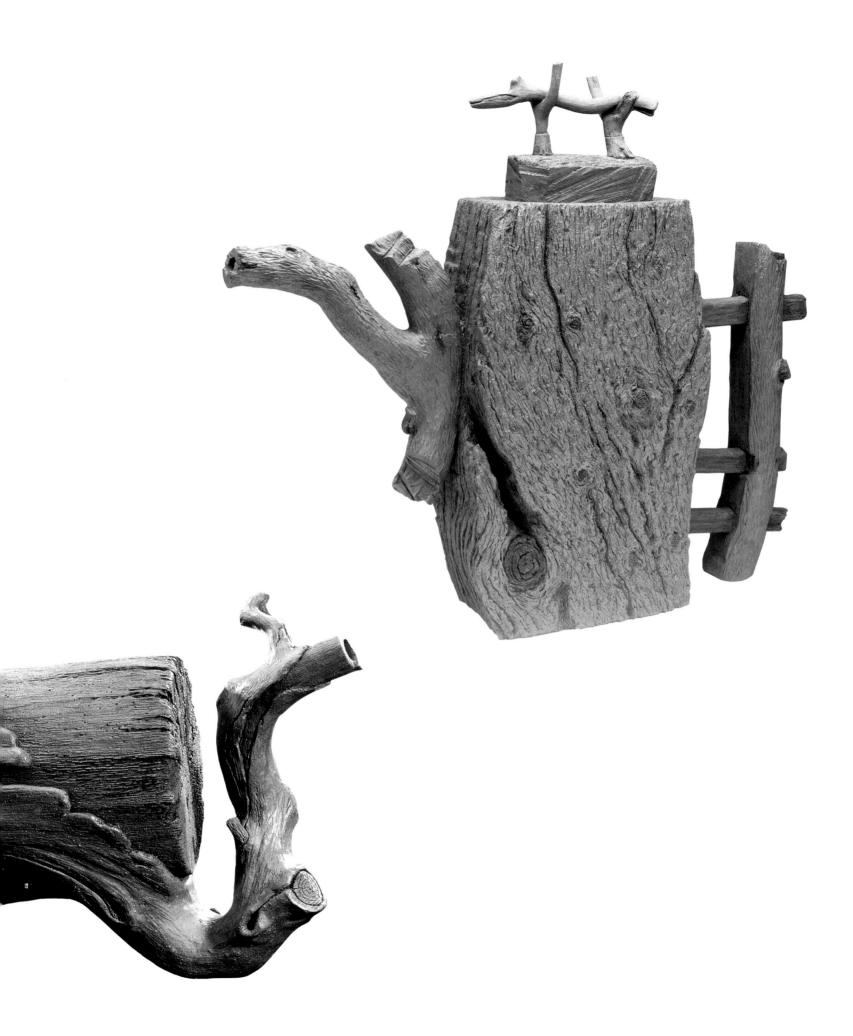

Chapter 7
Teapot Organicus

The potter's love of organic form goes back to man's first container when the gourds and baskets woven from bark, reeds, and grass were the examples of what clay vessels could be. Sometimes gourds and baskets were actually used to help the primitive potter mold the vessel shape before the potter's wheel arrived and altered the dynamics of form making. Although it is partly a fallacy, the ceramic world tends to see organic inspiration as the "natural" aesthetic for vessels made of clay, given its primal elements of mud, water, and fire. In fact there is no natural aesthetic for ceramics. It can take a classical cultural form as easily as one that derives from nature. But there is a special affinity here for the potter that has been explored and exploited for millennia.

Vegetables, fruit, rock, and wood have provided teapot makers with endless inspiration. Pomegranates covered in nuts (offering the blessing of numerous offspring to the teapot's owner), bundles of bamboo, peaches, and the citron fruit were favorites of the Yixing artisans. British potters quickly picked up on these themes and there are few 18th-century teapots that are more distinctive than the cabbage, pineapple, and cauliflower teapots produced around 1750 by Wedgwood, Greatbach, Whieldon, and scores of other potters in Stoke-on-Trent, Staffordshire.

The reason for the development of these teapots, and in particular the cauliflower teapot, is that the ceramic factories had developed a new palette – a brilliant green glaze and a new class of off-white earthenware that was known as creamware or Queensware. (The latter name came from a commission to Wedgwood from Queen Charlotte in 1765 to produce the first earthenware dinner service for British royalty. Earthenware was previously considered to be for peasant use while only gold, silver plate, and porcelain were fine enough for the royal table.)

In looking for something that would make sense for a palette of cream and green, English makers hit upon the cauliflower. As is so often the case in ceramics, aesthetic breakthroughs tend to be preceded by technical ones. In the early 19th century the growing popular interest in botany produced exquisite hand-painted tea services in porcelain and bone china with delicately china-painted, botanically correct renderings of flora. Sea life was also of interest and the Irish porcelain factory, Belleek, became famous for producing exceptional tea services based on sea shells that are frighteningly light, and thin-walled to the point of transparency, with a delicate edging in green to offset the quality of the white bone china.

By the end of the century, infatuation had turned from the scientific to the naturalistic, and then to the erotic with the advent of Art Nouveau. This was a sexually charged style with distinctive whiplash undulations that found favor in Continental Europe and in particular in Belgium and France where it originated. Albert-Louis Dammouse's lyrical undecorated teapot in the shape of fennel, designed for the French Sèvres Porcelain Manufactory, gives some sense of the fluid linearity of this short-lived but influential style.

Contemporary artists have taken to this subject matter in all of its expressions – part naturalism, part fantasy. Kathleen Royster's *Thorns* reminds us that nature's vegetal fecundity has a certain cutting edge and, while not expressing the full rapaciousness of *Little Shop*

Detail: Richard Allen Wehrs
**Tea Shrine # 3
(Artichoke)**
1998. Ceramic
22 x 15.5 x 9.5 in.
(55.9 x 39.4 x 24.1 cm)

of Horrors, this perfectly modeled ceramic piece has its own sense of fury, as does the spiky fugue that makes up Richard Allen Wehrs's *Tea Shrine,* an organic extravaganza of curling, armored leaves. The same sense of beauty and sexual unease can be seen somewhat more subtly in the work of Kim Dickey and Bonnie Seeman. On the other hand Adrian Saxe, the reigning master of postmodern excess, brings a hedonism to the lowly vegetable. His renditions of the cabbage and the ginger root show his affinity to the grandeur of 18th-century court porcelains.

Taken out of the kitchen and placed in the museum, these everyday vegetables take on an unaccustomed glamour. *Untitled Ewer (Gold Cabbage)* has three different gold glazes, each one more sumptuous than the last. The glaze on the main form is particularly remarkable and has the soft, powdery texture of newly applied gold leaf. The main form is studded with faux rubies, not just as an act of deliberate überkitsch, but also to designate the object as a thing of power and influence – the same role that early European porcelains played in the first half of the 18th century (the ownership of these porcelains indicated class and culture, and their purchase was also a means of gaining favors from the kings and princes who owned Europe's early porcelain houses).

Saxe's game with *Untitled Ewer (Ginger Root)* is a little different. Here the way that the various roots cast shade gives tonal variations to the overall glaze, creating shifting gold clouds across the surface. But by hanging small plastic fish on the work, the artist reminds us of

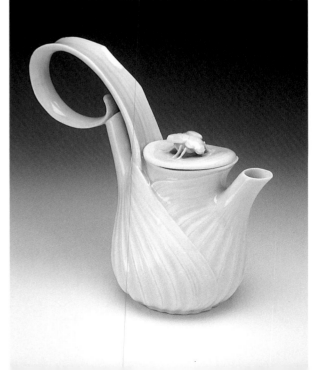

Opposite above:
Adrian Saxe
in his studio, Los Angeles

Opposite below:
Albert-Louis Dammouse
Fennel Teapot
c. 1898. Porcelain
6.9 x 7.6 x 3.6 in.
(17.5 x 19.3 x 9.1 cm)
Designed for Sèvres
Manufactory, France

Right: Belleek Porcelain
Factory, Ireland
Neptune Tea Set
c. 1880. Porcelain
Teapot: 5 x 8.4 x 5.25 in.
(12.7 x 21.3 x 13.3 cm)

the ginger root's similarity to coral growths – a witty transposition.

Mi-Sook Hur, Michael and Maureen Banner, and David Gignac all create a feeling of openness with their metal teapots – through spacious handles in the first three artists' work, and in the light base of metal twigs that holds Gignac's *Celestial Teapot* in the air. The latter teapot takes its title from a popular herbal tea, "Celestial Seasonings," and makes a truly celestial point: a hand-blown glass "moon" floats enigmatically through tree branches made of forged steel.

Kari Russell-Pool's teapot also has transparency but it is combined with extreme fragility. This teapot is unashamedly in pursuit of a delicacy and prettiness *sans* irony, *sans* paradox, *sans* symbolism or any other deep conceptual intent. The openwork glass is handled with breathtaking deftness, the tracery of green glass studded with pink roses and a bird perched at its center. It is a homage both to nature and to the decorative panache of glass, highlighting two of the art world's most controversial issues – beauty and craft skill.

Kathleen Royster
Thorns
1996. Ceramics
Teapot with tray:
5.75 x 10 x 9.5 in.
(14.6 x 25.4 x 24.1 cm)

Bonnie Seeman
Hojala (Rhubarb)
1997. Ceramic
5.5 x 7.5 x 6.25 in.
(14 x 19.1 x 15.9 cm)

Opposite: Richard Allen Wehrs
Tea Shrine # 3 (Artichoke)
1998. Ceramic
22 x 15.5 x 9.5 in.
(55.9 x 39.4 x 24.1 cm)

Right: Kim Dickey
The Fall Pot
1995. Porcelain
7 x 9 x 6 in.
(17.8 x 22.9 x 15.2 cm)

Below: Kari Russell-Pool
Untitled
1997. Lampworked glass
13.25 x 16.25 x 9.5 in.
(33.7 x 41.3 x 24.1 cm)

Adrian Saxe
Untitled Ewer
(Gold Cabbage),
1996. Porcelain
10.1 x 8.6 x 4.25 in.
(25.7 x 21.8 x 10.8 cm)

Opposite: Adrian Saxe
Untitled Ewer
(Ginger Root)
1995. Porcelain and
stoneware
19.5 x 10 x 6.5 in.
(49.5 x 25.4 x 16.5 cm)

David Gignac
Celestial Teapot
1999. Hand-blown glass,
forged steel
20.25 x 12.5 x 11 in.
(51.4 x 31.8 x 27.9 cm)

Above: Michael and
Maureen Banner
Melon
1997. Sterling silver
9.75 x 10 x 5 in.
(24.8 x 25.4 x 12.7 cm)

Left: Mi-Sook Hur
Winter Tree Teapot
1998. Pewter, maple
15.5 x 10 x 4.5 in.
(39.4 x 25.4 x 11.4 cm)

Chapter 8
Tannic Ark

The first "animal" to grace a teapot was the dragon. It appears in late Ming dynasty imperial porcelain teapots from Jingdezhen. This choice was particularly appropriate as in Chinese mythology the dragon lived in both water and clouds, and was the bringer of rain: liquid pouring from its mouth, then, was an elegant use of symbolism.

One of the dragon teapots shown here is part of an exotic silver service that is an over-the-top, fin-de-siècle tribute to the cult of Chinoiserie. Another teapot is made by one of the great legends of 20th-century ceramic art, Beatrice Wood. She began her art career in 1917 amongst the New York Dadaists, producing drawings in Marcel Duchamp's studio (he was briefly her lover). In 1932, at the age of forty, she decided to become a potter and soon established herself as the international queen of luster pottery, mastering an unpredictable but hedonistic technique in which she reigned supreme until her death in 1998 at the age of 105. Her animal figures reveal her casual approach to craft and her determination to remain what she termed "a sophisticated naïve."

The *Grotesque Figural Teapot* by Wallace Martin similarly belongs to the category of mythic beasts. Wallace was the eldest of the four eccentric Martin brothers, the British fin-de-siècle masters of salt-glazed pottery. Renderings of gothic creatures were popular in the Victorian era and Wallace developed an early taste for this aesthetic; while in his teens he served as an apprentice modeler for the Houses of Parliament in London, assisting in carving gargoyles and neo-Gothic ornament. The crouching beast shown here is the finest of his teapots, a form type that is rare within Wallace's oeuvre, dominated as it is by bird-shaped jars.

Other animal subject matter can be found imbedded deep in the long history of ceramic art. For instance Ken Ferguson's series of teapots exploring the parable of the tortoise and the hare arrived by a complex route. Ferguson, on his regular visits to the encyclopedic collection of British ceramics at the Nelson Atkins Museum of Art in Kansas City, had begun to notice the frequency with which the hare turned up in English slipware pottery of the medieval period. Then he noticed similar motifs of the springing hare turning up in Spanish slipwares, and in Japanese and Chinese porcelains. It was finally the nightly appearances of jackrabbits at his summer home in Wyoming that pushed him to use the hare in his own work. Drawn to the animal's power, grace, and virility, Ferguson saw that the leaping animal could be a handle on one of his pots or, in more static form, as in the teapot shown here, the long ears could support a vessel and become its base. The hare was long considered a suitable subject for pottery decoration because its long, lithe body allowed for quick, economic, and calligraphic rendering that suited the speed and simplicity of slip painting.

The lamb may be as charming a subject as the rabbit, but Mary Engel gives it a very different feeling to Ferguson's muscular creations; Engel's teapot is built out of plastic dice.

Akio Takamori's beast teapot, with its crouching figural finial, is a little more difficult to place. The shape is of an unspecific animal but drawn into the form is the figure of a naked woman looking out of the beast that encloses her.

Detail: Wallace Martin, Martin Brothers, Southall, England
Grotesque Figural Teapot
1896. Salt-glazed stoneware
6.75 x 12 x 6.75 in.
(17.2 x 30.5 x 17.2 cm)

Above: **Ken Ferguson**
in studio, Kansas City,
Kansas, 1990

Below: **Beatrice Wood**
at around 100 in her studio,
Ojai, California

Opposite clockwise from top
left: Belleek Porcelain Factory,
Dragon Teapot (also known
as the **Chinese Tea Urn** and

the **Dragon Kettle**)
c. 1880. Bone china and
overglaze with silk handle
15 x 11.2 x 9 in.
(38.1 x 28.4 x 22.9 cm)

Wallace Martin, Martin
Brothers, Southall, England
Grotesque Figural Teapot
1896. Salt-glazed stoneware
6.75 x 12 x 6.75 in.
(17.2 x 30.5 x 17.2 cm)

Beatrice Wood
Dragon
1980. Luster glazed earthenware
7.75 x 12.5 x 5.75 in.
(19.7 x 31.8 x 14.6 cm)

Kuhn and Komatz,
origin unknown
Dragon Tea Service
1900. Silver
Teapot: 9.2 x 8.7 x 7 in.
(23.4 x 22.1 x 17.8 cm)

Many animals bring with them a great deal of symbolism. We have conferred values, myths, and human characteristics upon the creatures with which we cohabit this world. Dogs and cats asleep at the hearth are as much a part of the domestic ambience as teapots. Dogs loom large and have an important role in Jack Earl's narrative sculpture and also in his teapot work. Jack Thompson's dogs are strictly surreal and have cabbage bodies and an eerie vulnerability. David Regan, on the other hand, covers his teapots in graphic sgrafitto images, cutting back through a layer of black slip on a white porcelain body, much as one would prepare a woodblock for printing, and illustrating complex narratives in which the dog plays a central part. Armilla Burden's poodle uses the dog-house as a finial and, in the case of Lynn Mattson's *Canine Tea*, feline and canine are blended into one artwork that denies the usually ambivalent and adversarial relationship that man's two best friends enjoy in real life. The cat serving as a mount for man is an unlikely but surprisingly frequent motif in teapots, with the animal providing the body and the human figure the lid, as in Sergei Isupov's surrealist feline.

Other creatures have found vogue amongst teapot makers simply because they suit the form. Birds, in particular, have this quality. Their plump bodies, beaks, and tails provide the main volumetric form, the spout, and the handle, while their heads often serve as the lids or finials. The feathered kingdom has inspired teapot transformations since the 18th century. French Art Deco designer Edouard-Marcel Sandoz created tea sets with Limoges Porcelain that are amongst the definitive ceramic designs of this playful jazz-age period. The Northern Californian artist Annette Corcoran has made a specialty of creating exquisitely resolved teapots that feature birds of every description – wrens, robins, parrots, owls, and turkeys, their plumage depicted with felicitous detail.

Monkeys were a popular subject matter in decorative arts of the mid- to late 19th century because of Charles Darwin. His theory of evolution created a fascination with the ape family that found decorative expression in ceramics, bronze statuary, and other media. The British craze for a new type of pottery called majolica (which had nothing to do with the tin glazed wares after

which it was named) produced some of the finest Victorian work in this genre. Striking a more contemporary note, Wayne Ferguson invokes the silver screen star of the ape family in *Kong Dynasty Teapot* with its banana spout.

Finally, food and frogs were for many years the core elements of a fantasy culture created by the playful artist David Gilhooly, one of Funk master Robert Arneson's first students. Before Gilhooly found art at college, he was first a biology and then an anthropology major; both elements coalesce in his work. In the teapot shown here, frogs and Oreo cookies gambol with gay abandon in a lively party that takes place in a pool of hot tea.

Ken Ferguson
**Tripod Teapot
with Turtle & Hare**
1997. Stoneware
21 x 14.6 x 11 in.
(53.3 x 37.1 x 27.9 cm)

Right: Mary Engel
Lamb Teapot
1997. Ceramic, dice
10.25 x 11 x 4.5 in.
(26 x 27.9 x 11.4 cm)

Below: Akio Takamori
**Man on Giant Beast
Teapot**
1990. Ceramic
11.25 x 12.75 x 4.75 in.
(28.6 x 32.4 x 12.1 cm)

Right: Jack Earl
Dog
1993. Glazed earthenware
10.75 x 11.75 x 6.125 in.
(27.3 x 29.8 x 15.6 cm)

Below: David Regan
Dog Head Teapot
1999. Porcelain
7.8 x 13.8 x 7 in.
(19.8 x 35.1 x 17.8 cm)

Opposite:
Armilla Marie Burden
Poodle Teapot
1995. Ceramic
14.1 x 8.75 x 6.25 in.
(35.8 x 22.2 x 15.9 cm)

Opposite:

Above: Jack Thompson
Whistling Capimorta
Teapot
1980. Whiteware, glaze,
acrylic paint
8 x 10 x 5.6 in.
(20.3 x 25.4 x 14.2 cm)

Below: Sergei Isupov
The Cat Walks Alone
for Herself
1997. Ceramic
13.5 x 20 x 8 in.
(34.3 x 50.8 x 20.3 cm)

Lynn Mattson
Canine Tea
1998. Mixed media,
shards, glass
Teapot: 15.6 x 13.5 x 6.4 in.
(39.6 x 34.3 x 16.3 cm)
Cup: 9.75 x 5 x 4 in.
(24.8 x 12.7 x 10.2 cm)

Annette Corcoran
Grey Bird Teapot
1985. Porcelain
4 x 6 x 4 in.
(10.2 x 15.2 x 10.2 cm)

Opposite:

Above: Edouard-Marcel
Sandoz
Bird Tea Set
c. 1925. Porcelain
Teapot: 6.4 x 6.5 x 4 in.
(16.3 x 16.5 x 10.2 cm)
Designed for Theodore
Haviland, Limoges, France

Below: Annette Corcoran
Parrot Head Teapot
1989. Porcelain
5.5 x 4.5 x 3.5 in.
(14 x 11.4 x 8.9 cm)

Opposite: Wayne Ferguson
Kong Dynasty Teapot
1997. Earthenware
12.25 x 11 x 7.5 in.
(31.1 x 27.9 x 19.1 cm)

David Gilhooly
Oreo and Frog Teapot
1990. Glazed earthenware
9 x 16 x 10 in.
(22.9 x 40.6 x 25.4 cm)

Chapter 9
Architectural Tea

Tea has its own tradition of architecture. The Japanese tea house, for instance, is one of the ultimate expressions of a minimalist, meditative structure. In the 19th century, British tea shops created their own cosy style of interior architecture. No lesser figure than Charles Rennie Mackintosh was attracted to this genre, producing his now famous Willow Tea Room in Glasgow. In the 1920s, vernacular architecture became popular and teapot-shaped buildings, often made cheaply and sited on heavily traveled highways, appeared in America, vying for attention with other, equally eccentric rest stops in the shape of dinosaurs, bears, and sombreros. Given this brief overview, it is no surprise that the subject of architecture has been one of the teapot's favorite targets.

Some of the earliest white salt-glazed house teapots in 18th-century British pottery are thought to have been modeled on the homes of the owners of the potteries or, in some cases, their wealthier patrons. Wedgwood created a majestic tea and dinner service for Empress Catherine the Great that was decorated with hand-painted views of England's stately homes and castles. More recently, the most enduring of the novelty teapots – a major craze in the 1920s and 1930s, as they still are today – has been the English cottage garden

teapot, which is still produced all over the world in vast quantities and unlimited variations.

Something about this subject matter, its innate Britishness, its rootedness, and charming domesticity struck a chord in the mass market that has resonated ever since, outselling the crinoline ladies, the Old Woman in the Shoe, Humpty Dumpty, and most of the other novelty teapots combined. Joan Takayama-Ogawa's *Rose Parade Float: Teatime at Great Aunt Tillie's* refers to both this tradition and the famed Pasadena Rose Parade in California but expands the garden and frees the form from its rigid rectangular mold.

The inventiveness of this format seems to be endless. When Newport Pottery was looking for a design that would appeal to the Canadian export market, Clarice Cliff hit upon a movable shelter – the Teepee or Wigwam teapot – which proved to be a great success.

Richard Allen Wehrs has created a temple or shrine for the teapot, lavishing on this object his usual obsessive detailing.

Lidya Buzio's trio of painted roofscape teapots come from a distinctive modernist lineage. This Uruguayan artist was raised in the Montevideo home and studio of the great South American painter Torres García, known for his geometric abstractions of cityscapes. Influenced by his work, she moved to New York City and began to paint the roofscapes of Soho, Wall Street, and Midtown on various vessel forms. She painted these directly onto the unfired clay with under-glazes and then burnished them. This is a process whereby the surface is rubbed continuously with a smooth object, a spoon or a small stone, until the clay surface has been compacted and a light sheen achieved. After the firing, Buzio added a final sealing coat of wax.

This is a technique frequently used in traditional and early South American pottery. Buzio's teapot forms are rare and have a particularly painterly quality,

Detail: Michael C. McMillen
Teapot Tower Sculpture
2000. Wood, metal
95 x 20 x 30 in.
(241.3 x 50.8 x 76.2 cm)

Right: **Michael C. McMillen**
in his studio

Below: **Lidya Buzio**
in studio, New York, 1987

Opposite above: three
of Gloria and Sonny Kamm's
five grandchildren in
a playhouse in the form
of a teapot: the largest teapot
in the Kamms' collection
108 x 120 x 96 in.
(274.3 x 304.8 x 243.8 cm)
Produced by Presley Homes
for HomeAid Auction

Opposite below: teapot-
shaped building near Seattle

integrating the handles and spouts into the urban
vista. The roofscapes often feature that leitmotif of
the New York skyline, the water tower. Raymon Elozua's
water towers are teapots more by default than intent.
They deal with a concern he has for ageing industrial
structures.

The same sensibility, but on a much grander
scale, can be found in the work of the sculptor Michael C.
McMillen. McMillen is a master of architectural nostalgia,
creating imaginary structures, painstakingly constructed
from wood and metal. They are made with a scaled-
down realism and careful attention to the smallest
detail. *Teapot Tower Sculpture* stands nearly six feet
high and is crowned by a water tower/teapot. McMillen's
works evince a precariousness and vulnerability not often
associated with architecture.

Robin Kraft's *Silver Silo: Indiana Archetype* and
Dan Anderson's *Teapot* both take on industrial buildings
but from a very specific industry – that of agriculture.
These works are drawn from the Midwestern "grain belt"
of America. While Kraft's buildings feel new and
optimistic, Anderson's cluster of corrugated iron

structures rendered in a handsome wood-fire palette give off a quite different mood. Anderson's teapot speaks of the decline of the small farmer in America. These agricultural buildings can be seen throughout America's rural landscape but are increasingly found rusted, dilapidated, and abandoned, as large-scale farming gobbles up family-owned tracts of land.

Finally the work of Sheila Ferri and Dennis Meiners takes us away from the gritty, decaying reality of Anderson into a realm where the house and the teapot seem to enter a landscape of dream, fantasy, and surreal abstraction – house, hearth, and teapot consumed into one entity.

Various manufacturers,
Staffordshire, England
English Cottage Teapots
c. 1930. Earthenware
From 5.6 x 8.2 x 5.8 in.
(from 14.2 x 20.8 x 14.7 cm)

Opposite

Above: Lidya Buzio
All burnished earthenware
Roofscape, 1993
4 x 11 x 7.5 in.
(10.2 x 27.9 x 19.1 cm)
Roofscape, 1990
8 x 9.75 x 6.75 in.
(20.3 x 24.8 x 17.1 cm)
Roofscape, 1991
4.5 x 9.125 x 6.75 in.
(11.4 x 23.2 x 17.1 cm)

Below: Joan Takayama-Ogawa
**Rose Parade Float: Teatime
at Great Aunt Tillie's**
1998. Ceramic
9.25 x 15.75 x 18 in.
(23.5 x 40 x 45.7 cm)

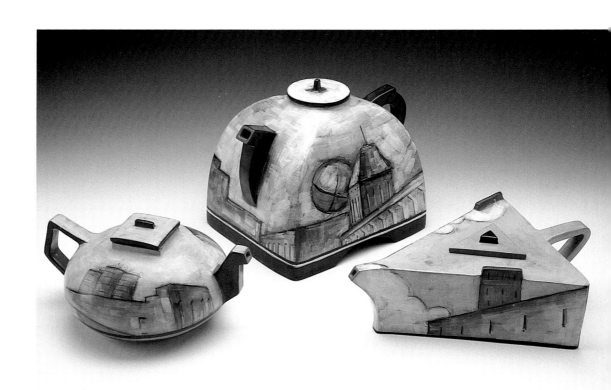

Opposite:

Left: Raymon Elozua
Water Tower
1999. Ceramic, metal
11.75 x 8 x 7.3 in.
(29.8 x 20.3 x 18.5 cm)

Right: Richard Allen Wehrs
Teapot Shrine # 1
1996. Ceramic
34 x 16.25 x 16.25 in.
(86.4 x 41.3 x 41.3 cm)

Michael C. McMillen
Teapot Tower Sculpture
2000. Wood, metal
95 x 20 x 30 in.
(241.3 x 50.8 x 76.2 cm)

Right: Dennis Meiners
Teapot
1992. Ceramic
22 x 15 x 7.7 in.
(55.9 x 38.1 x 19.6 cm)

Below: Daniel J. Anderson
Teapot
1992. Wood-fired stoneware
7.5 x 15.5 x 5 in.
(19.1 x 39.4 x 12.7 cm)

Right: Robin Kraft
**Silver Silo: Indiana
Archetype**
1998. Double-walled
oxidized silver
4.5 x 8.75 x 4.5 in.
(11.4 x 22.2 x 11.4 cm)

Below: Sheila Ferri
Wire
1999. Wire construction
11.5 x 8.75 x 7.7 in.
(29.2 x 22.2 x 19.6 cm)

Chapter 10

Tea on the Go

Tea is always a pleasure but as a tea drinker myself I know that one of the most romantic and delicious moments for imbibing comes when one is traveling. Tea served in a silver pot in the wood-paneled dining room of the Milan to Rome express train, or delivered by a uniformed steward on a cruise ship while one reclines on a deck chair soaking up the last rays of late afternoon sun, has an extra frisson. The tea seems to taste better, its aroma more evocative and its impact more brisk and refreshing. The recipe for this special quality is easy to define. It is an equal mix of the romance of tea with the romance of travel – a perfect tannic cocktail.

Real teapots designed for use by the traveler have already been discussed earlier. The teapots here represent the actual means of travel – planes, trains, and automobiles – and convert these vehicles into some of the most charming and whimsical of all the teapot shapes. Again, a certain convenience of form also gives this genre its design momentum. Teapots emerge quite happily out of tanks, battleships, saucers, and, remarkably, even scooters. Trains share with teapots an additional cipher, which is the emission of clouds of steam.

Cars have produced all kinds of teapot shapes, from the charm of the Sadler and Sons T42 Racing Car of the 1930s to its streamlined American version, a slinky,

abstracted red sedan produced by Hall China. The Russian artist Sergei Isupov enjoys working with the car as his "vessel" but, unlike the work of Sadler and Hall, his intent is not to charm. Isupov has evolved a narrative style of illustration, which he explores in both two and three dimensions, that is awash with psychological undercurrents. As Edward Kienholz demonstrated so graphically in his 1950s masterwork, *Back Seat Dodge*, the car is a potent symbol. It is linked to a host of issues of which transport is perhaps the least emotive: privilege, prestige, illicit sex, male aggression, phallic substitution, freedom of movement, speed, risk, road rage, and glamour.

Isupov, who now lives and works in the United States, makes exquisitely formed porcelain teapots with a radical spirit of invention. His teapots take on the form of cars, people, animals, and mythic beasts, and often combinations of all three. This is combined with a gift for tightly-etched painted illustration using sharp, acid colors. Isupov's two cars, *Cancelled Vacation* and *Businessmen Prowling*, are both charming and – when one begins to ponder more deeply the journeys involved and their end purpose – disturbing.

Tommy the Tank takes the shape of a World War I tank and was a popular novelty teapot in the 1920s and 1930s. Its bright orange and yellow coloration and cheerful looking driver make this mobile weapon seem almost endearing and non-military. When World War II broke out, the pottery noticed that "Billy," the nickname given to the driver, looked very much like Winston Churchill and so, despite the early vintage of the tank itself, the teapot found a renewed market in the 1940s as a patriotic symbol. George Walker's teapot tank, overloaded with passengers both under- and over-nourished, is at first glance a delightful and playful object. But the name of this piece, *Arms Dealer*, makes it clear that it is a critique of a cruel trade. The gun-barrel spout that emerges so rudely between the legs of the soldier is not meant to deliver tea so much as greed and death.

Detail: George Walker
Arms Dealer
1995. Ceramic
17.5 x 16.25 x 7.75 in.
(44.5 x 41.3 x 19.7 cm)

Sarsaparilla Deco Designs,
Japan
T42 Racing Cars
designed c. 1930. Ceramics
Each: 4.5 x 9.25 x 4.5 in.
(11.4 x 23.5 x 11.4 cm)
Replicas of original by
Sadler and Sons, England

The *Queen Mary* teapot is a handsome late-1930s entry to the novelty teapot world. It could be purchased on board the ship although the staff did not serve tea in this caprice. The official tea service on board was the Cube, illustrated on p. 76.

Marilyn Lysohir surprises with her large *Battleship Teapot*, which, while pretty enough in its pastel-colored camouflage, has a decidedly threatening and un-tea-like aura, bristling with guns and aggression. It seems appropriate that Lysohir, as a sideline, has created "Cowgirl Chocolates", which are rich and creamy but leave behind as their aftertaste the unexpected bite

of cayenne pepper. Susan Thayer, by contrast, does not perplex or challenge. She is a romantic and her work has a sentimental edge that evokes the busy decorative milieu of the Victorian era. Much the same mood of the *objet de vertu* can be sensed in the precious and refined use of various metals and wood in Jean Neeman's *Tea on the Go.*

David Damkoehler's *Fast Lane Teapot* and Brett Price's *Untitled Teapot* abstract the vehicle. Theirs is not a literal statement. What they do is explore the notions of beauty, power, and vigor of speed that vehicles project in the hearts of contemporary society.

Right: Sergei Isupov
Businessmen Prowling
1996. Porcelain, ceramic stain
9.25 x 13 x 6.4 in.
(23.5 x 33 x 16.3 cm)

Below: Sergei Isupov
Cancelled Vacation
1996. Porcelain, ceramic stain
6.5 x 11.5 x 3.75 in.
(16.5 x 29.2 x 9.5 cm)

Right: Carlton Ware, England
Red Baron
c. 1939. Ceramics
5.5 x 8.6 x 6.75 in.
(14 x 21.8 x 17.1 cm)

Below: Unknown
manufacturer, England
Tommy the Tank Teapot
c. 1935. Ceramic
6 x 9 x 4.75 in.
(15.2 x 22.9 x 12.1 cm)

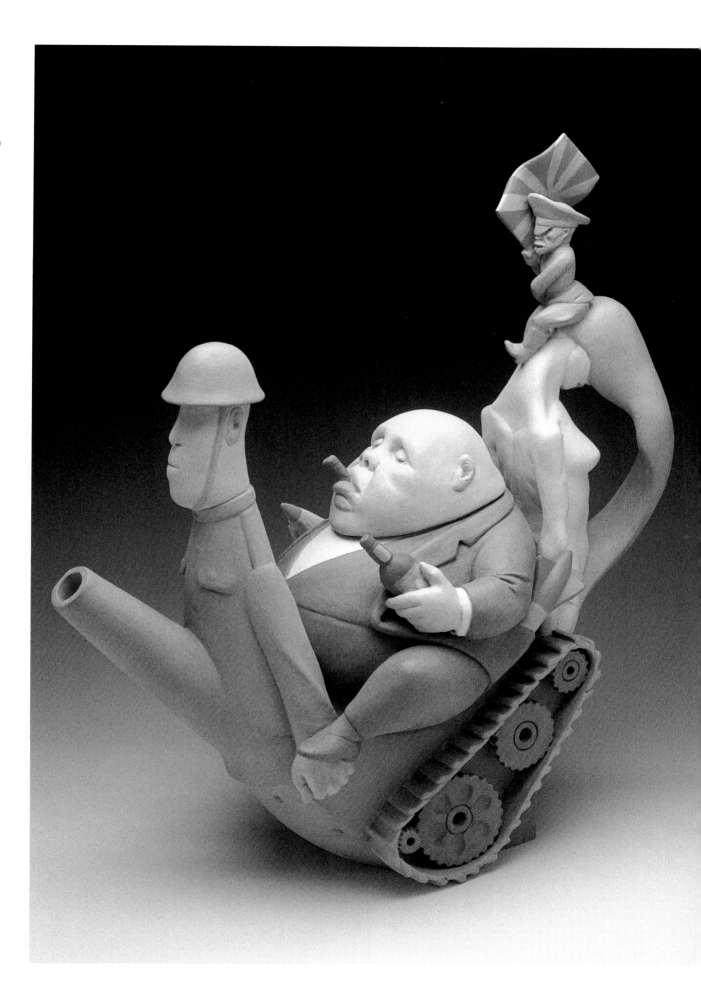

Right: tea being served
on the Queen Mary, c. 1940

Below: Midwinter
of Burslem, England
Queen Mary
1938. Ceramic
5 x 9.5 x 3.75 in.
(12.7 x 24.1 x 9.5 cm)

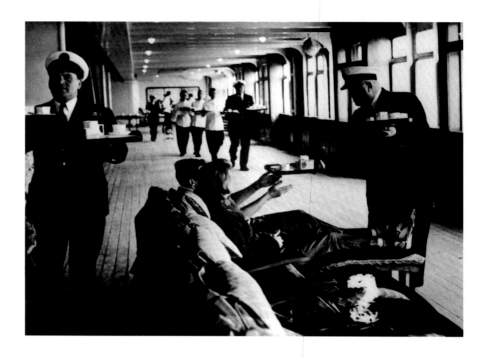

Right: Marilyn Lysohir
Battleship Teapot
1987. Ceramic
8.25 x 24 x 3.75 in.
(21 x 61 x 9.5 cm)

Below: Susan Thayer
Dream Boat
1999. Porcelain
7.25 x 11 x 4 in.
(18.4 x 27.9 x 10.2 cm)

Opposite: Jean Neeman
Tea on the Go
1994. Silver, wood,
copper, brass
8.4 x 7.75 x 4.5 in.
(21.3 x 19.7 x 11.4 cm)

Right: Brett Price
Untitled Teapot
1994. Chromed steel
12.6 x 17.5 x 5.25 in.
(32 x 44.5 x 13.3 cm)

Below: David Damkoehler
Fast Lane Teapot
1998. Stainless steel
10.9 x 19 x 7.1 in.
(27.7 x 48.3 x 18 cm)

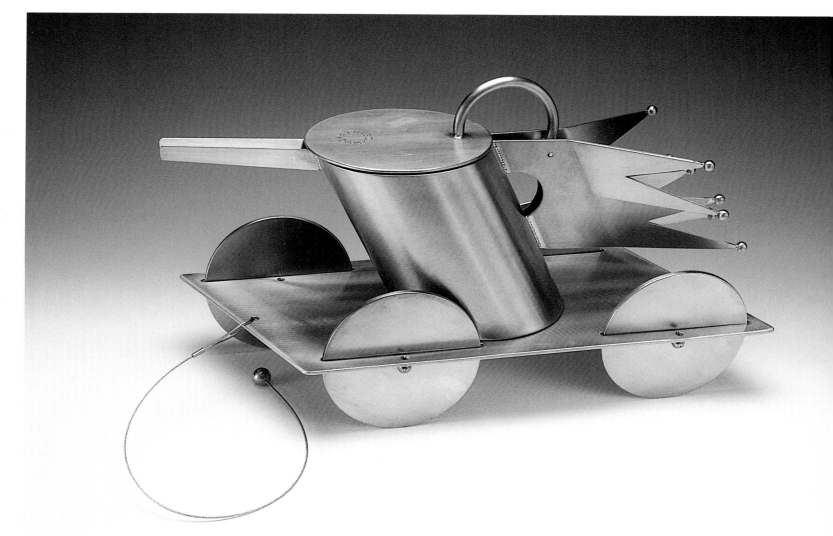

Chapter 11
I'm a Little Teapot

The "Teapot Song" sums up one of the strongest urges amongst artists who make teapots, which is to render this little pouring vessel in anthropomorphic form. Most believe that the song is a piece of Victorian folk music, conceived in some forgotten kitchen and passed on through the years. In fact, it was not composed until the spring of 1939 by George Harry Sanders, a musician and composer, and usurpers beware, is still in copyright. The story of the song and how it came to life is told charmingly by Richard Sanders, the composer's son, in his autobiography *Reflections of a Teapot* (New York, 1972). George Sanders was, like many New Yorkers in the music business in the 1930s, searching for ways to survive in a decade when the effects of the Depression had not yet passed. He wrote the song with the assistance of Clarence Kelley, his partner in their small music publishing enterprise on Broadway and 52nd Street. It was conceived with two goals – publishing and selling the ditty itself to the world at large, and assisting Kelley and his wife with a local problem they were facing at the dance school they ran for children.

The Kelley school taught the "Waltz Clog," an enormously popular tap routine that had the advantage of being easy to master, thus giving the young dancers the illusion of technical proficiency that made parents happy to pay the fees. However, the couple had many younger dancers, the "tots," for whom it was difficult to provide any sort of dance that would make it seem as though they were on their way to becoming Ruby Keeler or Fred Astaire. The school recital was coming up soon and this was of concern to Sanders as well because he was to be the piano accompanist for the event. "I'm a Little Teapot" proved to be the perfect solution for the tots, requiring minimal skill and exploiting the talent for pantomime with which most children seem to be born.

The "Teapot Tip" became all the rage in the thousands of dance schools in America and abroad, and Sanders had his hit. In the process, generations of girls and boys participated in this ritual of becoming spouted vessels. Of course this song did not kick off the craze of making human-shaped teapots – a fascination that dates back to the 18th century – but it did give the teapot its anthem, and certainly inspired Cheryl Frances's 21st-century visual riff – a wonderfully glitzy assemblage of metal and plastic. Christina Smith works exclusively in silver and her approach to the figure is more related to drawing, meticulously cutting her shapes and emphasizing silhouette over form. Over the centuries, tens of thousands of teapots have reflected this anthropomorphic urge and tea has poured from the fans of ladies of the court, out of the hollow legs of sailors, out of a corgi stuck into Queen Elizabeth II's ear, from noses, elbows, and other body parts that should remain unnamed.

The Chinese tended not to make teapots in human form. Animals, particularly the mythic dragon, were popular but using the human figure in this context presented them with problems of protocol. The West, on the other hand, was quick to embrace the idea. Meissen, the West's first "true" porcelain factory, founded in 1707 by King Augustus the Strong, made some memorable early works in this style, and these were copied throughout Europe. By the mid-18th century,

Detail: Cheryl Frances
I'm a Little Teapot
2000. Metal teapot, metal objects, doll parts, silver and other paint
11.5 x 9 x 7 in.
(29.2 x 22.9 x 17.8 cm)

the fascination with the teapot in human form had been launched and has remained a staple of teapots, whether for the purpose of use, novelty or art, ever since.

Staffordshire at the beginning of the 19th century was the largest center for ceramic production in the world and was producing these teapots in every shape, size, and gender. The most popular of the late 19th-century teapots were Minton's modestly scaled majolica pieces. These wares were developed by Minton's artistic director, Leon Arnoux. Lively sculptural forms were painted with colored glazes to give a vibrant polychromatic surface to the finely modeled teapots, most of which were designed by French sculptors who had fled France in the second revolution.

English majolica is widely collected and has been influential. Akio Takamori's teapot of a crouching man, with a painfully placed handle and spout that seem to run through his body, is a conscious homage to the Minton forms. Takamori's strong figural gesture is explored differently by Anthony Bennett's *Running Man with Greyhound* and Adrian Arleo's teapot of two layered figures. Takamori's *Multi-Figure Teapot*, in common with graffiti artist Keith Haring's *Spirit of Art*, creates a flurry of human activity.

Takamori is a Japanese ceramist who, after apprenticing as a production potter in Japan, came to the United States, studied with Ken Ferguson at the Kansas City Art Institute and at Alfred University in New York State. He remained in the United States, settling with his family in Seattle, and has become one

of the most respected and inventive ceramists in the country, known first for his melding of drawing, painting, and form in his so-called "envelope vessels," and later for his figurative sculpture.

Leslie Rosdol, John Frame, and John McNaughton all strike an edge of angst in their work. Rosdol's small liquidly glazed head is in anguish, Frame's figure is pensive and withdrawn (the spout can hardly be described as generous) while McNaughton's teapot, entitled *Where's My Bloody Tea*, strikes an irritable and intemperate note, out of keeping with the quietude of afternoon tea. The gritty work by Hungarian sculptor, Laszlo Fekete, and his *Resurrection of a Broken Teapot*, is similarly in a more serious vein. This piece, with its tower of thorny, fired, metallic clay concludes in two gnarled, blackened hands holding up a fractured teapot and assorted teapot parts that are pure and white. The work is a metaphor for the cultural wars that have wracked Hungarian society for over five hundred years.

For Joyce J. Scott, the performer and multi-media artist, the notion of culture wars have a different context. As both an African-American and a woman, many of her works take on both race and gender. The use of beads enables her to address both issues. Beadwork is generally, if wrongly, considered women's work. Beads also have connections to Africa. Zulu maternity aprons and Ndebele wedding aprons have been of particular inspiration to Scott. In African beadwork pieces, a system of communication codes through color and pattern has been set up that allows the women to sew beaded love letters to their intended suitors or new husbands. Writing of Scott's work in *Joyce J. Scott: Kickin' it with the Old Masters* (Baltimore, 2000), Mary Jane Jacob remarks that the artist manipulates beads "as a way of directly using color, of capturing and transmitting light, a way of creating representational image, a way of materializing sensual form," all within a medium that is universal and accessible.

While Michael Lucero's *Eye Ohr* teapots are designed to be shown high and mimic an old-fashioned optician's shop sign, his *Female Roman Statue* Reclamation Series, like Fekete's *Resurrection of a Broken Teapot*, is a rescuer, taking from the piles of cultural detritus we leave behind. In this series, Lucero finds broken works ranging from garden statuary to damaged African art and then "reclaims" the work, replacing the missing parts with a ceramic element of his own invention. Painting plays a major role in the impact of Lucero's work just as it does with Russian artist, Sergei Isupov, and Arizona ceramist, Kurt Weiser. The latter uses virtuoso china-painting skills on the teapot form to reprise a mood of the Magic Realists of the 1920s and 1930s. Weiser paints a vista of soft-core surrealism, exotic birds, jewel-like flowers, panoramas of lush tropical vegetation, and erotic figures. In other works he repaints canvases by masters of the German school and other painters he admires onto his teapots in a subdued sepia palette.

John de Fazio, a New York City artist with a love of kitsch and visual anarchy, also uses painting to bring his *Sincere Geisha Teapot* to life, adding for good effect a shocking pink wig to his bottle figure. This teapot has the rare distinction of having been exhibited at the Venice Biennale, an exalted high-art arena in which teapot sightings are rare.

Lastly, a spout is a spout is a spout. Or is it? In the 1930s another one of the novelty teapot hits was the crinoline teapot, which used the voluminous skirts of the 18th-century lady as a container for tea. In the 1970s and again in the 1990s Adrian Saxe returned to this idea and through strategic placement of the spout asked a number of questions about gender and the presumed female identity of the teapot (the dress on *The Little Shepherdess Teapot*, incidentally, is not that

of a shepherdess but is a reference to Marie Antoinette's penchant for playing this role). Rose Misanchuk takes two fine arts icons, Gainsborough's *Blue Boy* and Reynolds's *Pinkie*, and deals saucily with their spouts. The last word, however, belongs to the inventive Tony Bennett, whose *Red Devil* teapot provides a large-scale, exuberant, sculptural conclusion to this exploration.

In a sense the makers who produced this community of teapot people are a cross between tea masters and the Greek god Prometheus. Prometheus made men of clay and then stole fire from heaven to spark them into life. His fate for this activity was far from pleasant. Zeus had him chained to a mountain where every day a vulture ate his liver from his body only to have the liver grow back again at night. These latter-day Promethean artists have more humble goals. They no longer have to risk the ire of the gods when they play with fire, and they do not enrage by seeking flesh and blood life for their creations: they merely seek – and achieve – the vitality of animation.

Akio Takamori
in his studio, Seattle, Washington

Akio Takamori
Crouching Man
1989. Ceramic
6 x 8.5 x 4.25 in.
(15.2 x 21.6 x 10.8 cm)

Opposite:

Above: Keith Haring
Spirit of Art
c. 1990. Ceramic
8 x 8.5 x 5 in.
(20.3 x 21.6 x 12.7 cm)
Designed for Villeroy
& Boch, Germany

Below left: Minton, England
Chinaman Teapot
c. 1874. Glazed
earthenware (majolica)
5.25 x 7.5 x 3.75 in.
(13.3 x 19.1 x 9.5 cm)

Below right: Akio Takamori
Multi-Figure Teapot
1987. Porcelain
6.5 x 6.25 x 5 in.
(16.5 x 15.9 x 12.7 cm)

Right: Anthony Bennett
Running Man with Greyhound
1993. Whiteware
10.75 x 15.1 x 4 in.
(27.3 x 38.4 x 10.2 cm)

Below left: Adrian Arleo
Teapot
1995. Ceramic
7.5 x 15 x 4.5 in.
(19.1 x 38.1 x 11.4 cm)

Below right: Christina Smith
Untitled Teapot
1996. Sterling silver
7.9 x 5.5 x 5 in.
(20.1 x 14 x 12.7 cm)

Cheryl Frances
I'm a Little Teapot
2000. Metal teapot, metal
objects, doll parts, silver
and other paint
11.5 x 9 x 7 in.
(29.2 x 22.9 x 17.8 cm)

Opposite:

Above: Leslie Rosdol
Ariel
1991. Ceramic
7 x 4.5 x 2.25 in.
(17.8 x 11.4 x 5.7 cm)

Below: John W. McNaughton
Where's My Bloody Tea
c. 1993. Wood
25 x 16.5 x 16.25 in.
(63.5 x 41.9 x 41.3 cm)

John Frame
Untitled
2000. Wood, bronze,
steel, found objects
21.5 x 8 x 9 in.
(54.6 x 20.3 x 22.9 cm)

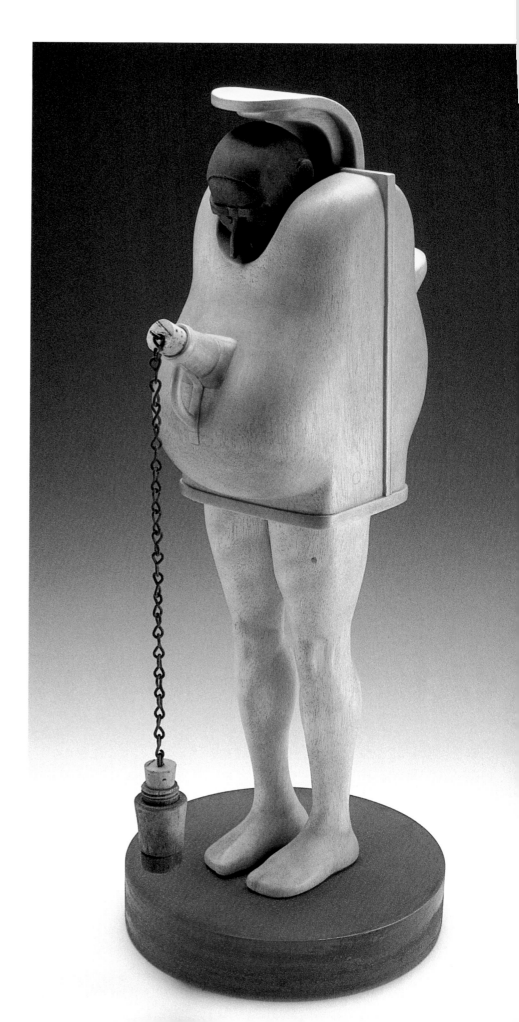

Laszlo Fekete
**Resurrection
of a Broken Teapot**
2000. Porcelain and
stoneware
26 x 11.5 x 11 in.
(66 x 29 x 27.9 cm)

Joyce J. Scott
Testicular Teapot
1997. Diagonal bead
weaving
11.5 x 9 x 6.75 in.
(29.2 x 22.9 x 17.1 cm)

Left: Michael Lucero
Eye Ohr, New World Series,
1993. Wheel-thrown and
altered glazed earthenware
Each teapot: 12 x 17 x 8 in.
(30.5 x 43.2 x 20.3 cm)

Below: Sergei Isupov
Invisible Support
1997. Porcelain, ceramic stain
14 x 10 x 8 in.
(35.6 x 25.4 x 20.3 cm)

Michael Lucero
Female Roman Statue,
Reclamation Series,
1996. Ceramic with glazes,
plaster with paint
47.5 x 16.4 x 12 in.
(120.7 x 41.7 x 30.5 cm)

Opposite: John de Fazio
Sincere Geisha Teapot
1989. Glazed, molded and
altered whiteware, nylon wig
24 x 20 x 12 in.
(61 x 50.8 x 30.5 cm)

Kurt Weiser
The Bird Merchant
1991. China-painted porcelain
11.25 x 13 x 4.4 in.
(28.6 x 33 x 11.2 cm)

Right: Anthony Bennett
Red Devil
1993. Whiteware with glazes
20 x 15 x 8 in.
(50.8 x 38.1 x 20.3 cm)

Below: Adrian Saxe
Muffy
1994. Porcelain with
artificial gems
9.5 x 7.75 x 6.5 in.
(24.1 x 19.8 x 16.5 cm)
The Little Shepherdess
Teapot
1973. Porcelain with
oxblood glaze
9.1 x 9.75 x 6.6 in.
(23.2 x 24.8 x 16.8 cm)

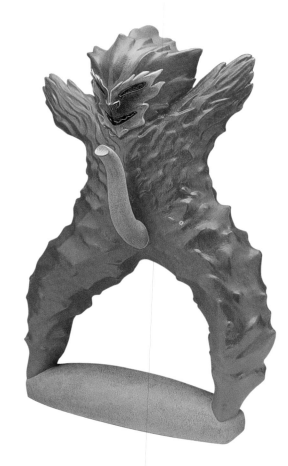

Right: Sadler and Sons Ltd.,
England
Yee Dainty Lady
(Crinoline Teapots)
c. 1935. Ceramic
7.25 x 7.1 x 5.2 in.
(18.4 x 18 x 13.2 cm)

Below: Rose Misanchuk
Blue Boy and Pinkie
1998. Ceramic
Blue Boy:
17.75 x 7.6 x 5.4 in.
(45.1 x 19.3 x 13.7 cm)
Pinkie:
16.5 x 7.75 x 8.75 in.
(41.9 x 19.8 x 22.4 cm)

Chapter 12
Celebrities and Clowns

Celebrities and clowns may seem to be an odd marriage, although the more cynical amongst us might argue that they are synonyms. What this title refers to is sub-genres of the figurative teapot: portraits of the rich, famous, and controversial, and at the other extreme of innocence, teapots inspired by the nursery and sometimes, but not always, directed towards children. In the latter section the clown looms large as subject matter.

In celebrity or portrait teapots, the motivations for immortalizing an individual as a pot, handle, and spout range from love to hate, with a sardonic halfway point between the two being the usual favored position. The *Aesthetic Teapot* by Royal Worcester Porcelain, arguably the most famous "portrait" teapot of all, comes from the darker side of this spectrum. It is a "depiction" of Oscar Wilde, even though the teapot does not directly resemble him in order to avoid any possibility of libel. However, the target of Worcester's porcelain missive is unquestionably Wilde. The teapot is said to have been designed as a gift for the composers of light operettas, Gilbert and Sullivan. They were amongst the most barbed and pointed of Wilde's satirists and skewered him as the lily-clutching Bunthorne in "Patience."

The iconography of this teapot is clear and malicious. Firstly, it is inspired by Wilde's epigram, "I find it harder and harder every day to live up to my blue china." (Wilde was a collector of ceramics.) Exactly why this statement should have been considered so scandalous and bothersome to Victorian society is difficult to understand today but there was something about its effeteness that deeply offended. Wilde was taken to task in an 1881 cartoon in the irreverent *Punch* magazine which directly inspired the Worcester teapot. In this drawing a wife and her groom, the latter clearly Wilde in this case, examine a teapot. The "Aesthetic Bridegroom" comments, "It is quite consummate, is it not?" and the "Intense Bride" answers, "It is indeed! Oh, Algernon, let us live up to it."

This is reflected in the printed legend that was applied to the foot of the teapot, parodying both Wilde's epigram and Darwin's Theory of Evolution: "Fearful consequences through the laws of natural selection and evolution of living up to one's teapot." The consequence appears to be androgyny as one side of the teapot is a man and the other side is a woman. One sports a lily and the other a sunflower, both symbols of the Aesthetic movement of which Wilde was an outspoken advocate. Together with the limp wrist, out of which the tea is poured, it is clear that the reference was to Wilde's not altogether secret bisexuality. Mean-spirited and homophobic as the teapot may have been in its time, age has leached it of its venom and, with its superb modeling, lively palette, and charming painting, it does capture the androgynous, playful, and decadent spirit of the Aesthetic movement.

At the beginning of the 20th century, Foley Pottery came up with a clever series of teapots featuring leading political figures. The design was very versatile. The same shape and color is used for all the series's subjects (shown here are President "Oom" Paul Kruger, who led

Detail: Royal Worcester Porcelain Company, Worcester, England
Aesthetic Teapot
(Oscar Wilde)
c. 1881-82. Porcelain
6.25 x 7 x 3.5 in.
(16 x 17.8 x 8.9 cm)

the South African Boer War against the British, and Lord Balfour, the former British prime minister) and over a dozen politicians were represented, each one painted in caricature. Margaret Thatcher, another British prime minister, and Ronald Reagan, the American president, are both caricatured in a series of recent teapots. They are designed by Fluck and Law (a.k.a. Luck and Flaw), responsible for "Spitting Image," a highly-rated and influential television series in England that used puppets to make fun of politics. Ronald Reagan looks suitably daffy and Margaret Thatcher's nose/spout has the required arrogance of the "iron lady" of British politics.

Yet another politician has found his way into the Teapot Hall of Fame via teapot-master Anthony Bennett, who depicts a sturdy, super-masculine, former American president, Teddy Roosevelt, mounted on his trusty steed, no doubt looking for large mammals to shoot.

Colonel Saunders, the junk food pioneer, takes on a bizarrely appropriate identity – part Southern entrepreneur and part plucked chicken – in John Revelry's *Kentucky Fried Teapot*, while Jack Earl's modern-day icon – Elvis Presley – is vividly depicted, right down to the curled lip and quiff. Noi Volkov, an artist-dissident from Russia, portrays one mythic and one real figure, using the ear as the handle for a teapot that shows

Vincent van Gogh on one side (infamous for cutting off his ear-lobe during a moment of despair) and on the other side Mona Lisa, perhaps the most famous face in the entire world, whose ears we have never seen.

Cindy Sherman is the master of disguise. Her art consists of photographs of herself dressed and made up to look like a variety of people past and present. When invited by Artes Magnus to create ceramics for their dinnerware project with the Limoges Porcelain factory, Sherman, after considerable research, decided to work with a replica of the plates, tureen, and tea service commissioned by the Marquise de Pompadour in 1756 from the Manufacture Royale de Sèvres. The Marquise was the mistress of Louis XV, who, in turn, was the founder of the Sèvres porcelain works. Sherman appears on the ceramics as Madame de Pompadour in what looks like a china-painted portrait with a traditional palette (apple green, bright yellow, royal blue, and rose) but the image is actually the result of a complex sixteen-screen printing process. As an added footnote to history, Sherman has chosen to surround the portrait with what looks like a scroll of leaves but is in fact a pattern made up of fish shapes, playing on "Poisson," the Marquise's maiden name, which means "fish" in French.

Then there is Mark Burns's sculptural assemblage *G's Affordable A*. For those outside the ceramic-world loop, the letter "G" refers to the author of this book and the "A" to the latter's working relationship with Adrian Saxe. The tower of teapots is covered in paste gems that crudely mimic Saxe's lushly beautiful teapots studded with faux gems. An example can be seen on p. 170. Even though I am portrayed as the standard 1950s huckster – a stock drawing used in newspaper advertisements to sell, among other things, used cars – the piece is an affectionate homage to a long friendship. No offence was intended and none was taken.

Beginning in the late Victorian period and continuing until World War II, nannies in upper-middle-class homes would prepare and serve a separate afternoon tea in the nursery for children. Amusing teapots directed towards youngsters made more fun of the event and encouraged them to eat a nourishing tea. Illustrators of children's books like Mabel Lucie Attwell designed services for children, and many of the denizens of fables and fairy stories ended up serving steaming cups of tea, including Humpty Dumpty and The Old Lady Who Lived in a Shoe. Then there were teapots made for children to use in mock tea ceremonies with their friends or dolls, serving colored water from cheap plastic sets such as the highly collectible Shirley Temple service illustrated here, itself a low-rent play on Wedgwood's famous Jasper wares.

Today it is a rare child who is served a formal afternoon tea (Jacqueline Kennedy, a tea devotee, was one of the few parents who maintained this tradition, regularly serving tea at the White House) so the contemporary work that harks back to this aesthetic is now designed for the child who lives within every adult. Even Mrs. Potts, Disney's maternal teapot character from the animated film *Beauty and the Beast*, is sold primarily to adults for decoration (it does not pour tea very well).

Clowns, cartoon figures, and comic figures abound in this genre. Robin Campo's *Mr. Spuds* is a teapot created from a child's toy; a lot of skill committed to a playful end.

Orange Pekoe, Michael Hosaluk's wood teapot with a manic, happy presence, is named after a particular type of tea. Hosaluk has created a fanciful creature that matches the perkiness of the name.

George Walker's large, cartoonish, and immaculately crafted teapots take on debates that are carefully considered, informed, and decidedly adult. *Pupil Correction III* deals with children but not in terms of nursery games. This piece critiques education and presents Walker's belief that teachers have a tendency to graft their values on to their students so that the student "sees" through the teacher's eyes rather than approaching the process of education as a more objective program designed to open the child's own eyes to the world.

Jim Lawrence's clown, meanwhile, has great charm but the crutches create a disturbing note. How does a clown become injured, one must ask? Did it happen in performance or is it a metaphor for the pathos and hidden pain of the jester?

Finally, Philip Maberry plays with a clown-like teapot in *Princess Cotton Candy*. It is doubtful whether the artist's tea cosies/wigs would do a good job of insulation. Moreover, few of us would have the courage to actually brew tea in this hilarious drag-extravaganza of overdone make-up and theatrical hair.

Cartoon on Oscar Wilde's aestheticism, *Punch*, 1881

Opposite above: Foley
Pottery, England
**President Kruger and
Lord Balfour Teapot**
c. 1904. Ceramic
4.5 x 8 x 3.75 in.
(11.4 x 20.3 x 9.5 cm)

Opposite centre:
Luck and Flaw
Ronald Reagan
c. 1986. Porcelain,
10 x 7.5 x 5 in.
(25.4 x 19.1 x 12.7 cm)
Hall China, USA
Margaret Thatcher
c. 1986. Porcelain
8.25 x 11.6 x 6.8
(21 x 29.5 x 17.3 cm)
Cardew, UK

Opposite below: Royal
Worcester Porcelain Company,
Worcester, England
Aesthetic Teapot
(Oscar Wilde)
c. 1881–82. Porcelain
6.25 x 7 x 3.5 in.
(16 x 17.8 x 8.9 cm)

Left: Anthony Bennett
Teddy Roosevelt Teapot
1986. Earthenware
10.75 x 10 x 3.5 in.
(27.3 x 25.4 x 8.9 cm)

Right: detail of Cindy Sherman's **Madame de Pompadour (née Poisson) Tea Service** 1990

Below: Cindy Sherman **Madame de Pompadour (née Poisson) Tea Service** 1990. Porcelain
Teapot: 7.8 x 7.6 x 4.7 in. (19.8 x 19.3 x 11.9 cm)
Limited edition of 75 designed for Artes Magnus, New York, produced by the Limoges Porcelain Factory

Right: Jack Earl
Elvis
1994. Ceramic
10.25 x 9.75 x 5.6 in.
(26 x 24.8 x 14.2 cm)

Below: John Revelry
Kentucky Fried Teapot
1979. Earthenware
5 x 7 x 4.5 in.
(12.7 x 17.8 x 11.4 cm)

Left: Noi Volkov
Mona Lisa/Van Gogh
1999. Earthenware
17.25 x 13.25 x 5.6 in.
(43.8 x 33.7 x 14.2 cm)

Below: reverse side
of Noi Volkov's
Mona Lisa/Van Gogh

Opposite: Mark Burns
G's Affordable A
1995. Earthenware,
metal, glaze
31.5 x 28.5 x 8 in.
(80 x 72.4 x 20.3 cm)

Right: Lingaard Pottery,
England
Humpty Dumpty
c. 1930. Ceramic
7.1 x 8.8 x 4.5 in.
(18 x 22.4 x 11.4 cm)

Below: Lingaard Pottery,
England
**The Old Lady Who
Lived in a Shoe**
c. 1930. Ceramic
6 x 9.25 x 4.3 in.
(15.2 x 23.5 x 11 cm)

Right: Mabel Lucie Attwell
Tea Set
c. 1930. Ceramic
Teapot: 5 x 7.25 x 5.25 in.
(12.7 x 18.4 x 13.3 cm)
Designed for Shelley, England

Below: Ideal Novelty and
Toy Company, USA
Shirley Temple Tea Set
c. 1935. Plastic
Teapot: 6.25 x 5.75 x 3.75 in.
(16 x 14.6 x 9.5 cm)

Left: Robin Michael Campo
Mr. Spuds
1997. Ceramic
9 x 8 x 3.3 in.
(22.9 x 20.3 x 8.4 cm)

Below: Michael Hosaluk
Orange Pekoe
1996. Wood
8 x 8 x 5 in.
(20.3 x 20.3 x 12.7 cm)

Opposite: George Walker
Pupil Correction lll
1995. Ceramic
17.625 x 16.75 x 5.5 in.
(44.8 x 42.5 x 14 cm)

Left: Jim Lawrence
Teapot
1998. Wood, paint
16.5 x 11.5 x 4.75 in.
(41.9 x 29.2 x 12.1 cm)

Opposite: Phillip Maberry
Princess Cotton Candy
2000. Earthenware, acrylic wig
21 x 15 x 10 in.
(53.3 x 38.1 x 25.4 cm)

I look for a door, that
I have been through
before, that opens into
another world, a place
of stillness where time
and the rules of this
world stop. There is a
small child that lives here
who seems familiar with
this door.

Chapter 13
Tea Tales

When Henry James noted in his book, *Portrait of a Lady*, that "there are few hours in life more agreeable than the hour dedicated to the ceremony of afternoon tea," he might have added that there were also few hours where the exchange of human intelligence (i.e. gossip) was more intense. Freed from the tyranny of men, this was the time of day when women gathered – long before telephones and later the ubiquitous e-mail – to compare notes and pass on the latest tidbits of scandalous rumor. But it was also a time for family news to be exchanged, for problems to be confided, and advice sought. It seems appropriate therefore that the teapot has acquired a special role amongst artists as regards playing with both language and narrative. It is also worth noting that in this realm of the domestic confessional, it is women artists who dominate and feel most at ease revealing often private and intimate moments in their lives.

Aside from formal games with language itself, such as Adrian Saxe's witty *Ampersand* teapot, which was inspired by 19th-century Chinese porcelain wine pots in the shape of Chinese characters offering benedictions such as "good luck" or "good health,"

or Dina Angel-Wing's use of the word "TEA," teapots can take on a more complex role, expressing revelations from dreams, resolving emotional conflicts, pushing propaganda, or even explaining the history of tea itself. Constance Roberts also plays with "tea," naming each of her tea bags with a play on the word – "Chasti-tea," for instance. Jeannot Blackburn, on the other hand, uses the letter "T" as a distraction. In this case it stands for Saint Teresa. This teapot is part of a series depicting Catholic saints.

Sometimes the message is conventional and blunt. The Edwardian period *Sayings* teapot by Doulton and Co. of England reads as a primer for suffragettes, noting that "The Best of Men are Only Men at Best," while the "War Against Hitlerism" teapot brews patriotism as well as tea. The teapot has a particular virtue in the narrative role. It is first of all associated with maternal ceremony and thereby with nurturing. The moment one picks up one of these objects to read it, one is already partly enveloped in that aura of home and hearth, and so one drops one's defenses and is perhaps more receptive to the message the object contains. Moreover, the object is in our hands, a few inches from our face, occupying what artist Viola Frey terms "personal space."

What one reads can surprise one, particularly if the context is surprising. I have watched grown men turn pale when reading the teapots of Anne Kraus, the master of this genre. What they see and pick up is a cup, a teapot or a vase with charming decoration, exquisite color, painted images, and minutely detailed texts. Once they begin to read, and some of her pain is transferred, it is clear that these objects have an emotional bite. Kraus's work is drawn from her dreams and explores moments of life that are often fraught with anxiety and self-doubt. The great film maker Karel Reisz, one of Kraus's most fervent collectors, once

Detail: Anne Kraus
I Look for a Door
1999. Whiteware
9.25 x 11 x 8.25 in.
(23.5 x 27.9 x 21 cm)

Crown Ducal, England
War Against Hitlerism,
c. 1940. Ceramic
5.5 x 8.5 x 6 in.
(14 x 22 x 15.2 cm)
Text on the back of the
teapot reads: "'War Against
Hitlerism'. This Souvenir
Teapot was made for Dyson
& Horsfall of Preston to
replace aluminium stocks
taken over for Allied
Armaments, 1939.
'That Right Shall Prevail'
'Liberty and Freedom.'"

described collecting her work as like receiving pages torn illicitly from a private diary.

This is both insightful and accurate. The work derives from dream diaries and has an hermetic intensity. The production of Kraus's ceramics has ebbed and flowed with occasional dramatic highs and lows that directly parallel the transitions and transactions in the artist's life, expressed through a mix of painted underglaze imagery and carefully printed and poignant texts. For some, this relationship between her life and work is too personal. For others it is exactly the kind of interior vision, integrity, and courage they find too often lacking in art. "More than just amusing in postmodern pastiche," writes *New York Times* art critic Ken Johnson, "her works are little monuments to significant moments or crises in the artist's spiritual biography."

Cindy Kolodziejski, who works from a small studio in Venice, California, presents paradoxical, ironic narratives without words. As Stephen Lueking wrote in a recent monograph on her work, "Her narratives supply the lion's share of irony especially in the conjunction of vessel form and underglazed imagery. Kolodziejski's most frequent strategy is to exploit the recto/verso division of the pot created by handle and spout. Typically she places two images, one on each side, which cannot be viewed simultaneously. She thus coerces a back-and-forth, dichotomous viewing of the images. Good narrative art, like that of Kolodziejski, is analogous to good literature. Beneath the skilled structure and the masterful imagery lies the real work."

This sense of being on the cusp of literature is very much a central theme that runs through three other artists's work: Ellen Wieske's *History of Tea*, Ellen Jantzen's *Tea for Two Fables,* and Margaret Wharton's *Caddy*. Wieske's teapot is made up of what is almost a ticker tape of short statements about tea's history, written with telegraphic economy, the words impressed in light relief on thin ribbons of copper that are then woven into a wire frame. Jantzen's teapot *is* a book. It opens up to present two parables. Wharton, on the other hand, makes her teapot *from* a book: it is her raw material, cut, carved, and reshaped.

The term "caddy" refers to a lockable box in which jars or tea containers are placed. The term is often used incorrectly for the container in which the tea is kept. The term comes from the Chinese tea trade's measure of weight, the "catti." During the 18th century, when tea was valued at the equivalent of $2,500 a pound, being able to lock up the tea was an essential part of housekeeping security. In Wharton's case the caddy contains not tea but a teapot, wonderfully and expressively crafted with a curious defacing tenderness, a rich sense of texture, and implied literary content.

Royal Doulton, England
Sayings tea set,
c. 1925. Ceramic
Teapot: 5 x 7.25 x 5.25 in.
(12.7 x 18.4 x 13.3 cm)
The legend on this teapot, delivered by what appears to be a rendering of an old maid, reads: "The Best of Men are Only Men at Best."

Right: Adrian Saxe
Ampersand
1988. Porcelain
10.25 x 9.1 x 2.75 in.
(26 x 23.1 x 7 cm)

Below: Jeannot Blackburn
T-pot
1990. Earthenware
8 x 11 x 3.5 in.
(20.3 x 27.9 x 8.9 cm)

Right: Dina Angel-Wing
"T" "E" "A" teapots
1997. Ceramic
"T": 8.75 x 6.75 x 3.5 in.
(22.2 x 17.1 x 8.9 cm)
"E": 8.75 x 5.5 x 3.25 in.
(22.2 x 14 x 8.3 cm)
"A": 8.75 x 9.75 x 3.1 in.
(22.2 x 24.8 x 7.9 cm)

Below: Constance Roberts
Var-1-E-Tea
1997. Wood
Teapot: 9.4 x 11.5 x 6.75 in.
(23.9 x 29.2 x 17.1 cm)

Right: Anne Kraus
Shattered Dreams
1988. Glazed whiteware
10 x 10 x 6 in.
(25.4 x 25.4 x 15.2 cm)
The text reads: "People
had warned you against
your ideals, now there you
lie dead in the snow. So I
will now carry this dream
until one day I fall and it
shatters once again."

Below: Anne Kraus
Don't Give Up the Dream
1986. Whiteware
10.1 x 7.5 x 3.75 in.
(26.7 x 19.1 x 9.5 cm)

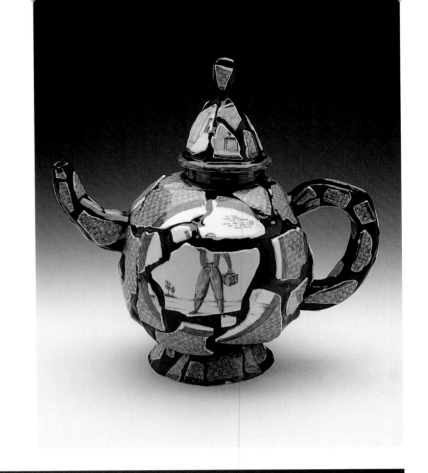

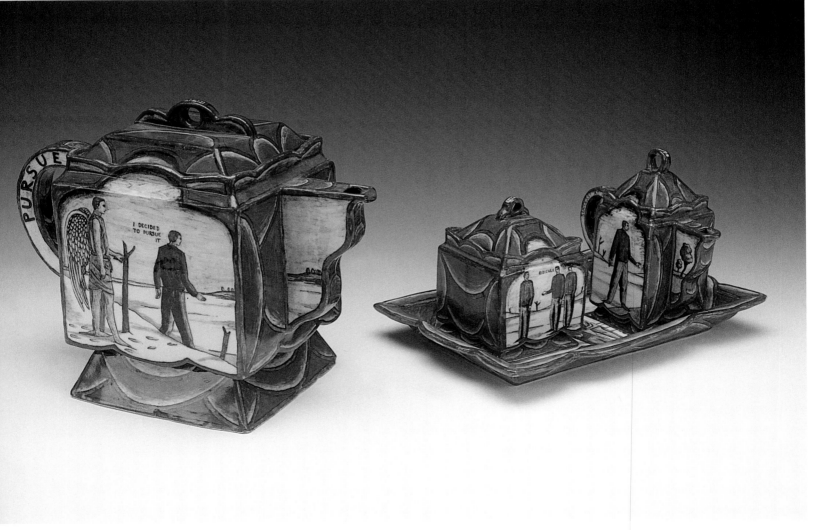

Anne Kraus
I Look for a Door
1999. Whiteware
9.25 x 11 x 8.25 in.
(23.5 x 27.9 x 21 cm)

I look for a door, that I have been through before, that opens into another world, a place of stillness where time and the rules of this world stop. There is a small child that lives here who seems familiar with this door.

Left: Cindy Kolodziejski
Harvest
1994. Whiteware
10.75 x 8 x 4.25 in.
(27.3 x 20.3 x 10.8 cm)

Below left: reverse side
of Cindy Kolodziejski's
Harvest

Below right: Cindy
Kolodziejski
Geisha
1995. Whiteware
Teapot: 9.75 x 7 x 3.25 in.
(24.8 x 17.8 x 8.3 cm)

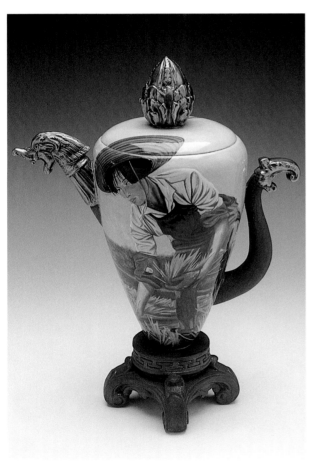

Right: Margaret Wharton
Caddy
2000. Found book, tea, glass
cup handles, mixed media
9 x 11 x 12 in.
(22.9 x 27.9 x 30.5 cm)

Below: Margaret Wharton's
Caddy closed

Opposite: Ellen Wieske
History of Tea
1999. Copper
10.5 x 10.6 x 5.75 in.
(26.7 x 26.9 x 14.6 cm)

Opposite: inset: detail
of Ellen Wieske's
History of Tea

Ellen Jantzen
Tea for Two Fables
1999. Reformed paper
pulp, wood filler, brass
Open (90°): 9.4 x 11 x 9 in.
(23.9 x 27.9 x 22.9 cm)

Chapter 14
Tea for Art's Sake

Kasimir Malevich, the Russian who in 1915 founded the non-objective art movement Suprematism, is famous for his statement that "if it is useful it cannot be art." It also happens that he is famous for a teapot design that seems to directly challenge the veracity of his statement. Malevich's *Suprematist Teapot* is an icon of modernism. When the director of the Lomosov Porcelain Factory in Leningrad contacted the artist with the message, "Mr. Malevich, your teapot does not pour well," the latter supposedly replied, "Mr. Director, it is not a teapot, it is the *idea* of a teapot." This was the early clarion call for the teapot to enter the modern fine arts as an iconic object or image.

Arman, the sculptor, painter and, with Yves Klein, one of the founders of Nouveau Réalisme, calls the teapot "one of the great fetish objects of our time." Of all of the artists in this book it is arguably Arman who best understands the common obsession with teapots. He was raised from birth in a milieu of accumulation, his father being an antiques- and second-hand-goods dealer, and a dedicated, precise cataloger of things. So when, in 1960, Arman burst onto the art scene with his exhibition "Le Plein" at the elegant Galerie Iris Clert in Paris, it was with a crowded assembly of what most observers would have considered junk; Arman, however, presented it as a kind of instant archeology. He has subsequently made his work from collections of oil paint tubes, violins, flat irons, coffee grinders, reading lamps, supermarket carts, and cars. There is even an Arman peace sculpture in Beirut, seven floors high, made from captured and destroyed tanks. As one critic wrote, he has "embraced the raw materials of life."

Renowned for his formidable scholarship in a wide array of cultural specializations from blue and white china and African art to Samurai armor, the artist first worked with teapots in 1964 when he made *Accumulation of Sliced Teapots*, now in the collection of the Walker Art Museum, Minneapolis. In the early 1990s he was invited by Artes Magnus to take part in a project creating limited edition artworks in porcelain, along with Cindy Sherman, Dan Flavin, Roy Lichtenstein, and others. This resulted in *As in the Sink (II)*, cut and assembled teapots, and other crockery in pristine white Limoges porcelain.

Then, in 1994, working with Ceramica Gatti in the pottery town of Faenza, Italy, he made another three series of teapot-themed sculptures, *La Prima Opera*, *Barrissement* (the French term for the sound an elephant makes when trumpeting, an amusing recognition of the multitudinous spouts that emerge with erect urgency from the piece), and *Pellerinage*, a masterwork that creates a procession of one-inch-wide teapot "filets", cut from the center of still wet teapot forms, glazed white, and assembled to create an optically complex vision of moving forms.

The transparency of this piece is echoed here in several works that one way or another remove the materiality of the teapot body: Leopold Foulem does it by covering chicken wire in slip and firing his openwork teapot; Brian Peshek works similarly with his ethereal, luminous *White Mice* in thin wire; and John McQueen turns a hand into an abstracted teapot with the thumb as a spout, all made from woven twigs. There are other ways to dematerialize a teapot. Tony Marsh takes the

Detail: Karen Estelle Koblitz
Still Life with Teapots
1996. Low-fire ceramic
Assembled:
6 x 14.75 x 14.75 in.
(15.2 x 37.5 x 37.5 cm)

Above left: **Arman** working on ceramic in Ceramica Gatti, Faenza, 1994

Above right: **Leopold Foulem** in studio, Montreal, 1992

basic form, divides it into its component parts, drills holes to destroy its physical density, and assembles the parts in a bowl. Pamela Gazalé takes the opposite approach, retaining all the mass by carving a teapot shape into a solid, luminous piece of rock salt. Marek Cecula slices his *Divided Teapot* into three sections.

Polish-born Cecula, one of the most fascinating and inventive artists currently working in ceramics in a visionary Post-Industrial style, also produced *Collection* in 1997. This is part of a series entitled "Violations." Each work contains a violation of one kind or another. In one work, conventionally beautiful teapots displayed in a museum-style cabinet spout tumors and warts. In *Collection* sixteen teapots are displayed, crammed into tight shelves, claustrophobically compressed and minus their lids. *Separate*, by Jeannie Quinn, is in essence about the opposite. It is about two or more objects becoming one, in which the strength of the pieces comes from two different elements. One is the way in which an everyday form – the teapot – takes on a Siamese-twin shape, when doubled, that is surprisingly different and unexpected. The second force in Quinn's work is the dramatic way in which the discourse between positive and negative space becomes multiplied by these conjunctions.

Belgian polymath Piet Stockmans has created *Twenty-Five Teapots,* but the teapots in this collection are deflated and collapsed, lying one on top of the other in simple, grid-like, collapsed bladders. The overlapping objects sport Stockmans's distinctive material signature of white slip-cast porcelain and blue dip.

Nicholas Homoky plays an interesting game with form and graphics. His teapots are half-real, half-drawn,

creating a dynamism between 2-D and 3-D. His teapot forms exist both in their own right and as white grounds to hold his drawings. Although Edward Eberle employs the same basic device as Homoky, the aesthetic result in *Teapot Study*, his torn and reconstructed teapot, is very different. It is covered in drawing and pattern but unlike Homoky's ceramics, where surface and form work in dynamic opposition to each other, Eberle's surface and form meld into a jumble of extraordinary energy and movement. The piece is kinetic, powerful, and sculptural.

In the realm of the fine arts, the teapot has made many appearances in still lifes, sitting demurely on checked tablecloths between apples and oranges. It is the still life canvasses of early modernist masters such as Picasso, Braque, and Matisse that inspired the 1978 work shown here by Andrew Lord. This traditional assembly of a tea service was carefully and subtly painted on the surface to capture the tonal impact of a specific lighting set-up so that the surface becomes a controlled tapestry of light and shade. By comparison, Karen Estelle Koblitz's *Still Life with Teapots* could not be more different in sensibility. In contrast to Lord's primal and reductive spirit, Koblitz takes the still life as deeply into the jungles of pattern and color as she can, with an explosion of decorative elements making her work seem like the teapot equivalent of a Technicolor dance sequence by Carmen Miranda. Much the same decorative mood, although with a more abstracted vision of the teapot, can be found in John Garrett's *Teatime with Jay,* a wild assembly of computer parts, cloth, enamel, wire, beads, and sequins.

Roy Lichtenstein's limited edition tea service for Rosenthal features ben-day dots, the tonal stippling once used in printing to reduce a photographic image to a printable entity – a precursor of the pixilated world of the computer. Lichtenstein's sophisticated highlights play graphically on the plain white teapot – one of the most joyful and definitive Pop icons to come from the imagination of this great artist.

Peter Shire's large, skeletal, metal vessel presents the inner scaffolding of the teapot, removed of function, decoration, and volume. It is to teapots what stick figures are to figure drawing.

Nicolai Diulgheroff's rare *Futurist Tea Set* was made in a program to produce ceramics in the spirit of the Italian Futurist movement, working to a manifesto co-written by the movement's founder, Filippo Tommaso Marinetti, and the founder of its ceramic arm, Tullio d'Albisola. The unusual form and decorative color of Diulgheroff's work make it a precursor of the later postmodern movement in Italy.

Ron Nagle was the *enfant terrible* of the so-called Abstract Expressionist Ceramics group - the most important avant-garde movement in the ceramic arts. Against all odds, Nagle has kept his youthful quality some forty years later. Influenced by Ken Price's cups and a 1963 Giorgio Morandi exhibition of paintings and prints, he took the decision that if Morandi could spend his entire life painting a dozen or so domestic objects on a tabletop, he could devote himself to one modest but primary form – the cup. *Untitled Teapot # 1*, the small,

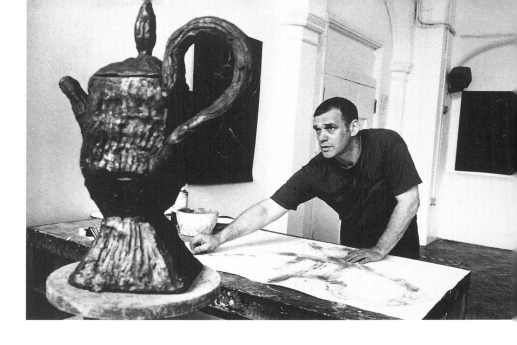

jewel-like vessel shown here, is Nagle's first departure from the cup, and his very first teapot. He brings to this form the same reductive elemental quality that he has lavished on the cup for four decades. This plump object, only five inches high, is a compression of everything that the teapot is about – its sturdiness, its pregnant volume, its matronly sense of gravity. The appendages – handle and spout – are represented as contracted, vestigial forms that have surprising sculptural power. Finally there is the superb depth of color, achieved by numerous layers of china paint that make the piece glow with inner light.

While this is the largest survey ever taken of the artist-made teapot it still only touches the surface, not only of Sonny and Gloria Kamm's collection but also of the full range of this engaging and animated form. We have not seen the last of teapots standing on the sculpture plinth nor have we seen the last reinvention of the functional form. It will continue to fascinate sculptors, painters, and photographers for the century that has just begun and probably long thereafter. There is something about this shape and its social baggage that has bonded itself to the human soul. It sums up turbulent history, evinces domestic comfort, and lends itself to all kinds of exploratory caprices. It enters our lives through the back door to pour tea and the front door to charm our eye. It is swathed in steamy mists of legend, from the bloodied eyelids of Bodhidharma to the fortunes that are told from the leaves that it brews. Plump and stout, it has found a universal, permanent, and comfortable place in our material culture.

Above: **Andrew Lord**
in studio, New York, 1995

Below: **Edward Eberle**
in studio, Pittsburgh, 1988

Left: Kasimir Malevich
**Suprematist Teapot
and Three Cups**
designed c. 1923. Porcelain
Teapot: 6.5 x 9.5 x 3.6 in.
(16.5 x 24.1 x 9.1 cm)
Limited production by Robert
M. Bozak, Canada, 1988, of
original by Leningrad State
Porcelain Factory

Below: Arman (Armand
Fernandez)
Pellerinage
1994. Earthenware
11 x 61 x 20 in.
(27.9 x 154.9 x 50.8 cm)
Produced at Ceramica
Gatti, Faenza, Italy

Opposite: Arman
(Armand Fernandez)
As in the Sink (II)
1996. Porcelain
9 x 21 x 19 in.
(22.9 x 53.3 x 48.3 cm)
Designed for Artes
Magnus, New York, and
manufactured by Limoges
Porcelain, France

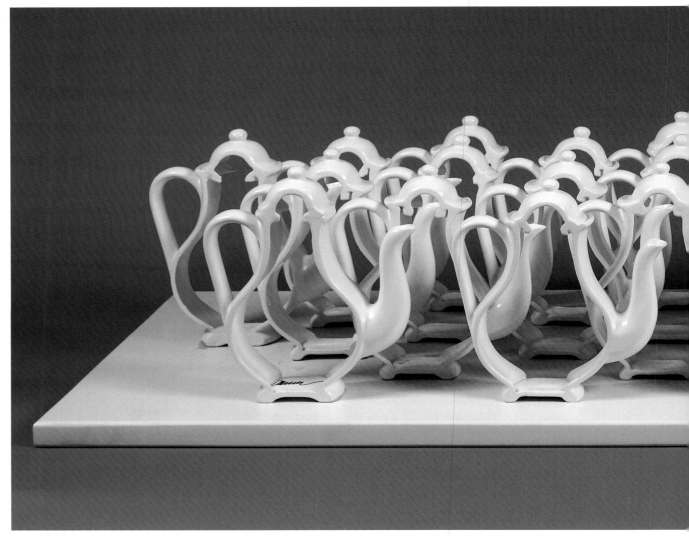

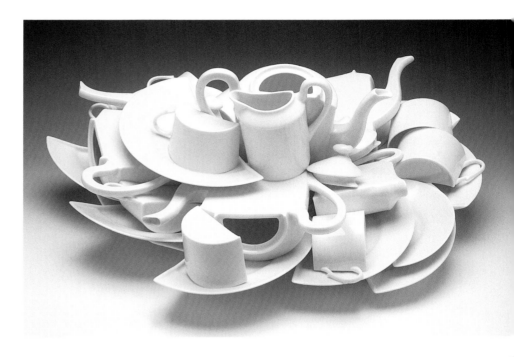

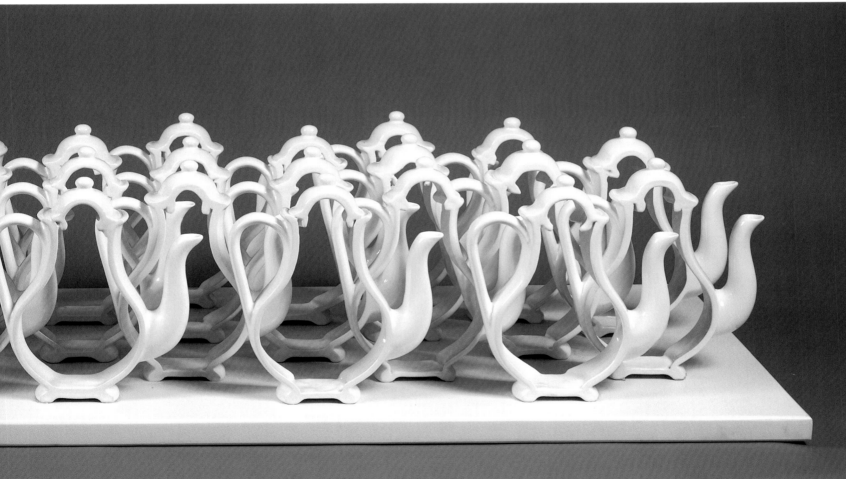

Opposite: John McQueen
Teaser-Vice
1999. Twigs and string
22 x 20 x 9.25 in.
(55.9 x 50.8 x 23.5 cm)

Right: Leopold Foulem
Théière
1987. White glazed
ceramic on wire
10.25 x 10.25 x 6 in.
(26 x 26 x 15.2 cm)

Below: Brian Peshek
White Mice
1991. Wire mesh
6 x 13.9 x 7.75 in.
(15.2 x 35.3 x 19.7 cm)

Left: Pamela Gazalé
Teapot Sculpture
1999. Carved rock salt
5 x 9.5 x 7.8 in.
(12.7 x 24.1 x 19.8 cm)

Below: Tony Marsh
**Round Open Basket
with Deconstructed
Teapot Parts**
1999. Earthenware
Basket: 5.5 x 20 x 20 in.
(14 x 50.8 x 50.8 cm)

Opposite: Jeannie Quinn
Separate
1995. Ceramic
22.75 x 19 x 8.5 in.
(57.8 x 48.3 x 21.6 cm)

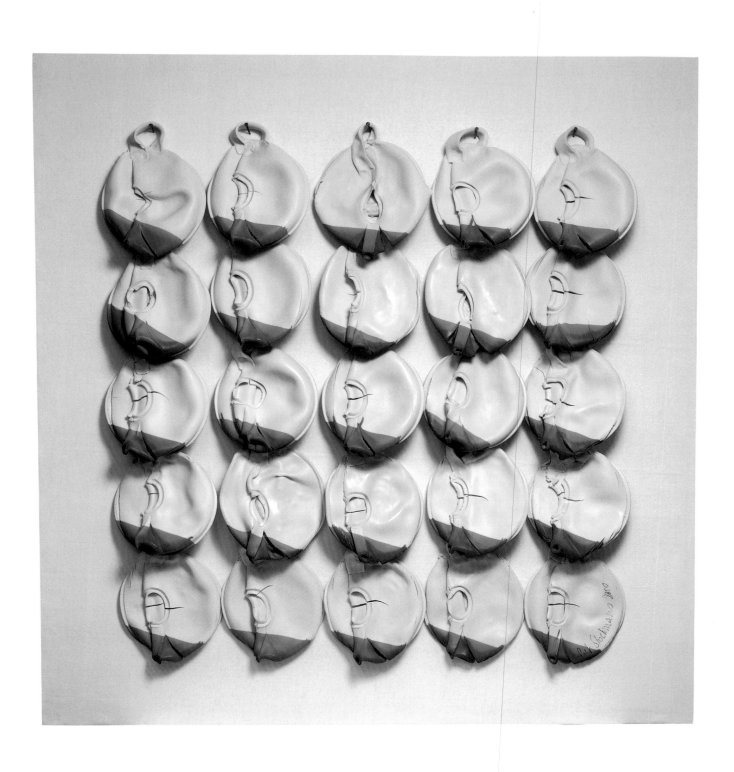

Opposite: Piet Stockmans
Twenty-Five Teapots
2000. Porcelain and
blue slip dip
36 x 36 x 5 in.
(91.4 x 91.4 x 12.7 cm)

Right: Marek Cecula
3-piece Divided Teapot
1990. Glazed ceramic
Assembled:
7.625 x 10.4 x 12 in.
(19.4 x 26.4 x 30.5 cm)

Below: Marek Cecula
Collection
1997. Porcelain, wood
41 x 29 in.
(104.1 x 73.7 cm)

Right: Andrew Lord
Tea Set Still Life
1978. Ceramic
Teapot: 8.5 x 10.75 x 5.25 in.
(21.6 x 27.3 x 13.3 cm)

Below: Nicholas Homoky
Group of five teapots
c. 1981-83. Porcelain
From 2.8 x 5.4 x 3.5 to
4.9 x 3.625 x 3.625 in.
(From 7.1 x 13.7 x 8.9
to 12.4 x 9.2 x 9.2 cm)

Karen Estelle Koblitz
Still Life with Teapots
1996. Low-fire ceramic
Assembled:
6 x 14.75 x 14.75 in.
(15.2 x 37.5 x 37.5 cm)

Left: Roy Lichtenstein
Porcelain Tea Service
1984. Porcelain
Height 7 in.
(17.8 cm)
Designed for Rosenthal
Porcelain, Studio Line,
Germany: number 96
in an edition of 100

Below: Nicolai Diulgheroff
Futurist Tea Set
c. 1932. Glazed earthenware
Teapot: 6.8 x 6.6 x 4.1 in.
(17.3 x 16.8 x 10.4 cm)
Designed for Giuseppe
Mazzotti Pottery, Albisola
Mare, Italy

Right: Edward Eberle
Teapot Study
1992. Porcelain
9.9 x 10.5 x 5.75 in.
(25.1 x 26.7 x 14.6 cm)

Below: Ron Nagle
Untitled Teapot # 1
1999. Earthenware, glaze,
china paint
4.75 x 6 x 4.75 in.
(12.1 x 15.2 x 12.1 cm)

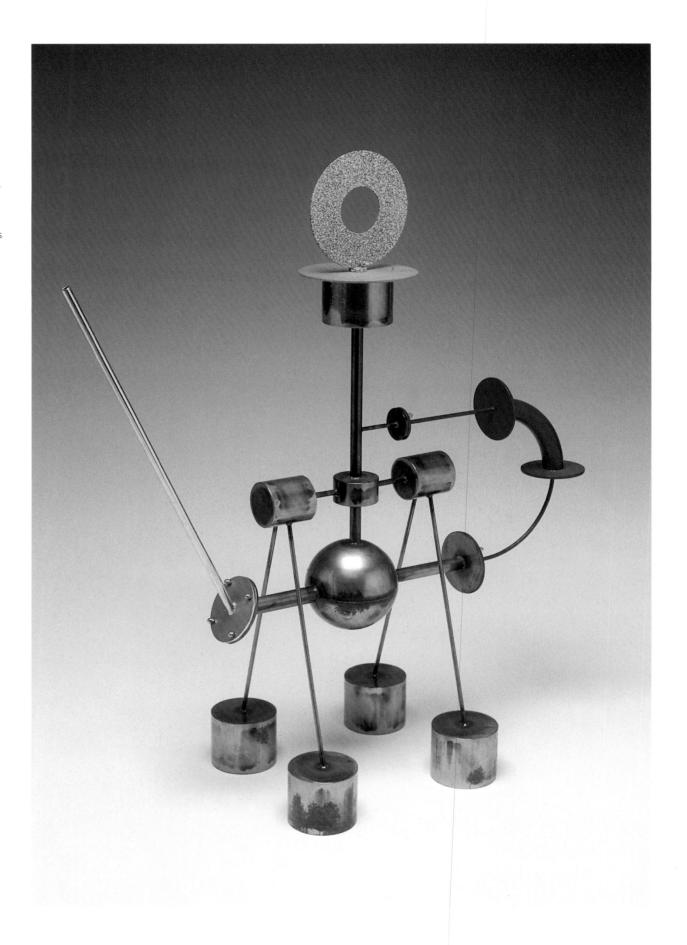

Right: Peter Shire
Small Torso
1992. Gold plated steel,
enamel
28.5 x 26 x 9.75 in.
(72.4 x 66 x 24.8 cm)

Opposite: John Garrett
Teatime with Jay
1999. Aluminum computer
parts, hardware, cloth,
oil-based enamel, plastic-
coated wire, beads, sequins
18 x 8.75 x 8.75 in.
(45.7 x 22.2 x 22.2 cm)

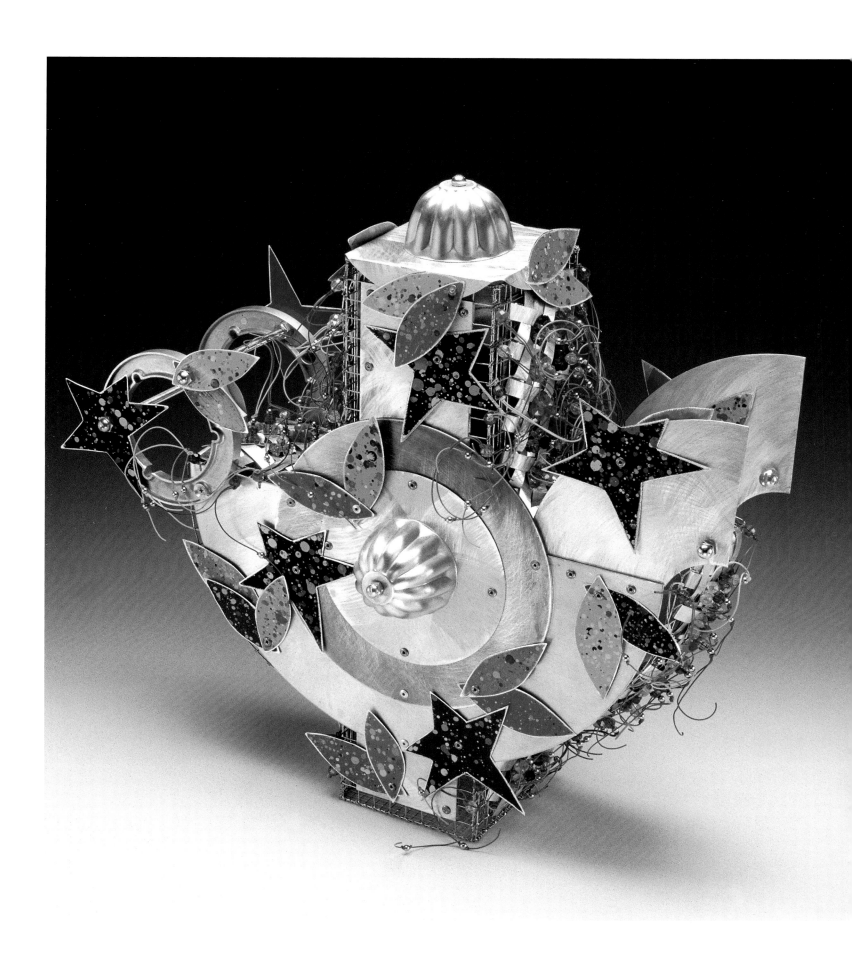

Biographies
Compiled by Garth Clark, Mark Del Vecchio and John Pagliaro

DANIEL J. ANDERSON b. St. Paul, MN, USA, 1945. Anderson received his BS from the University of Wisconsin, River Falls, in 1968 and his MFA in 1970 from Cranbrook Academy of Art, Bloomfield Hills, MI. The recipient of a record number of Illinois Arts Council Fellowships (1975, 1979, 1981, 1984, 1985, 1987, 1988, 1989, 1991, 1996, 1999), a Ford Foundation Grant (1979) and an Individual Art Fellowship from the NEA (1990), Anderson has been Professor and Head of Ceramics at Southern Illinois University, Edwardsville, since 1970. The effect of wood-fire on his often brightly glazed "architectural" pots mutes and subdues their tonality, and makes them approximate the weathered surface of real farm buildings. Often grouped together in ways that recreate their actual appearance in the landscape, Anderson's pots become "utilitarian sets" through proximity and interplay. Since 1968 he has had over forty one-person exhibitions and participated in hundreds of group shows, including recent exhibitions at Babcock Gallery, New York, NY; Garth Clark Gallery, New York, NY; Gallery WDO, Chicago, IL; Works Gallery, Philadelphia, PA; and SOFA Chicago, IL. Anderson's work is in the collections of the Philadelphia Art Museum, Philadelphia, PA; Charles A. Wustum Museum of Fine Arts, Racine, WI; Everson Museum of Art, Syracuse, NY; Mint Museum of Craft and Design, Charlotte, NC; and Carnegie Museum of Art, Pittsburgh, PA. See: Tony Merino, "Midwestern Clay: Anatomy and Architecture," *Ceramics: Art and Perception* (Issue 12, 1993) and Mark Del Vecchio, *Postmodern Ceramics* (London: Thames & Hudson, 2001).

KATE ANDERSON b. St. Louis, MO, USA, 1953. Anderson studied painting at Webster University, St. Louis, but the turning point in her education came in 1996 when she took a knotting course with Jane Sauer at the Craft Alliance in St. Louis. Since then her work has appeared in over twenty exhibitions, including "New Baskets: Expanding the Concept" (Craft Alliance, St. Louis, MO, 1997), "Muse of the Millennium" (Nordic Heritage Museum, Seattle, WA, 1998), and "Social Fiber: Untangling the Message" (Society of Arts and Crafts, Boston, MA, 1999). See: Ruth Billie Sudduths, *Baskets: A Book for Makers and Collectors* (Madison: Hand Books Press, 1999).

DINA ANGEL-WING b. Haifa, Israel, 1944. Angel-Wing studied ceramics with Wayne Horuchi at Stanford University, Palo Alto, CA, and raku with Andree Thompson at the University of California, Berkeley. She has exhibited her work widely, including shows at: del Mano Gallery, Los Angeles, CA; Toki Gallery, Berkeley, CA; Langmann Gallery, Philadelphia, PA; Vesperman Gallery, Atlanta, GA; Ferrin Gallery, Northampton, MA; Nancy Margolis Gallery, Portland, ME; and Craft Alliance, St. Louis, MO.

Her work has also appeared at Los Angeles County Museum of Art, Los Angeles, CA; Philadelphia Museum of Art, Philadelphia, PA; Ohio Craft Museum, Columbus, OH; and Oakland Museum of Art, Oakland, CA. See: Charlotte F. Speight and John Toki, *Make It In Clay* (Mountain View: Mayfield, 1997).

ADRIAN ARLEO b. Tarrytown, NY, USA, 1960. Arleo studied an interesting mix of art and anthropology at Pitzer College, Claremont, CA, and received her BA in 1983. She also studied at the American University of Rome, Italy, and the Hoko River Archaeological Field School, Pullman, WA. Arleo was awarded an MFA in Ceramics from the Rhode Island School of Design, Providence, RI, in 1986, but spent an isolated year of study at the University of Massachusetts, Amherst, two years prior to this. She was a visiting instructor at the University of Montana, Missoula, in 1995, and has given countless workshops and held visiting artist positions nationally. Her work has remained an imaginative mixture of figuration and symbol, whereby the body often becomes the structure that enables a deeper story. She has great adeptness with the female figure and, in her evocative animal/human interplays, builds compelling narrative imagery. Her figures are lyrically rendered by use of complex, polychrome, sgrafitto surfaces and other richly layered treatments. Arleo's work has been widely exhibited, in both solo and group shows, and shown principally by Works Gallery, Philadelphia, PA; David Beitzel Gallery, New York, NY; Society for Contemporary Crafts, Pittsburgh, PA; and Ferrin Gallery, Northampton, MA. See: Leslie Ferrin, *Teapots Transformed* (Madison: Guild Books, 2000); Robert Pipenburg, *The Spirit of Clay* (Farmington Hills, MI: Pebble Press, 1996); "Portfolio," *American Craft* (Feb./Mar. 1991).

ARMAN (Armand Fernandez) b. Nice, France, 1928. Arman studied briefly in Paris at the Ecole des Arts Decoratifs and the Ecole du Louvre. In 1957 he founded the Nouveau Réalisme movement, together with Yves Klein, making art out of assemblages of junk. (Arman's father was a dealer in antiques and second-hand goods, and a compulsive cataloger of object types.) In the 1960s Arman moved to New York and has lived between this city and France ever since. In New York he became friends with Andy Warhol and other artists in the Pop movement with whom he shared an affinity for the everyday. He first worked with the teapot form in 1964 (*Installation of Sliced Teapots* in the collection of the Walker Art Center, Minneapolis, MN). He later worked with Artes Magnus, creating a series of amusing ceramic pieces, and in 1994 he worked with Ceramica Gatti in Faenza, Italy. His major series of ambitious pieces include three teapot-themed works, *La Prima*

Opera, Pellerinage and *Barrissement.* See: Henry Martin and Umberto Eco, *La Ceramica Di Arman* (Bologna: Edizioni Maggiore, 1994).

MABEL LUCIE ATTWELL b. London, England, 1879; d. Fowey, Cornwall, England, 1964. Known foremost as an illustrator of children's books, Attwell began designing nursery wares for Shelley Potteries in 1926. Her three-dimensional pieces portraying cherubic infants have been a source of delight to several generations of British children. The sense of whimsy and wit that was always apparent in her designs made them popular and much anticipated during the Depression years, and the continued interest in her light-hearted motifs has encouraged collection of her work up to the present day. See: Karen McCready, *Art Deco and Modernist Ceramics* (London: Thames & Hudson, 1995).

RALPH BACERRA b. Garden Grove, CA, USA, 1938. In 1961 Bacerra received his BFA from the Chouinard Art School in Los Angeles, CA, and after two years of military service returned there to head the Ceramics Department until the school's closure in 1972. He later joined the Ceramics Department at the Otis/Parsons School of Art in Los Angeles, CA, where he taught until the department was closed in 1998. Best known by his students as "Mr. Perfection," Bacerra has an ability to create highly complicated surface treatment in keeping with traditional Japanese Imari works but always with his own contemporary spin. In 1998 he received the Outstanding Achievement Award from the National Council on the Education of Ceramic Art. Bacerra is also a Fellow of the American Crafts Council. His work is in the collections of the Cooper-Hewitt National Design Museum, New York, NY; Kohler Arts Center, Sheboygan, WI; Long Beach Museum of Art, Long Beach, CA; Museum of Contemporary Ceramic Art, Shigaraki Ceramic Cultural Park, Shigaraki, Japan; American Craft Museum, New York, NY; Los Angeles County Museum of Art, Los Angeles, CA; National Museum of American Art, Smithsonian Institution, Washington, DC; and Victoria and Albert Museum, London, England. See: Garth Clark, *American Ceramics* (New York: Abbeville Press, 1987); Jo Lauria, *Color and Fire* (New York: Rizzoli, 2000); Garth Clark and Oliver Watson, *American Potters Today* (London: Victoria and Albert Museum, 1986); and a recent monograph by Garth Clark, *Ralph Bacerra: A Survey* (New York: Garth Clark Gallery, 1999).

MICHAEL J. AND MAUREEN ARNOW BANNER Michael b. Kalamazoo, MI, USA, 1939; Maureen b. Chicago, IL, USA, 1946. Michael holds a BS from Western Michigan University and has also studied at the Cleveland Institute of Art. Maureen studied at Northern Illinois University and Evanston Art Center. The Banners' many awards include a 1999 Massachusetts Cultural Council Artist Fellowship, and they have exhibited their work in many venues, including Tesoro Gallery, Los Angeles, CA; Swan Gallery, Philadelphia, PA; Incorporated Gallery, New York, NY; Charles A. Wustum Museum of Fine Arts, Racine, WI; Carnegie Museum of Art, Pittsburgh, PA; and Downey Museum of Art, Downey, CA. The couple have work in the permanent collections of the Renwick Gallery, National Museum of American Art, Smithsonian Institution, Washington, DC; Art Institute of Chicago, Chicago, IL; and Mint Museum of Craft and Design, Charlotte, NC. See: "Acquisitions," *American Craft* (Feb./Mar. 1998).

RON BARON b. Springfield, MA, USA, 1957. Baron holds a BS in Art from the University of Wisconsin, Madison (1984) and took an MFA from the University of California, Davis, in 1987. He has been the recipient of numerous awards and honors, including a 1992 Mid Atlantic Artist's Fellowship, NEA, and a 1998 Greenwall Foundation Fellowship for Art in the Public Realm from the Public Art Fund. Baron works with accumulations of found objects. His ceramic work consists mainly of "vase" shapes made by piling industrial plates of varying diameters one above another to create the silhouette of a traditional vessel. His work has been widely exhibited, including shows at: Anna Kustera Gallery, Chassie Post Gallery, Sculpture Center, Gracie Mansion Gallery, Garth Clark Gallery, and Milford Gallery, all New York, NY; Gallery Joe, Philadelphia, PA; Mint Museum of Craft and Design, Charlotte, NC; Brooklyn Museum, Brooklyn, NY; and Museum Het Kruithuis, 's-Hertogenbosch, Netherlands. See: Bill Arning, "Ron Baron at Anna Kustera Gallery," *Time Out* (Apr. 1997) and Charlotta Kotik, *Domestic Transformations* (Brooklyn: Brooklyn Museum, 1999).

JEROEN BECHTOLD b. Eindhoven, Netherlands, 1953. Bechtold trained as a teacher at the Academie voor Beeldende Vorming, Amersfort, Netherlands, and in 1981 he graduated from the Rietveld Academy. Recently identified as a "virtual" ceramic artist, Bechtold has also exhibited internationally in a more traditional capacity, as a ceramic artist making paper-thin porcelain works. He was the proprietor of his own gallery – JBK – in Amsterdam, Netherlands, and has also had solo shows at Spiegeling Gallery, Amsterdam. Bechtold's research and practice have made him an aficionado of the interface between technology and the fine arts. His virtual teapots have been translated from computer designs to reality by craftsmen in Yixing, China, which he has visited on several occasions on tours organized by Ah Leon (q.v.).

SUSAN BEINER b. Newark, NJ, USA, 1962. Beiner received her BFA in 1985 from the Mason Gross School of the Arts, Rutgers University, New Brunswick, NJ. After a year of Graduate Studies in Ceramics at Arizona State University, Tempe (1989), she took her MFA in Ceramics at the University of Michigan School of Art, Ann Arbor, in 1993. Beiner is currently the Chair of the Ceramics Department at California State University, San Bernadino. Her work with functional forms could be said to have an obsessive edge. She typically adorns the outside of her pots with dense clusters of (slip-cast) found objects, both industrial and organic, so that her pieces convey the sense of being made wholly out of the objects at their surface. Though she sometimes draws a sense of conflict and danger by casting objects that subvert the form they construct, at other times her 3-D surfaces stand to augment or play with her repertoire of forms, as in her homage to Victorian forms (mantlepiece jars, etc.) created largely from floral elements. Beiner has participated in both solo and group shows, including exhibitions at the Sybaris Gallery, Royal Oak, MI; Los Angeles County Museum of Art, Los Angeles, CA; SOFA New York, NY (Ferrin Gallery, 1999); and Charles A. Wustum Museum of Fine Arts, Racine, WI. See: Leslie Ferrin, *Teapots Transformed* (Madison: Guild Books, 2000); Jo Lauria, *Color and Fire* (New York: Rizzoli, 2000); and "Portfolio," *American Craft* (Oct./Nov. 1997).

ANTHONY BENNETT b. Evesham, Worcestershire, England, 1949. Bennett received his Diploma in Art and Design in 1971 from Wolverhampton Polytechnic and an MA in 1974 from the Royal College of Art, London. Wolverhampton was one of the first schools outside the US to acknowledge American Funk ceramics, which were a strong influence on Bennett. He evolved a style of carefully drawn, cartoon-like surreal images. An exceptional modeler, Bennett has also been commissioned by the Royal Geological Museum and British Museum of Natural History to create Neanderthal figures for dioramas. Bennett has exhibited internationally, in both solo and group exhibitions, at the Garth Clark Gallery, New York, NY, and Los Angeles, CA; Dolphin Gallery, Kansas City, MO; Los Angeles County Museum of Art, Los Angeles, CA; Rye Art Gallery, Rye, England; and Museum of Contemporary Ceramic Art, Shigaraki, Japan. His work is in the collections of Auckland Museum, Auckland, New Zealand; Hastings Museum, Hastings, England; Melbourne Museum, Melbourne, Australia; Shigaraki Ceramic Cultural Park, Shigaraki, Japan; Los Angeles County Museum of Art, Los Angeles, CA; and Ulster Museum, Belfast, Northern Ireland. See: Garth Clark, *The Eccentric Teapot* (New York: Abbeville Press, 1989); Jo Lauria, *Color and Fire* (New York: Rizzoli, 2000); and Mark Del Vecchio, *Postmodern Ceramics* (London: Thames & Hudson, 2001).

HARRIETE ESTEL BERMAN b. Harrisburg, PA, USA, 1952. Berman studied at Syracuse University, Syracuse, NY, earning a BFA in 1974 in Metalsmithing and Fiber, and an MFA from the Tyler School of Art, PA, in 1980. As Charlotte Moser writes, "Using the household appliance as a metaphor for women's utilitarian position in society, she [has] created true-to-life facsimiles of household gadgets called *The Family of Appliances You Can Believe In*, that shows the artist's ambivalence about the role of women in the suburban American dream." Berman is an activist on many levels – for women's rights in her work and as a volunteer for social and professional issues. She has worked for Earth Day, established a critique group for Bay Area metalsmiths, and created a neighborhood watch group in San Matheo, CA. She also works on a volunteer art education program at grade school level in the California Public School System, where art is no longer offered as part of the regular curriculum. Berman has exhibited in numerous group shows, and exhibits with Sybaris Gallery, Royal Oak, MI, and Mobilia, Cambridge, MA. Her work is in the collections of the Detroit Institute of Art, Detroit, MI; National Museum of American Art, Smithsonian Institution, Washington, DC; and Temple University, Philadelphia, PA. See: Charlotte Moser, "Harriete Estel Berman," *Metalsmith* (Summer 1995).

JEANNOT BLACKBURN b. Dunham, Quebec, Canada 1959; d. Montreal, Canada, 1996. Blackburn was a member of the so-called "Quebecois Clay," a small group of like-minded ceramists headed by Leopold Foulem (q.v.) and including Paul Mathieu and Richard Milette (q.v.). Their work was emphatically contemporary, strong on irony, and highly literate in references to the history of the ceramic medium. Blackburn's work was more whimsical than the other artists' and a little more playfully camp as well. He had solo exhibitions at Interaction, Montreal (1985), Galerie Barbara Silverberg, Montreal (1987, 1993), and Garth Clark Gallery, New York, NY (1989). His work was also shown in many group shows at galleries and museums, including the Everson Museum of Art, Syracuse, NY; the Shigaraki Museum of Ceramic Art, Shigaraki, Japan; and the American Craft Museum, New York, NY. His work is in the collections of the Shigaraki Museum of Ceramic Art and the Burlington Cultural Center, Burlington, Ontario. See: Thomas Piche, *Four Quebecers in Syracuse* (Syracuse: Everson Museum of Art, 1993).

ARMILLA MARIE BURDEN b. Portsmouth, OH, USA, 1945. Burden is primarily a self-taught ceramist but she did apprentice with Jack Earl (q.v.) from 1993 to 1994, learning techniques in sculpture and painting. Since 1984 she has taught ceramic classes at Indian Lake Ceramics, Russell Point, OH. She has taken part in many exhibitions, including at the Works Gallery, Philadelphia, PA; Studio B. Lancaster, OH; and the Arts Space, Lima, OH.

MARK BURNS b. Springfield, OH, USA, 1950. Burns received his BFA in 1972 from the College of the Dayton Art Institute, OH, with a major in Ceramics. He received his MFA in 1974 at the University of Washington, Seattle, under Howard Kottler and Patti Warashina. He has taught at the College of the Dayton Art Institute; the University of Washington; the Factory of Visual Arts, Seattle, WA; the State University of New York at Oswego; the Philadelphia College of Art, PA; and California State University, Chico. Since 1991 he has been Professor and Head of the Ceramics Department at the University of Nevada, Las Vegas. Burns employs bizarre, exotic, and sadomasochistic imagery in his immaculately crafted works. In 1977 he held the first of numerous one-man exhibitions at the Drutt Gallery, Philadelphia, PA, and subsequently in New York, NY, as well. In 1984 he was commissioned by the Pennsylvania Academy of the Fine Arts to create an installation as a homage to the architect Frank Furness. The Society for Art in Craft, Verona, PA, organized a mid-career survey of his work in 1986 entitled "Mark Burns – Decade in Philadelphia." Burns's sculptures are in the public collections of the Everson Museum of Art, Syracuse, NY; Philadelphia Museum of Art, Philadelphia, PA; Stedelijk Museum, Amsterdam, Netherlands; and Montreal Museum of Decorative Art, Montreal, Canada. See: Dave Hickey, "Mark Burns: Venetian America," *American Craft* (June/July 1998).

GAIL BUSCH b. Tucson, AZ, USA, 1958. Busch received her BFA from the Kansas City Art Institute, MO, in 1981. Prior to this she spent two years studying at the Philadelphia College of Art, PA. In 1986 Busch took her MFA at Montana State University, Bozeman. Initially working with functional forms and scales, she has since taken to making "stacks" that are highly decorated, miniature groupings of several fused pots. Her off-scale pot clusters conspire to build diminutive towers, wherein the grandeur of each form is strangely pronounced by curious scale shifts within a single small stack. Her formal influences draw from a broad range of contemporary and historical sources, and her love of complex surface and decoration has been influenced by her time in Thailand. Busch's broad exhibition history encompasses group shows at the American Craft Museum, New York, NY; Clay Studio, Philadelphia, PA; Ferrin Gallery, Northampton, MA; and Garth Clark Gallery, New York, NY. See: Peter Dormer, *The New Ceramics* (London, Thames & Hudson, 1994) and Leslie Ferrin, *Teapots Transformed* (Madison: Guild Books, 2000).

LYDIA BUZIO b. Montevideo, Uruguay, 1948. Buzio studied painting and drawing with Horacio Torres, José Luis Montes, and Guillermo Fernández from 1964 to1966, and in 1967 she studied ceramics with José Collell. Later that year she moved to the US and set up a studio in New York. After her move she found herself drifting towards cityscapes, creating slab-built burnished pots with rooftop images. Her work is in numerous public collections including: Brooklyn Museum of Art, New York, NY; Los Angeles County Museum of Art, Los Angeles, CA; Nelson Atkins Museum of Art, Kansas City, MO; and Victoria and Albert Museum, London, England. From 1983 she exhibited her work at the Garth Clark Gallery in New York, NY, and Los Angeles, CA. She has recently stopped working in ceramics and is currently working in wood, but still within her specialty of urban architecture. See: John Beardsley, Jane Livingston, and Octavio Paz, *Hispanic Art in the United States: Thirty Contemporary Painters and Sculptors* (Houston: Museum of Fine Arts, 1987); Garth Clark, *Ceramic Echoes: Historical References in Contemporary Ceramics* (Kansas City, MO: Contemporary Art Society, 1983); and Oliver Watson, *American Potters Today* (London: Victoria and Albert Museum, 1986).

ROBIN MICHAEL CAMPO b. Baton Rouge, LA, USA, 1958. Campo holds a BFA in Ceramics from Louisiana State University, Baton Rouge (1984). In 1988 he received his MFA, also in Ceramics, from the University of Wisconsin, Milwaukee. Campo has been an art instructor at Spruill Art Center, Dunwoody, GA, since 1995. In addition to this, he serves as Director of the Ceramics Department at the center. He has exhibited his work at venues including the Swan Coach House and Signature Gallery, both Atlanta, GA; Ferrin Gallery, Northampton, MA; Craft Alliance Gallery, St. Louis, MO; I.O. Gallery, New Orleans, LA; and Fletcher Challenge Awards, Auckland, New Zealand.

MICHAEL CARDEW b. Wimbledon, London, England, 1901; d. Truro, Cornwall, England, 1983. Cardew learned to throw pottery from W. Fishley Holland of Braunton Pottery in Devon while on a summer vacation. He studied at Exeter College, Oxford, from 1916 to 1920, and worked with Bernard Leach (q.v.) at the St. Ives Pottery in Cornwall from 1920 to 1923. Cardew established Winchcombe Pottery in 1924 and, inspired by early English slipwares, made his distinctive decorated earthenware pots there until 1938. In 1939 he established Wenford Bridge Pottery in Cornwall. Unable to make a go of it under wartime restrictions, he accepted a post to teach pottery at Achimota College on the Gold Coast of Africa (now Ghana) and to set up a production pottery to supply the British army's requirements in Africa. When the war ended Cardew remained and founded the Vume Pottery. In 1947 he was appointed Senior Pottery Officer in Nigeria and brought stoneware pottery to West Africa, though as another option and not as a replacement for indigenous low-fire pottery. He remained in Nigeria until 1970, when his health forced him to return to Wenford Bridge, where he made pots, taught, and conducted workshops. Cardew was also the author of *Pioneer Pottery*, one of the most influential pottery manuals ever written. Originally published by Macmillan, London, in 1968, it was reissued by A. C. Black in 2001 to mark the anniversary of Cardew's 100th birthday, an event also celebrated with an international conference in Aberystwyth, Wales. In 1976 the British Craft Council organized a retrospective exhibition that traveled to Europe. In 1981, Garth Clark's Institute for Ceramic History organized Cardew's only American retrospective, held as part of that year's NCECA conference. See: Garth Clark, *Michael Cardew* (Tokyo: Kodansha International, 1976); Michael Cardew, *A Pioneer Potter: An Autobiography* (London: Collins, 1988); and Ron Wheeler, *Winchcombe Pottery: The Cardew Finch Tradition* (Oxford: White Cockade Publishing, 1998).

JEAN-JOSEPH CARRIES b. Lyons, France, 1855; d. 1894. Carries trained in sculpture at L'Ecole des Beaux-Arts, Lyons, and from 1874 worked in Paris. Inspired by the Japanese display of pottery at the 1878 Exposition Universelle, he moved to Saint-Armand-en-Puisaye in 1888 to study the region's specialty in stoneware, and showed his first ceramic work a year later at his Paris studio. He evolved a rustic, organic style of pottery, using dipped and trickled glazes that were remarkably free and expressive for their time. He also sculpted dramatic heads and masks, often half-animal and half-human, in glazed stoneware. By the time of his death he had become, in a very short period, one of the most gifted ceramists in France and certainly the most expressive. He attracted a loyal cadre of students and followers that included Georges Hoentschel (who purchased Carries's Saint-Armand workshop from his estate), the gifted Paul Jeanneney, Abbé Pierre Pacton, Jean Pointu, and Patrick Nordstrom. Carries's work can be seen at the Musée des Arts Decoratifs in Paris and in numerous other decorative art collections throughout France and Europe. See: Patrice Bellanger, ed., *Jean-Joseph Carries* (Paris: Galerie Patrice Bellanger, 1997).

MAREK CECULA b. Kielce, Poland, 1944. Cecula studied and was apprenticed in Israel. Since 1977 he has worked in New York, NY. He is the head and coordinator of the Ceramics Department at Parsons School of Art, New York. Cecula was known primarily as a ceramics designer both for industry and for his own low-volume production unit. His turnaround came after working on new ideas at the European Ceramic Work Centre in 's-Hertogenbosch, Netherlands, in 1994. The works from this experimental period were shown for the first time at the Garth Clark Gallery in New York under the title "Scatology." Cecula has subsequently brought out one groundbreaking body of work after another: "Hygiene" in 1996 and "Violations" in 1998. His work is in the collections of the Los Angeles County Museum of Art, Los Angeles, CA; Mint Museum of Craft and Design, Charlotte, NC; Museum of Fine Arts, Boston, MA; and Cooper-Hewitt National Design Museum, New York, NY. See: Lydia Tugendrajch, *Marek Cecula: Scatology Series* (New York and Rotterdam: Garth Clark Gallery and Galerie Maas, 1994); Gabi Dewald, *Marek Cecula: Hygiene* (New York and San Francisco: Garth Clark Gallery and Modernism, 1996); and Jozef A. Mrozek, *Marek Cecula* (Warsaw: Centre for Contemporary Art, 1999).

DAVID K. CHATT b. Sedro Wooley, WA, USA, 1960. Chatt studied at Western Washington University, Bellingham, where he received a BA in Design in 1989. In 1994 and 1995 he took courses at the Pilchuck Glass School in Stanwood, WA, with Felice Nittolo and Hank Murta. His imaginative beadwork has been shown at many exhibitions since 1992, including "Rebellious Bead" (an exhibition traveled by the Bellevue Art Museum, 1995-2000) and "Beadz: Contemporary Bead Artists" (American Craft Museum, New York, 1999-2000). Chatt's work is in the collection of the Charles A. Wustum Museum of Fine Arts, Racine, WI, and other institutions. He is represented by Mobilia Gallery, Cambridge, MA. See: Kathlyn Moss and Alice Scherer, *The New Beadwork* (New York: Abrams, 1993).

MICHAEL COHEN b. Boston, MA, USA, 1936. Cohen received his BFA from the Massachusetts College of Art in 1957 and attended graduate school at the Cranbrook Academy in 1960. He has taught at Penland School of Crafts, NC; Haystack School of Crafts, ME; and Ohio State University; and has received two grants from the NEA (Craftsman Fellowship 1974, Master Craftsman/Apprentice 1975). A full-time studio potter since 1961, Cohen has also recently devoted some time to professional slide photography. Throughout the past three decades he has shown his work at numerous galleries, including Clay Place, Pittsburgh, PA; Ferrin Gallery, Northampton, MA; and Benson Gallery, Bridgehampton, NY. His work is in the permanent collections of the Museum of Modern Art, Design Collection, New York, NY; Everson Museum of Art, Syracuse, NY; American Craft Museum, New York, NY; and Walker Art Center, St. Paul, MN.

ANNETTE CORCORAN b. Inglewood, CA, USA, 1930. Corcoran received her BA from the University of California, Berkeley, in 1952. She also attended courses at Long Beach State University, California Polytechnic State University, Saddleback College, and the College of Marin. Having achieved mastery of underglaze on porcelain, Corcoran has evolved a highly stylized, trompe l'oeil form of teapot and her image repertoire covers a broad range of members of the avian world. As her strongly refined graphic realism jumps between 2-D surface and volumetric form, she exacts a stunning degree of realism in terms of her subject's plumage, and even aspects of personality and gesture proper to the species. Elements from the bird's surroundings often figure somewhere on the surface or in the structure of the teapot (perhaps as a handle or spout), and these elements reinforce the artist's acute refinement of both form and surface in the compelling overall image of the pot. Corcoran has shown in solo shows at the Dorothy Weiss Gallery, San Francisco, CA; Joanne Rapp Gallery, Scottsdale, AZ; and Swan Gallery, Philadelphia, PA. Her work is in many private collections, and also in the collections of numerous museums, including Los Angeles County Museum of Art, Los Angeles, CA; Everson Museum of Art, Syracuse, NY; and Charles A. Wustum Museum of Fine Arts, Racine, WI. See: Garth Clark, *The Eccentric Teapot* (New York: Abbeville Press, 1989) and Leslie Ferrin, *Teapots Transformed* (Madison: Guild Books, 2000).

DAVID DAMKOEHLER b. Oconto, WI, USA, 1943. Damkoehler earned his BA from the University of Wisconsin, Oshkosh, in 1963. He took his MFA in 1969 at Kent State University, Kent, OH. His broad teaching experience includes his post as Professor of Environmental Design at the University of Wisconsin, Green Bay, held for the past six years. Damkoehler's metalwork has been widely exhibited, including shows at the Sybaris Gallery, Royal Oak, MI; Perimeter Gallery, Chicago, IL; Mobilia Gallery, Cambridge, MA; AIA Gallery, Seattle, WA; Gallery Ra, Amsterdam, Netherlands; SOFA New York, NY, Miami, FL, and Chicago, IL; American Crafts Museum, New York, NY; Charles A. Wustum Museum of Fine Arts, Racine, WI; and Milwaukee Art Museum, Milwaukee, WI. His work is in the permanent collection of the American Crafts Museum, New York, NY. See: Leslie Ferrin, *Teapots Transformed* (Madison: Guild Books, 2000) and Frank Lewis, "The Fortuitous Encounters of David Damkoehler," *Metalsmith* (Fall 2000).

ALBERT-LOUIS DAMMOUSE b. Paris, France, 1848; d. Paris 1926. Dammouse studied at the Ecole des Arts Decoratifs and Ecole des Beaux-Arts in Paris. In 1869 he apprenticed with L. M. Solon, the Sèvres master of *pâte-sur-pâte*, a technique of decoration with thin layers of slip on porcelain. Dammouse joined the studio of Charles Haviland, working with the *eminence grise* of French decorative art, Felix Bacquemond, and the pioneer of French studio pottery, Ernest Chaplet, until the studio closed in 1881. Together with his brother, Edouard-Alexandre Dammouse, he established a studio in Sèvres producing stoneware and, after 1898, glass, notably *pâte de verre* and *pâte d'émail*. Dammouse's work can be seen at the Musée des Arts Decoratifs, Paris, and numerous other collections of decorative art in Europe. See: Gabriel P. Weisberg, *Art Nouveau Bing: Paris Style 1900* (New York: Abrams, 1986) and Geneviève Becquart and Dominique Szymusiak, *Du Second Empire a l'Art Nouveau: La Création Ceramique* (Saint-Armand: Musée de Saint-Armand-les Eaux, 1987).

JOHN DE FAZIO b. Reading, PA, USA, 1959. In 1981 De Fazio earned a BFA in Ceramics at Philadelphia College of Art, PA, and took an MFA in Sculpture at San Francisco Art Institute three years later. He has been a visiting artist and lecturer at both the University of Nevada, Las Vegas, and University of Washington, Seattle (both 1998). The artist's awards include an NEA Visual Art Fellowship (1986) and a New York Foundation for the Arts Fellowship (1991). De Fazio works with molded readymades – mostly items considered to be kitsch – transforming them with irony and humor. His many commissions include a massive ceramic and glass table for the boardroom of MTV in New York. His work has been widely exhibited, including shows at the Harrison Gallery, Philadelphia, PA; Garth Clark Gallery, New York, NY; Dolphin Gallery, Kansas City, MO; American Craft Museum, New York, NY; Baltimore Clayworks, Baltimore, MD; San Angelo Museum, San Angelo, TX; and Museum of Contemporary Ceramic Art, Shigaraki, Japan. His work appears in the collections of, among others, Honolulu Art Museum, Honolulu, HI; Museum of Contemporary Ceramic Art, Shigaraki, Japan; and Mint Museum of Craft and Design, Charlotte, NC. See: Dave Hickey, *Stardumb*, illustrated by John de Fazio (San Francisco: Artspace, 1999); Mark Del Vecchio, *Postmodern Ceramics* (London: Thames & Hudson, 2001); and Ezra Shales, "The Unprudish Moment," *American Ceramics* (13/2, 1999).

KIM DICKEY b. White Plains, NY, USA, 1964. Dickey received a BFA in Ceramics from Rhode Island School of Design, Providence, RI, in 1986 and an MFA from New York State College of Ceramics at Alfred University, Alfred, NY, in 1988. Dickey currently holds an assistant professorship at the University of Colorado, Boulder, where she has taught since 1999. Over the past decade she has been a visiting artist at nearly twenty colleges and universities, and has held visiting professorships at six institutions. Her work has been widely exhibited, including shows at the Garth Clark Gallery, Thomas Healy Gallery, Jack Tilton Gallery, Jane Hartsook Gallery, and Bronwyn Keenan Gallery, all New York, NY; Rule Modern and Contemporary, Denver, CO; Museum of Contemporary Art, Denver, CO; and Everson Museum of Art, Syracuse, NY. Dickey's work is in the public collections of the Museum of Contemporary Art, Honolulu, HI, and the Everson Museum of Art, Syracuse, NY. See: Garth Clark, *The Eccentric Teapot* (New York: Abbeville Press, 1989).

NICOLAI DIULGHEROFF b. Kiustendil, Bulgaria, 1901; d. Torino, Italy, 1982. Diulgheroff, the son of a typographer, emigrated to Italy in 1926 and six years later graduated from the Architecture School of the Accademia Albertina di Belle Arti, Turin. It was there that he first gained an awareness of Futurism. While focusing his energies on painting, he also designed furniture, lamps, crystal, and ceramics during this period. In 1928 he was a participant in the Futurists' display at the XVI Venice Biennale, and was also represented in the Futurist Pavilion at the Esposizione Internazionale in Turin. From 1931 to 1932 he was employed at the Casa Mazzotti in Albisola by Tullio d'Albisola, who was developing "Aeroceramica" or Futurist ceramics with the movement's founder, Filippo Tommaso Marinetti. While employed in this position Diulgheroff incorporated decorative elements into his work, the thrust of which was to realize solutions to the problems of function previously associated with ceramics. At the same time, he insisted upon innovation within a context of modern style. See: Enrico Crispolti, *La Ceramica Futurista da Balla a Tullio D'Albisola* (Florence: Centro Di, 1982) and Karen McCready, *Art Deco and Modernist Ceramics* (London: Thames & Hudson, 1995)

PAUL DRESANG b. Appleton, WI, USA, 1948. Dresang earned a BA in Art from the University of Wisconsin, Oshkosh, in 1970, and an MFA from the University of Minnesota, Minneapolis, in 1974. He has guest lectured and given workshops at colleges and universities across the US. He has also received an NEA Visual Artist's Fellowship Grant (1988) and the Illinois Art Council Fellowship Finalist Grant (1999). Recently his work has involved variations of the teapot form, concealed but suggested beneath trompe l'oeil leather, replete with zippers and clasps, whose number and placements draw a mood of fetish about these objects. Dresang has exhibited his work in many venues, including the Nancy Margolis Gallery, New York, NY; Ferrin Gallery, Northampton, MA; The Clay Studio, Philadelphia, PA; American Craft Museum, New York, NY; The Weisman Art Museum, Minneapolis, MN; and the Los Angeles County Museum of Art, Los Angeles, CA. His work is in the permanent collections of Los Angeles County Museum of Art, Los Angeles, CA;

Renwick Gallery, Smithsonian Institution, Washington, DC; and Mint Museum of Craft and Design, Charlotte, NC. See: Leslie Ferrin, *Teapots Transformed* (Madison: Guild Books, 2000) and Mark Del Vecchio, *Postmodern Ceramics* (London: Thames & Hudson, 2001).

CHRISTOPHER DRESSER b. Glasgow, Scotland, 1834; d. London, England, 1904. Dresser entered the School of Design at Somerset House, London, in 1847. He soon emerged as the star pupil and began lecturing on botany. In 1858 his influential treatise "Botany as Adapted to the Arts and Art Manufactures," influenced both by A. W. N. Pugin and Owen Jones, was published in *Art Journal*. He also published several books, including *The Principles of Decorative Design* (1873) and his major work, *Japan, its Architecture, Art and Art Manufactures* (1882). He was one of the first industrial designers to take a very different, pro-industry stance from the leading reformers of the time, such as William Morris. Dresser designed in various materials, producing textiles, carpets, wallpaper, ceramics, glass, and metalwork. Although his ceramic design work is extensive (his designs were manufactured by Watcombe Terra Cotta, Linthorpe Pottery, Minton and Co, and Wedgwood), he is best known for his exceptional teapots and pouring vessels in silver plate and other metals. These elegant, modernist, and visionary objects prefigure a similar Bauhaus aesthetic that only emerged twenty years after Dresser's death. However, as Simon Jervis writes in *The Penguin Dictionary of Design and Designers* (1984), Dresser's style is better understood "as an extreme version of the High Victorian geometric style, which also provided a disciplined framework for his abstract explorations of polychromatic ornament and his wide usage of an extraordinarily wide range of historic and exotic prototypes, even including Peruvian pottery." See: Stuart Durant, *Christopher Dresser 1834–1904* (London: Richard Dennis, 1972) and Widar Halen, *Christopher Dresser* (Oxford: Phaidon/Christie's, 1990).

MICHAEL DUVALL b. Grand Rapids, MI, USA, 1950. From 1972 to 1974 Duvall was a Ceramics major at Wayne State University, Detroit, MI. He has operated his studio full-time since 1975. This ceramist's broad exhibition record includes shows at the Joy Horwich Gallery, Chicago, IL; Garth Clark Gallery, New York, NY, and Los Angeles, CA; Works Gallery, Philadelphia, PA; Ferrin Gallery, Northampton, MA; Crafts Alliance, St. Louis, MO; American Crafts Museum, New York, NY; Museum Het Kruithuis, 's-Hertogenbosch, Netherlands; Victoria and Albert Museum, London, England; and Columbus Museum of Art, Columbus, OH. His work appears in the collections of Newark Museum, Newark, NJ; Museum Het Kruithuis, 's-Hertogenbosch, Netherlands;

and Victoria and Albert Museum, London, England. See: Mark Del Vecchio, "Michael Duvall" in Gert Staal, ed., *Functional Glamour* ('s-Hertogenbosch: Museum Het Kruithuis, 1989).

JACK EARL b. Unipolis, OH, USA, 1934. Earl received his BA at Bluffton College, OH, in 1956, and returned to school in 1964 to take an MA at Ohio State University in Columbus. From 1963 to 1972 he taught at the Toledo Museum of Art, where the magnificent collection of ceramics exhibited had a strong impact on his work and perfectionist craftsmanship. A one-man survey was held at the Museum of Contemporary Crafts in New York, NY, in 1971 and there have been over one hundred exhibitions at both galleries and museums since then. Earl's work swings between two poles. On the one hand he is almost a folk artist, creating narratives about his dog and life in the Corn Belt; at other times he is a sophisticated Pop artist, creating large, superbly styled portraits of celebrities both real (Abraham Lincoln) and fictional (Dick Tracy). He is represented by the Perimeter Gallery, Chicago, IL, and Nancy Margolis in New York, NY. Public collections of his work include the Art Institute of Chicago, IL; Delaware Art Museum, Wilmington, DE; Everson Museum of Art, Syracuse, NY; and National Museum of American Art, Smithsonian Institution, Washington, DC. See: Lee Nordness, *Jack Earl: The Genesis and Triumphant Survival of an Underground Ohio Artist* (Chicago: Perimeter Press, 1985).

EDWARD S. EBERLE b. Tarentum, PA, USA, 1944. Eberle took a BS from Edinboro State College, PA, in 1971 and an MFA from New York State College of Ceramics, Alfred University, Alfred, NY, in 1976. The artist's voluminous, lidded, porcelain vessels draw vague allusions to houses and architecture. His elaborate sgraffitto imagery narrates, with lively parades of people, the interior life of his "houses." The imagery fluctuates deftly between tonal representations of bodies in space and graphic surface pattern which serves to reinforce the formal structure of the pot. Many influences can be found in Eberle's work, from black and white Mimbres pottery to painting and decoration on early Greek vases. The artist directs the eye between the lavish, lyrical, narrative imagery and the 2-D line of the form the imagery moves around. Eberle's accolades include a Visual Artist's Fellowship from the NEA in 1987. He has exhibited his work widely, in both solo and group shows, at venues including the Garth Clark Gallery, New York, NY; Perimeter Gallery, Chicago, IL; Temple Gallery, Philadelphia, PA; Joanne Rapp Gallery, Scottsdale, AZ; Northern Clay Center, Minneapolis, MN; and Museum of Art, Carnegie Institute, Pittsburgh, PA. His work is in the collections of the Museum of Art, Carnegie Institute, Pittsburgh, PA;

Charles A. Wustum Museum of Fine Arts, Racine, WI; and Detroit Institute of Art, Detroit, MI. See: Janet Koplos, "Edward Eberle at Garth Clark," *Art in America* (May 1996) and Mark Del Vecchio, *Postmodern Ceramics* (London: Thames & Hudson, 2001).

RAYMON ELOZUA b. Stuttgart, West Germany, 1947. Elozua studied at the University of Chicago and has been an invited lecturer at colleges and universities throughout the US since 1979. He has taught Ceramic Sculpture at New York University, NY (1982–86), Rhode Island School of Design, Providence, RI (1983), California College of Arts and Crafts, Oakland, CA (1983), and Pratt Institute of Design, Brooklyn, NY (1984–85). He has been the recipient of NEA fellowships in painting and sculpture (1980, 1981, 1987) as well as of a New York Foundation for the Arts Fellowship in Ceramics (1988). His solo exhibitions include shows at Pfizer Gallery, New York, NY; Garth Clark Gallery, New York, NY; Habatat-Shaw Gallery, Detroit, MI; Braunstein Gallery, San Francisco, CA; OK Harris, New York, NY; and Carlo Lamagna Gallery, New York, NY. Elozua's work is in the collections of the American Craft Museum, New York, NY; Everson Museum of Art, Syracuse, NY; Los Angeles County Museum of Art, Los Angeles, CA; Mint Museum of Craft and Design, Charlotte, NC; and Charles A. Wustum Museum of Fine Arts, Racine, WI. See: Garth Clark, *American Ceramics* (New York: Abbeville Press, 1987); Garth Clark, Mary F. Douglas, Carol E. Mayer, Barbara Perry, Todd D. Smith, and E. Michael Whittington, *Selections from Allan Chasanoff Ceramic Collection* (Charlotte: Mint Museum of Craft and Design, 2000); Mark Del Vecchio, *Postmodern Ceramics* (London: Thames & Hudson, 2001); and Jo Lauria, *Color and Fire* (New York: Rizzoli, 2000).

MARY ENGEL b. Chicago, IL, USA, 1963. Engel received her BS in 1988 from Illinois State University, Normal, and her MFA from the University of Georgia, Athens, in 1993. Engel's work has made broad strides away from its early basis in pots and wood-fire. Her newer work is centered in her love of lavishly adorned surfaces, built from a selection of found objects. She embeds things in an almost obsessive manner to achieve a surface of both visual and historical depth. Her new work draws on a range of historical sources: American outsider art, with its obsessively patterned surface, and African funerary jars, whose embellished surfaces speak of personal histories lodged amidst mundane artifacts. Lately her favorite subjects have been dogs and other animals, about which Engel has developed a strong empathetic curiosity. She has been represented by Dorothy Weiss Gallery, San Francisco, CA, and has shown in both solo and group exhibitions at the Marcia Wood Gallery and Dorothy McRae Gallery, Atlanta, GA; Georgia Museum of Art, Athens, GA; Macon

Museum of Arts and Sciences, Macon, GA; and Asheville Museum of Art, Asheville, NC. See: Pamela Bloom Leonard, "Visual Arts," *Atlanta Journal Constitution* (Dec. 13, 1996) and Anna Brutzman, "Memories in Clay," *Atlanta Homes and Lifestyles* (Jan. 1997).

ZHOU DING FANG b. Yixing, China, 1965. Ding Fang is one of two students of Xu Xiu Tang, a "National Craft Master" of China. Ding Fang has herself earned the rank of "Craft Master" and works within the established traditions of Yixing-ware: teapots, small sculpture, and literati objects known for trompe l'oeil effects and their general degree of exacting detail. Her work has been published in China, Hong Kong, Taiwan, and Singapore, and has also appeared in a series of Chinese postage stamps featuring famous Yixing pots. Ding Fang has shown at Garth Clark Gallery, New York, NY, and her work is in the collections of the British Museum, London, England; Asian Art Museum of San Francisco, CA; Mint Museum of Craft and Design, Charlotte, NC; and Beijing Art Museum, Beijing, China. See: Mark Del Vecchio, *Postmodern Ceramics* (London: Thames & Hudson, 2001) and Lee Jingduan, ed., *Charm of Dark-Red Pottery Teapots* (Nanjing: Yilin Press, 1992).

LASZLO FEKETE b. Budapest, Hungary, 1949. Fekete studied at the Budapest Academy of Applied Arts from 1969 to 1974. As was typical amongst artists during the Communist era, he focused mainly on international juried exhibitions and won a slew of medals, prizes, and diplomas for his work from the Hungarian Cultural Ministry, the French Cultural Ministry, the Mino Triennial and the Academy of International Ceramics. Since 1994 Fekete has exhibited with the Garth Clark Gallery, New York, NY. His work takes on a grand theme – the layered cultural detritus of five hundred years of successive regimes in Hungary, each of which attempted to wipe out traces of the previous power. In some of his work Fekete collaborates with the Herend Porcelain factory, using their seconds to assemble sardonic commentaries on taste and culture. His work is in the collections of the Mint Museum of Craft and Design, Charlotte, NC; Budapest Museum of Decorative Art, Budapest, Hungary; and Mino Triennial, Mino, Japan. See: Garth Clark and Laszlo Fekete, *Laszlo Fekete* (New York: Garth Clark Gallery, 1997); Garth Clark, Mary F. Douglas, Carol E. Mayer, Barbara Perry, Todd D. Smith and E. Michael Whittington, *Selections from Allan Chasanoff Ceramic Collection* (Charlotte: Mint Museum of Craft and Design, 2000); and Mark Del Vecchio, *Postmodern Ceramics* (London: Thames & Hudson, 2001).

KENNETH FERGUSON b. Elwood, IN, USA, 1938. Ferguson studied at the American Academy of Art, Chicago, IL, and at the Carnegie Institute of Technology, Pittsburgh, PA, where he received his BFA in 1952. In 1954 he was awarded his MFA from Alfred University, Alfred, NY. He has taught at various institutions, including the Carnegie Institute, Alfred University, and the Archie Bray Foundation in Montana. Since 1964 he has headed the Ceramics Department of the Kansas City Art Institute, and in 1996 he became Professor Emeritus of Ceramics. Under Ferguson's influence KCAI has become one of the most important ceramics schools in the country. His students from the 1970s now dominate the leading edge of the American ceramics world: Richard Notkin (q.v.), Chris Gustin, Akio Takamori (q.v.), Kurt Weiser (q.v.), and others. Ferguson's work is included in numerous public collections including the Everson Museum of Art, Syracuse, NY; Los Angeles County Museum of Art, Los Angeles, CA; Mint Museum of Craft and Design, Charlotte NC; Carnegie Museum, Pittsburgh, PA; and Charles A. Wustum Museum of Fine Arts, Racine, WI. In 1995 his legacy both as an artist and as a teacher was surveyed in two exhibitions: "Ken Ferguson: Retrospective" at the Nelson/Atkins Museum, Kansas City, MO, and "Keepers of the Flame: Ken Ferguson's Circles" at the Kemper Museum of Contemporary Art, Kansas City, MO. See: Ed Lebow, *Ken Ferguson* (Kansas City: Nelson Atkins Museum of Art, 1995) and Garth Clark and Vicky Clark, *Keepers of the Flame: Ken Ferguson's Circles* (Kansas City: Kemper Museum of Contemporary Art, 1995).

WAYNE FERGUSON b. Chattanooga, TN, USA, 1946. Ferguson studied at the University of Kentucky, Lexington. He has lectured and instructed at colleges and schools around the Southeastern US. He was the recipient of the Al Smith Fellowship from the Kentucky Arts Council. The influence of Native American vessel ceramics is apparent in his hand-built bowl forms and pots. He has great adeptness at the "corrugated" technique of coil built pots, curiously matched with a facility at rendering animals of many kinds. He has exhibited his work widely, including shows at Lil Street Gallery, Chicago, IL; Images Friedman Gallery and Kentucky Art and Craft Gallery, both Louisville, KY; Plantation Gallery, Key West, FL; Los Angeles County Folk Museum, Los Angeles, CA; Owensboro Museum of Fine Art, Owensboro, KY; and Huntington Museum, Huntington, WV.

SHEILA FERRI b. Philadelphia, PA, USA, 1951. Ferri received her BFA from the Tyler School of Art, Philadelphia, PA, in 1973, and her MFA from the Rhode Island School of Design (RISD), Providence, RI, in 1976. She then went on to earn an MAT from RISD in 1977. Initially, Ferri's sculptural wireworks were done as reliefs. They later served to support glass inclusions – almost like hammocks – that were slumped into the woven infrastructure. Sometimes her organic wire tangles supported ceramic forms. Now her wire sculptures almost "weave themselves" into reductive house forms and other domestic iconography (cups, saucers, etc.) It's not a stretch to read her imagery autobiographically – not only does she have her own family but she has also devoted nearly two decades to teaching art to children at the Horace Mann School in Riverdale, NY. Her glass- and wire-based sculptures have been exhibited nationally and internationally, in both public and private collections at the Glas Museum, Ebeltoft, Denmark; Kanazawa Chamber of Commerce and Industry, Kanazawa, Japan; Delaware Art Museum, Wilmington, DE; and ASI Gallery, San Francisco, CA. See: *Neues Glas* (Dusseldorf, 2/88).

LEOPOLD FOULEM b. Bathurst, New Brunswick, Canada, 1945. He received his BA from the Alberta College of Art, Calgary, Alberta, and his MA from the Indiana State University in 1988. Foulem works with ceramics from a decidedly conceptual point of view and has been the inspiration for a group of Canadian artists with a similar bent, known loosely as "Quebecois Clay:" Richard Milette (q.v.), Jeannot Blackburn (q.v.), and Paul Mathieu. Foulem writes and lectures extensively on ceramics as well as being an active exhibitor. He has had numerous solo exhibitions since 1969, most recently with Prime Gallery in Toronto and Garth Clark in New York, NY. He has shown at 42 museums and been in 180 group exhibitions. His work is in many collections, including that of Los Angeles County Museum of Art, Los Angeles, CA. In 1999 he received one of Canada's top accolades, the Jean A. Chalmers National Crafts Award. See: Paul Bourassa, *Phantasses et Soucoupes: Ceramics by Leopold L. Foulem* (Saint-Laurent: Musée d'Art Saint-Laurent, 2000).

JOHN FRAME b. Colton, CA, USA, 1950. In 1975 Frame earned a BA in Literature from San Diego State University, CA, and went on to receive an MFA from Claremont Graduate School, CA, in 1980. The artist's awards include two NEA Visual Artist's Fellowship Grants (1984 and 1986) and a J. Paul Getty Museum Individual Artist's Fellowship (1995). Frame's work has been exhibited widely for over two decades, including shows at the Kohn/Turner Gallery, Koplin Gallery and Garth Clark Gallery, all Los Angeles, CA; Francine Seders Gallery, Seattle, WA; LewAllen Gallery, Santa Fe, NM; Los Angeles County Museum of Art, Los Angeles, CA; and Nevada Institute of Contemporary Art, Las Vegas, NV; Hunsaker/Schesinger Gallery, Los Angeles, CA. His work appears in the permanent collections of Los Angeles County Museum of Art, Los Angeles, CA, and the Renwick Gallery, National Museum of American Art, Smithsonian Institution, Washington, DC. See: Edward Lucie-Smith, *Zoo: Animals in Art* (New York: Watson-Guptill, 1998).

CHERYL FRANCES b. Berwyn, IL, USA, 1958. Frances holds an AS in Commercial Art from Honolulu Community College, Honolulu, HI, 1989, and a BA in Liberal Studies (Summa Cum Laude) from the University of Hawaii at Monoa, Honolulu, 1991. Frances took her MA in Fine and Performing Arts at Southern Oregon State College, Ashland, 1995 (Summa Cum Laude) and received both a Juror's Award and People's Choice Award, *Metal Art*, 2000. Her recent line of work – reconfigured spoons and other domestic objects – makes use of both found and fabricated parts, and exploits her facility with a broad range of media. About her work she writes: "By recombining elements associated with femininity and domesticity in a playful fashion, I hope to release these roles from their prescribed expectations." Her exhibition record includes shows at the Arkansas Center for the Arts, Museum of Decorative Arts, Little Rock, AR; Ellen Noel Art Museum, Odessa, TX; Andy Sharkey Gallery, Royal Oak, MI; and Ferrin Gallery, Northampton, MA. She has work in the collection of the Arkansas Center for the Arts, Museum of Decorative Arts, Little Rock, AR.

KEIKO FUKAZAWA b. Tokyo, Japan, 1955. In 1979 Fukazawa earned her BFA at Musashino Art University, Tokyo, Japan. Her 1986 MFA in Ceramics is from Otis/Parsons, Los Angeles, CA, where she studied under Ralph Bacerra (q.v.). Between her degrees, Fukazawa went to Shigaraki, Japan, and studied other regional pottery styles and techniques, independently, throughout the country. Since 2000, she has taught at Loyola Marymount University, Los Angeles, CA. She has also taught in the California State Prison system for more than eight years, and her dedication to this work has perhaps shaped her personal oeuvre more than any other single force. Fukazawa describes literally breaking her traditional vessels as an evolutionary catalyst away from her foundations in such form and process. While using this same exercise with her student wards, she has become the ultimate assimilator of imagery. Her almost flagrantly juxtaposed cultural pastiche is born from a sense of spontaneity and graphic irreverence. A collage of student graffiti, commercial pop images (Japanese, American, and otherwise) and historical reproductions are "cut and pasted" into a "scrapbook" surface. The bright palette of her plates and pots augments their bold graphic terms, and heightens our view of their cultural kaleidoscope. Her many exhibitions include six one-person shows at Garth Clark Gallery, Los Angeles, CA, Kansas City, MO, and New York, NY. Group shows include exhibitions at Los Angeles County Museum of Art, Los Angeles, CA; California African-American Museum, Los Angeles, CA; American Craft Museum, New York, NY; Forum for Contemporary Art, St. Louis, MO; and Dorothy Weiss Gallery, San Francisco, CA. Her work is in the permanent collections of the National Museum of History, Taipei, Taiwan; Los Angeles County Museum of Art, Los Angeles, CA; and Charles A. Wustum Museum of Fine Arts, Racine, WI. See: Susan Peterson, *Contemporary Ceramics* (New York: Watson-Guptill, 2000).

JOHN GARRETT b. El Paso, TX, USA, 1950. Garrett holds a BA (1972) from Claremont College, Claremont, CA, and an MA (1976) from the University of California, Los Angeles. Between 1972 and 1989, he held numerous teaching posts, primarily in California. His awards include two NEA fellowships (1983 and 1995). Garrett's work has virtually reconfigured our contemporary conception of the basket. His forms often begin as a matted weave of found metal objects within a prefabricated matrix, or as grids woven from the objects themselves. The artist then forms these "synthetics" – by crimping, riveting or weaving them – into basket and vessel forms. Drawn to the patina of surfaces that comes only from time and use, Garrett challenges himself to bring new life to the castaway detritus of our industrial, consumer society. He has exhibited widely for nearly three decades, including shows at: R. Duane Reed Gallery, Chicago, IL; Goldesberry Gallery, Houston, TX; Mobilia Gallery, Cambridge, MA; Quay Gallery, San Francisco, CA; Sybaris Gallery, Royal Oak, MI; Snyderman/Works Gallery, Philadelphia, PA; Whitworth Art Gallery, Manchester, England; The Jewish Museum, San Francisco, CA; Charles A. Wustum Museum of Fine Arts, Racine, WI; American Craft Museum, New York, NY; and Netherland Textile Museum, Tilburg, Netherlands. See: Kari Lonning, *The Art of Basketry* (New York: Sterling, 2000).

PAMELA GAZALE b. Washington, DC, USA, 1962. Gazalé studied at the Rhode Island School of Design, Providence, earning her BFA in 1987, and then at the Tyler School of Art, Temple University, Elkins Park, PA, from 1987 to 1988. Interested in using unusual material, Gazalé recently wrote about how she was inspired by a documentary on Sahara desert salt traders. "Rich in history, metaphor, and life itself, the element of salt is like no other. I have dedicated nine years of my life to the study of it and the sculpture is the result of my findings. I have chosen to hand carve the material in the same manner as classical marble sculpture. The irony is the similarity of appearance." She has had various solo shows, including "Halite" (Esther Claypool Gallery, Seattle, WA, 2000); "Matière Saline" at the Fuel Gallery, Seattle; and a show at the Kitteridge Gallery, University of Puget Sound, Tacoma, WA, 1994. Her numerous group shows include "Tabletops" at the California Center for the Arts Museum, Escondido, and "Maryland's Best" at the Rockland Art Center, Ellicott City. Gazalé has received several awards, including the Betty

Bowen Special Recognition Award from the Seattle Museum in 1993, and the Silver Award from the Kristallnacht Project at the American Interfaith Institute, Philadelphia, PA. Her work is in the collections of the Liberty Museum, Philadelphia, PA, and the Museum of American Glass, Millville, NJ. See: Steve Kemper, "Salt of the Earth," *Smithsonian* (Jan. 1999) and Elizabeth Bryant, "Review," *Artweek* (Vol 26, No 3, 1995).

DAVID R. GIGNAC b. Alfred, NY, USA, 1967. Gignac received his BFA from the New York State College of Ceramics, Alfred, NY, in 1991. In the same year he worked at the Pilchuck Glass School, Stanwood, WA, and taught at the University of Illinois, Champaign. Gignac's principal materials are steel and glass, which his sculptural works combine in ways that produce surreal overtones. At the same time his references play very much off the familiar. His forms are often architectural or industrial, but sometimes incorporate hyper-organic motifs. Using recycled materials, Gignac may work within an established form (the teapot) and, while his renditions often preclude functionality, their references are to the infrastructure of production (factories, water towers). His work has been exhibited at Kimzey Miller, Seattle, WA; West End Galleries, Corning, NY; and Museo, Langley, WA. See: Meagan Corwin, "History of Objects," *Metalsmith* (Winter 2000) and Leslie Ferrin, *Teapots Transformed* (Madison: Guild Books, 2000).

DAVID GILHOOLY b. Auburn, CA, USA, 1963. Gilhooly had a peripatetic childhood, living throughout the Caribbean. In 1961 he enrolled at the University of California, Davis, as a biology major, switching to anthropology and then to art after he took a ceramics class with Robert Arneson, the father of Funk, "to impress a girl," and instead fell in love with clay. After graduation Gilhooly stayed on for another three years to take an MA, and by 1968, had become a popular member of an emerging Funk sensibility in ceramics. Gilhooly began to exhibit with the Candy Store Gallery in Folsom, CA – one of the first advocates of this iconoclastic approach to ceramic art – and with Hanssen Gallery in San Francisco, CA. In 1969 he began to work with his invented frog culture, the body of work with which he is most closely identified. His work has been shown in hundreds of exhibitions, both solo and group, at the Whitney Museum of Art, New York, NY; Los Angeles County Museum of Art, Los Angeles, CA; and numerous other public institutions. He currently shows with John Natsoulas Gallery in Davis, CA, and the Sherry Frumkin Gallery, Los Angeles, CA, but no longer makes ceramics. See: Peter Selz, *Funk* (Davis: University of California Press, 1967) and Kenneth Baker et al., *David Gilhooly* (Davis: John Natsoulas Gallery, 1992).

ISMAEL GONZALEZ b. Havana, Cuba, 1952. Gonzalez studied at the San Alejandro Art School, Havana, but a call to military service prevented him from graduating. In 1979 he won political asylum in Madrid, Spain. In the same year, with assistance from the Red Cross and Cuban organizations, Gonzalez realized his aspiration of coming to the USA. In 1980 he settled in Los Angeles, CA, where he eventually gained citizenship and a degree in computer and electronic technology. This training figures heavily in his functional art designs, which include clocks, lamps, and teapots, but his broad talents range to acrylic painting and collage as well. Gonzalez's art reflects his Cuban/American cultural heritage, but often with his uniquely humorous approach. He exhibits his work at the del Mano Gallery, Pasadena and West Los Angeles, CA. See: Wilma J. Camacho, "An Exploration of Cuban Culture," *Saludos Hispanos* (Sept./Oct. 1999).

MICHAEL GRAVES b. Indianapolis, IN, USA, 1934. Graves studied in the architecture program at the University of Cincinnati, OH, and the Graduate School of Design at Harvard University, Boston, MA, graduating in 1959. After a brief stint as a studio artist in New York, he went on to study at the American Academy in Rome, Italy (1960–62). He taught at Princeton University, NJ, becoming Schirmer Professor of Architecture (1972), and from 1964 ran a private practice as well. In 1969 his participation in a group show at the Museum of Modern Art, New York, NY, elevated his career by establishing him as one of the "New York Five." Graves, however, was quick to resist his placement within the Modern Movement and its philosophical underpinnings, and moved towards a more whimsical design sensibility in terms of his use of color and eclectic historical influences. Later furniture designs extrapolated elements of Art Deco and other established genres, and brought Graves recognition. His architecture, however, did not take off with the same vigor until the early 1980s. Graves is best known for his decorative and design work of the 1980s – including jewelry, ceramics, and numerous items made for Alessi in Italy – and for his current work for the Target stores. Among his many awards are nine AIA National Honor Awards, fourteen Progressive Architecture Design Awards, 52 New Jersey Society of Architecture Awards, and six honorary doctorates. See: Alex Buck and Matthias Vogt, *Michael Graves: Designer Monographs 3* (Frankfurt: Ernst & Sohn, 2001).

PETER GRIEVE b. London, England, 1936. Grieve was educated at the Bromley College of Art and at the Royal Academy Schools, both in London, England. His international exhibition record includes shows at the Ann Nathan Gallery, Chicago, IL; Hahn Ross Gallery, Santa Fe, NM;

Kouros Gallery, New York, NY; Holdsworth Contemporary Galleries, Sydney, Australia; Harcourts Contemporary, San Francisco, CA; Zolla/Lieberman Gallery, Chicago, IL; and Air Gallery, London, England. His work is in the collection of the Arkansas Arts Center, Little Rock, AR.

WALTER GROPIUS b. Berlin, Germany, 1883; d. Boston, MA, USA, 1969. Gropius studied from 1903 to 1905 at the Technische Hochschule, Munich, and from 1905 to 1907 at the Technische Hochschule, Berlin. He then worked for Peter Behrens (1908–10) in furniture and office design. In 1919, under his directorship, the Hochschule für angewandte Kunst was united with the Kunstakademie, Weimar, into the Staatliches Bauhaus. Gropius's directorship of this institution lasted nearly a decade, until 1928, and he was insistent upon precepts of unity within the arts. Upon the Bauhaus's move to Dessau in the early 1920s, its conceptual framework transformed to accommodate general trends towards industrial modernization. Gropius emigrated to London in 1934, where he worked in partnership with E. Maxwell Fry for three years, before moving to the USA. There he became Professor of Architecture at Harvard University, Boston, MA. Gropius founded The Architects Collaborative (TAC) in 1945 to undertake architectural and design projects. In 1968, while designing new buildings for Rosenthal, he was commissioned to produce the *TAC1* tea service. This was not entirely new ground. While in London, Gropius had designed an aluminum electric teapot. Louis McMillen is often cited as the *TAC1* collaborator but has denied involvement. Research reveals that it was a little-known employee, Katherine De Sousa, who played a central role in *TAC1*'s development. See: Bernt Fritz, *The Tea Service TAC1 by Walter Gropius* (Frankfurt: Verlag form, 1998).

GERALD GULOTTA b. Rockford, IL, USA, 1921. Gulotta was an instructor of Industrial Design at Pratt Institute from 1955 to 1970. He was also an adjunct professor of industrial design from 1970 to 1985. Now an independent, international design consultant specializing in ceramics, glass, stainless steel, and silver, Gulotta works with manufacturers in the US, South America, Europe, and Asia. He has served as Design Education Consultant to the Portuguese Ministry of Economics and, in 1974, he organized and directed "Industrial Design Workshop" in Portugal, to provide introductory training to advanced students of art and architecture. Gulotta also served as Design Education Consultant to the University of Guadalajara, Mexico, where he developed the foundation curriculum in industrial design for their new School of Design. He has been a guest lecturer at the Central School of Arts and Crafts, Beijing, China (1982) and in 1987 was invited by the China National Arts and Crafts Import Export Corporation to design a collection of miniature teapots for the Violet Sand Factory, Yixing, China. His work appears in the collections of Cooper-Hewitt National Design Museum, New York, NY; Brooklyn Museum of Art, Brooklyn, NY; Dallas Museum of Art, Dallas, TX; and Newark Museum, Newark, NJ.

KEITH HARING b. Kutztown, PA, USA, 1958; d. New York, NY, USA, 1990. Haring first attended the Ivy School of Professional Art in Pittsburgh in 1977 but soon realized that he did not want to be a commercial artist. He then sat in on classes at the University of Pittsburgh and became involved with the Pittsburgh Arts and Crafts Center. Inspired by a lecture given by Christo, Haring decided to seek a more public forum for his own work. In 1978 he moved to New York, NY, as a scholarship student at the School of Visual Arts, where he began to attract attention for his subway drawings. Shows at PS 122 and Club 57 gave him greater visibility and in 1982 he had his first solo show with Tony Shafrazi Gallery. By the mid-1980s Haring was a bona-fide international art star with shows in Rotterdam, Tokyo, London, Cologne, Milan, Basel, Munich, and Amsterdam. His work began to grow expensive and to counter this he opened his Pop Shop in 1986, selling inexpensive multiples. Haring died in 1990 of AIDS, one of hundreds of New York artists to succumb to the disease. He only produced two bodies of ceramic work. In 1984 he made a series of huge terracotta amphora that he decorated with felt-tipped pens. His tea services, produced by the Belgian firm of Villeroy & Boch, were produced posthumously and derived from his drawings. In 1997 the Whitney Museum of American Art in New York opened a major retrospective of his work that traveled internationally through 2000. See: Elizabeth Sussman, Keith Haring, et al., *Keith Haring* (New York: Whitney Museum of American Art, 1997).

ANNE HIRONDELLE b. Vancouver, WA, USA, 1944. Hirondelle came to ceramics by a circuitous route. After receiving her BA in English from the University of Puget Sound in Tacoma, WA, she took an MA in Counseling Psychology at Stanford University, CA. After trying law school, she began attending classes at the Factory of Visual Arts in Seattle, WA. This stimulated her interest in clay, and she completed her BFA in Ceramics at the University of Washington, Seattle, in 1976. Encouraged by Robert Sperry and others, she set up a studio in Port Townsend. Martha Drexler Lynn, writing in *Clay Today*, comments that "all of her pieces are tied to the reality of function; only her use of oversized forms makes it clear that they are, in fact, for contemplation."

Hirondelle's work is in many public collections, including the Los Angeles County Museum of Art, Los Angeles, CA. See Gretchen Adkins, "The Aquarta Art of Anne Hirondelle," *Ceramic Art and Perception* (Issue 31, 1998) and Christine Hemp, "Anne Hirondelle," *American Crafts* (Dec. 2000/Jan. 2001).

DAVID HOCKNEY b. Bradford, Yorkshire, England, 1937. Hockney studied at the Royal College of Art, London (fellow students included Allen Jones and R. B. Kitaj) and, by the time he graduated in 1962, he had already been identified as a leader of the British Pop art movement. His first solo exhibition was held in 1963 at the John Kasmin Gallery. He first drew attention for his paintings, drawings, and prints and then for his photographic collages and stage design at Glyndebourne. There are numerous books on Hockney's art, in addition to his own writings, *David Hockney by David Hockney* (London: Thames & Hudson, 1977) and *That's the Way I See It* (London: Thames & Hudson, 1993).

NICHOLAS HOMOKY b. Sarvar, Hungary, 1950. Homoky's family emigrated to England in 1956. He attended Bristol Polytechnic, Bristol, England, from 1970 to 1973, and the Royal College of Art in London from 1973 to 1976. He studied painting, sculpture, graphics, and draftsmanship, all of which are evident as elements in his subsequent work in ceramics. Homoky comments that he "finally chose to work with clay because it seemed to be the only medium capable of being as purely expressive as it was functional." Fascinated with opposites – black versus white, line versus form, and the appearance of function versus the lack of function – Homoky's work has been included in numerous exhibitions worldwide and is in the collections of the Los Angeles County Museum of Art, Los Angeles, CA; the Victoria and Albert Museum, London, England; and Boijmans van Beuningen Museum, Rotterdam, Netherlands. See: John Fowles and Nicholas Homoky, *Nicholas Homoky* (Yeovil: Marston House, 1997).

MICHAEL HOSALUK b. Invermay, Saskatchewan, Canada, 1954. Hosaluk studied Cabinet Making and Millwork at the Kelsey Institute of Applied Arts and Sciences, Saskatoon, Saskatchewan (1974). He was responsible for organizing the first annual Saskatchewan Woodworkers show in 1979 and, since 1982, has taught and given workshops throughout the US and Canada. Hosaluk was also instrumental in starting and maintaining the American Association of Wood Turners and the Furniture Society. Among innumerable awards and distinctions, he has received the Premier's Prize from the Saskatchewan Craft Council (2000) and Arts Grant B, Saskatchewan Arts Board, Regina, SK (1991,

1994, 1997). His broad exhibition record includes shows at the Craft Alliance, St. Louis, MO; Mobilia Gallery, Chicago, IL; del Mano Gallery, Los Angeles, CA; Hodges Taylor Gallery, Charlotte, NC; Gallery of Fine Woodworking, Seattle, WA; and Mint Museum of Craft and Design, Charlotte, NC. His work is in the public collections of the Los Angeles County Art Museum, Los Angeles, CA; Royal Ontario Museum, Toronto, ON, Canada; Detroit Museum of Art, Detroit, MI; and Mint Museum of Craft and Design, Charlotte, NC. It is also in the private collections of Queen Elizabeth II at Buckingham Palace, London, England. See: Bonita File and Mike Mendelson, *The Fine Art of Wood* (New York: Abbeville Press, 2000) and Ray Leier, Jan Peters, and Kevin Wallace, *Contemporary Turned Wood* (Madison: Hand Books Press, 1999).

MI-SOOK HUR b. Seoul, Korea, 1965. Hur received her BFA in Metalsmithing and Jewelry Design from Seoul National University in 1987. In 1998 she took her MFA in the same field from the University of Wisconsin, Madison, and has been lecturing at the School of Art, East Carolina University, Greenville, NC, since 1999. She has shown at the Seoul Metalsmiths Biennial, Korea; Vincenza Oro II, Vincenza, Italy; and at World Gold Council, Seoul, Korea. Hur has also shown at the John Michael Kohler Arts Center, Sheboygan, WI, in conjunction with her residency there. She has been reviewed by and written for numerous metals and jewelry magazines in Seoul and Hong Kong.

DAVID HUTCHINSON b. Albuquerque, NM, USA, 1940. Hutchinson holds a BFA in Painting and Drawing from the University of New Mexico. Originally known for his stoneware pottery, produced under the name of Ground-Work Pottery, Hutchinson has more recently developed a line of (functional) earthenware pots influenced by indigenous pottery styles of the Southwestern US. His use of bold colors and animal imagery make his designs contemporary at the same as referencing older traditions. He is represented by Off the Wall Gallery, Santa Fe, NM.

SERGEI ISUPOV b. Stavrapole, Russia, 1963. Isupov studied at the Ukranian State Art School, Kiev (1982) and took both his BA and MFA (1990) in Ceramics at the Art Institute of Tallinn, Estonia. In 1993, Isupov emigrated from Estonia to the USA, and has since made Kentucky his home and workplace. His pieces are complex unions of articulated figuration, conjoined with less resolute forms that contort to meet their resting surface. They are animated and upright, while still appearing painfully subjected to some oblique, diffuse gravity. All of his formal convolutions are reinforced by a stark, surreal surface, in both image and color. Man becomes beast, body becomes face, and the

artist's ability to express human (animal) sexual appetite and its complex social component leaves us with saturated narratives that are essentially deep questions, despite their level of visual completeness. Isupov's gymnastic imagery melds 2-D narrative onto hyper-gestural narrative figures, and these pictorial surfaces alternately recede into, then overwhelm, his refined forms. Isupov has given workshops and lectured widely since 1990, including at the Rhode Island School of Design, Providence, RI, and Penland School of Crafts (both 2000). He has also received the Smithsonian Craft Show Top Award for Excellence (1996). Isupov's work has been widely exhibited, including shows at SOFA Chicago, IL, New York, NY, and Miami, FL (Ferrin Gallery); Connell Gallery, Atlanta, GA; Dorothy Weiss Gallery, San Francisco, CA; Los Angeles County Museum of Art, Los Angeles, CA; Mint Museum of Craft and Design, Charlotte, NC; and Charles A. Wustum Museum of Fine Arts, Racine, WI. His work also appears in the collections of the Tallinn Museum of Applied Art, Estonia; Museum of Applied Art, Tuman, Russia; Museum of Contemporary Ceramics, Summe, Ukraine; Oslo Museum of Applied Art, Oslo, Norway; Mint Museum of Craft and Design, Charlotte, NC; and Los Angeles County Museum of Art, Los Angeles, CA. See: Leon Nigrosh, "Erotica in Ceramic Art, Sexual, Sensual and Suggestive," *Ceramic Art & Perception* (# 38, 1999); Mark Del Vecchio, *Postmodern Ceramics* (London: Thames & Hudson, 2001); and Leslie Ferrin, *Teapots Transformed* (Madison: Guild Books, 2000).

ELLEN JANTZEN b. St. Louis, MO, USA, 1946. Jantzen received an AA in Graphic Arts from St. Louis Junior College District, 1966. She also attended Southern Illinois University in 1969, where she studied Ceramics and Weaving with a Fine Arts major. She graduated Summa Cum Laude from the Fashion Institute of Design and Merchandising, Los Angeles, CA (1992). Between 1992 and 1994 she worked as a project designer for Mattel Toys and, while she still pursues freelance work in a similar capacity, Jantzen has engaged in her own creative, sculptural work since 1994. She has taught Product Design at the Art Center College of Design, Pasadena, CA (1998–2000), and earned four patents (US Patent and Trademark Office) for her product designs. Her work has been exhibited at del Mano Gallery, Pasadena, CA; Chiaroscuro Gallery, Chicago, IL; Ariana Gallery, Royal Oak, MI; Orlando Museum of Art, Orlando, FL; The Society of Arts and Crafts, Boston, MA; Oakland Museum of Art, Oakland, CA; and Vancouver Museum, Vancouver, BC, Canada.

WALTER KEELER b. London, England, 1942. Walter Keeler trained at the Harrow School of Art under Victor Margrie and Michael Casson. He has taught at Harrow School of Art, London; Central School of Art,

London; and Bristol Polytechnic, Bristol, England. He was inspired by Bernard Leach (q.v.) and his *A Potter's Book*. In the late 1960s Keeler was introduced to salt-glazed pottery, prompting him to work with this demanding technique. Committing himself to only working in salt glazes, he also found inspiration in traditional British functional pottery as well as in archaeology, oil containers, and other industrial artifacts. In 1965 he set up a studio in Bledlow Ridge, Buckinghamshire, and in 1976 moved to Penally in Wales. His latest work has moved into low-fire glazes in the tradition of early Staffordshire masters such as Whieldon, Greatbach, and Wood. See: Oliver Watson, *British Studio Pottery* (London: Phaidon 1990) and Martha Drexler Lynn, *Clay Today* (San Francisco: Chronicle Books, 1990).

KAREN ESTELLE KOBLITZ b. Hollywood, CA, USA, 1951. Koblitz first became interested in ceramics while studying at California State University, Northridge, in 1968. In 1970 she traveled to Florence, Italy, and was introduced to Renaissance maiolica and Della Robbia ware. In 1973 she took her BFA from the California College of Arts and Crafts in Oakland. After graduation she traveled to Japan, where she visited the Tatsmura Silk Company in Kyoto. In 1974 she moved to Madison, WI, where she studied with Don Reitz. She also learned mold making from Bruce Breckenridge. After teaching for a number of years, she decided to return to California and support herself through her art. She completed a large commission in 1987 for the Cranston Securities Company of Los Angeles – a two-part wall mural made of tiles inspired by Mimbres pottery. Koblitz continued to make smaller table and wall pieces as well. Her work carries traces of the work of a number of ceramic and non-ceramic artists, including Robert Arneson, Bernard Palissy, Paul Cézanne, Gustav Klimt, and Henri Matisse. See: Martha Drexler Lynn, *Clay Today* (San Francisco: Chronicle Books, 1990), and Jo Lauria, *Color and Fire* (New York: Rizzoli, 2000).

CINDY KOLODZIEJSKI b. Augsburg, Germany, 1962. Kolodziejski received her BFA from Otis Art Institute, where she studied under Ralph Bacerra (q.v.), and her MFA from Long Beach State University under Tony Marsh (q.v.). She uses her highly refined painter's skill to create irreverent and intimate images on her cast vessel forms. Whether drawn from her own personal experience or from art history, the works tell stories that are startling and provocative. Lately, a mirrored distortion has crept into the scenes. Faux metal bases and handles add to the overall impression of consummate skill. She has exhibited in solo and group exhibitions since 1988, and her work is in the public collections of the American Craft Museum, New York, NY; Los Angeles County Museum of Art, Los

Angeles, CA; Mint Museum of Craft and Design, Charlotte, NC; National Museum of History, Taipei, Taiwan; and Shigaraki Ceramic Cultural Park, Shigaraki, Japan. See: Jo Lauria, "Pluperfect – The Painted Narrative Vessels of Cindy Kolodziejski," *Ceramics: Art and Perception* (Issue 19, 1995), Stephen Luecken, *Cindy Kolodziejski* (New York and Los Angeles: Garth Clark Gallery and Frank Lloyd Gallery, 1999).

ROBIN KRAFT b. Chicago, IL, USA, 1955. Kraft holds a BA from the University of Illinois, Chicago (1978). She earned her MFA at Kent State University, Kent, OH. An assistant professor at Purdue University, West Lafayette, IN, from 1993 to 1998, Kraft has been an associate professor of art there since 1999. She has been the recipient of an Individual Artist Grant, Indiana Arts Commission (2000) as well as an Individual Artist Fellowship, Ohio Arts Council (1994). Her work has been widely exhibited, including shows at Galeria Mesa, Mesa, AZ; Steinbaum Krauss Gallery, New York, NY; SOFA Chicago, IL, and New York, NY; Mobilia Gallery, Cambridge, MA; Facere Gallery, Seattle, WA; American Craft Museum, New York, NY; Wichita Center for the Arts, Wichita, KS; National Ornamental Metal Museum, Memphis, TN; and Evansville Museum of Arts and Sciences, Evansville, IN. See: Leslie Ferrin, *Teapots Transformed* (Madison: Guild Books, 2000) and Anne Allen, "Penchant for Pendants," *Metalsmith* (Winter 1997).

ANNE KRAUS b. Short Hills, NJ, USA, 1956. After a BA in Painting at the University of Pennsylvania, Kraus earned a BFA from Alfred University, Alfred, NY, in 1982. Her love of painting continues today, as she creates narrative scenes on ceramic vessels. On a single artwork many different images appear with meticulously printed text. Together they explore stories depicting man's tenuous balance between reality and the unknown – a psychological state Kraus mines in all her work. A recent development is her use of the large, wall-hung, tile picture, drenched in color. Kraus keeps an active dream journal as an idea source. Her work is in numerous public collections, including the Los Angeles County Museum of Art, Los Angeles, CA; Houston Museum of Fine Art, Houston, TX; Newark Museum, Newark, NJ; Carnegie Museum, Pittsburgh, PA; Everson Museum of Art, Syracuse, NY; Museum of Contemporary Ceramic Art, Shigaraki, Japan; and Victoria and Albert Museum, London, England. See: Jo Lauria, *Color and Fire* (New York: Rizzoli, 2000) and Garth Clark, *Anne Kraus: A Survey* (New York: Garth Clark Gallery, 1998).

NATHALIE KREBS b. Copenhagen, Denmark, 1895; d. Copenhagen, 1978. Krebs worked for Bing and Grondahl from 1919 to 1929. For a brief time she shared a studio with Gunnar Nyland before moving to Helrev and opening her own workshop, Saxbo, in 1930. Influenced by Japanese wares, Krebs became known for her simple, modernist forms and textured glazes with soft tonal gradations of color. Her classic teapot and pear-shaped jug, with a split neck forming the handle and spout, are two of Krebs's most renowned designs. In addition to her own work she collaborated at Saxbo with a number of leading Scandinavian designers and sculptors, including Eva Staehr-Nielsen, Hugo Liisberg and Olaf Staehr-Nielsen. See: Jennifer Hawkins Opie, *Scandinavian Ceramic and Glass in the Twentieth Century* (New York: Rizzoli, 1990).

RICK LADD b. Syracuse, NY, USA, 1958. Ladd earned his BFA in Painting from the Art Institute of Chicago in 1982. He went on to an MFA in the same field at the Pratt Institute, Brooklyn, NY, which he completed in 1986. Ladd has exhibited widely at various venues, including the Empire State Building, New York, NY; American Primitive Gallery, New York, NY; Jayne Baum Gallery, New York, NY; Aaron Packer Gallery, Chicago, IL; and Gallery of Functional Art, Santa Monica, CA. See: Suzanne Slesin, "The Latest in Bottle-Cap Marquetry," *New York Times* (Mar. 12, 1992).

GEO LASTOMIRSKY b. Fairfield, CT, USA, 1953. Lastomirsky earned his BFA in Ceramics at Kansas City Art Institute, Kansas City, MO, 1983. He also attended the University of Bridgeport, Bridgeport, CT (1971–73), New York State College of Ceramics at Alfred University, Alfred, NY (1979–80) and the University of Washington, Seattle, WA (1985). Lastomirsky was a guest at the 1st Yixing International Ceramic Art Conference, Yixing, China; Alfred China Ceramic Summer Workshop and Tour; Jingdezhen Ceramic Institute, Jingdezhen, China; and other workshops in Asia. His solo exhibitions include shows at the Joanne Rapp Gallery, Scottsdale, AZ; William Traver Gallery, Seattle, WA; and Charles Wright Academy, Tacoma, WA. He has also shown in numerous group exhibitions at venues including Los Angeles County Museum of Art, Los Angeles, CA; American Craft Museum, New York, NY; Tacoma Art Museum, Tacoma, WA; Craft Alliance, St. Louis, MO; Pewabic Pottery, Detroit, MI; Ferrin Gallery, Northampton, MA; Margo Jacobsen Gallery, Portland, OR; Jeroen Bechtold Keramiek Gallery, Amsterdam, Netherlands; Dorothy Weiss Gallery, San Francisco, CA; and Swidler Gallery, Royal Oak, MI. His work is in the collections of the Los Angeles County Museum of Art, Los Angeles, CA; Jingdezhen Ceramic Institute, Jingdezhen, China; and JINRO Cultural Foundation, Seoul, Korea. See: Jo Lauria, *Color and Fire* (New York: Rizzoli, 2000).

JIM LAWRENCE b. Independence, OR, USA, 1944. Lawrence holds a BFA from Portland Art School, OR, and also studied at Reed College, Portland. His carved wood figures convey complex psyches within complex narratives. They certainly alienate us from our sense of entitlement to an "easy reading" of the story in which the works engage us. Lawrence's depiction of puppet-like figurines is disarming in its narrative starkness and formal absurdity. For the past few years he has been represented by Koplin Gallery, Los Angeles, CA, and he has exhibited his work at the Jan Baum Gallery, Los Angeles, CA; Ruth Siegel Ltd., New York, NY; Galerie Brusberg, Berlin, Germany; Cirrus Gallery, Los Angeles, CA; Van Straaten Gallery, Chicago, IL; Gagosian Gallery, Los Angeles, CA; California Center for the Arts Museum, Escondido, CA; and Taipei Fine Arts Museum, Taipei, Taiwan. See: Jeff Kelley, "Jim Lawrence," *Artforum* (Sept. 1984).

JAMES LAWTON b. USA, 1954. Lawton received a BS in Constructive Design (Ceramics and Enamels) from Florida State University, Tallahassee, in 1976, and an MFA in Ceramics from Louisiana State University, Baton Rouge, in 1980. Lawton has held various teaching posts since 1986, in Chicago, IL; Alfred, NY; and Baton Rouge, LA. He is currently Associate Professor of Ceramics at CVPA University of Massachusetts, Dartmouth. Among his numerous awards are two Visual Art Fellowships (1984, 1986) from the NEA. Since 1979 Lawton has given over forty workshops throughout the US and Europe. His keen sense of design and balance are always evident within the formal lyricism of his pots. Elements within his pieces ground them squarely in the realm of potterly traditions, their flawless craftsmanship and fluid construction least among these. While his surface motifs are often strongly graphic, their subtle hue and halos melt pattern into the clay surface, and confound our sense of the graphicness existing separately from the pot's "skin." Lawton's broad exhibition record includes shows at the Clay Works Gallery, Philadelphia, PA; Mobilia Gallery, Cambridge, MA; Gallery 1021, Chicago, IL; Garth Clark Gallery, Los Angeles, CA, New York, NY, and Kansas City, MO; Everson Museum of Art, Syracuse, NY; Northern Clay Center, St. Paul, MN; and Museum of Contemporary Ceramic Art, Shigaraki, Japan. His work is in the permanent collections of the Los Angeles County Museum of Art, Los Angeles, CA; Victoria and Albert Museum, London, England; Mint Museum of Craft and Design, Charlotte, NC; and Georgia Museum of Art, Athens, GA. See: Jo Lauria, *Color and Fire* (New York: Rizzoli, 2000) and Susan Peterson, *Contemporary Ceramics* (New York: Watson-Guptill, 2000).

BERNARD LEACH b. Hong Kong, 1887; d. St. Ives, Cornwall, England, 1979. Leach, the so-called father of studio pottery, was the son of a

High Court judge and lived in Asia as a child, moving from Hong Kong to Japan and then to Singapore. In 1897 he went to Windsor, England, to attend Beaumont Jesuit College. In 1903, at the age of sixteen, he entered the Slade School of Art, studying drawing under Henry Tonks. After a brief stint as a clerk at the Hong Kong and Shanghai Bank, he joined the London School of Art to study etching under Frank Brangwyn. In 1909 he moved to Japan to teach etching, and made friends with Kenchichi Tomimoto and with the founder of the Mingei movement, Soetsu Yanagi. In 1911 he attended a party at which the entertainment was making raku pottery and he immediately fell in love with the medium. Leach and Tomimoto studied with Ogata Kenzan, the sixth "inheritor" of the once-noble Kenzan tradition. Leach earned his "densho" from his master, thus making this tweed-suited Edwardian Englishman the seventh Kenzan. In 1920 Leach returned to England and set up a pottery in St. Ives, a seaside resort with something of a reputation as an artists' retreat. Shoji Hamada was his first apprentice, followed by Michael Cardew (q.v.), Katherine Pleydell Bouverie, Norah Braden, and dozens more over the years. Leach was fired with an evangelical zeal and offered a vision of pottery inspired by the classic periods of Asian ceramics, by the directness and honesty of English medieval slipwares, and by the notion of function as the root of all beauty. He wrote many books and articles, and traveled worldwide lecturing on ceramics. His artist's manual, *A Potter's Book*, is the most successful and popular book of its kind. First published in 1940, it is still reverentially referred to in the field as the "bible." By 1950 Leach was arguably the most influential potter in the world. He was revered in Japan and there were legions of adherents to his Anglo-Oriental school in America, Canada, South Africa, and Australia. Europe, however, never impressed by the British obsession with utility, remained largely untouched by this gifted polymath. He died at 92, having lived to see his beliefs challenged and rejected. Today the Leach presence looms large in British ceramics – an ambivalent mixture, hostile to modernity, and yet, more than any other visual artist, Leach imbued the field with a dignity and sense of its aesthetic worth. His work can be found in museums throughout the world but a particularly fine collection has been assembled by the Victoria and Albert Museum, London, England. See: Bernard Leach, *A Potter's Book* (London: Faber and Faber, 1940); Carol Hogben, ed., *The Art of Bernard Leach* (London: Faber and Faber, 1978); Oliver Watson, *Bernard Leach: Potter and Artist* (London: Crafts Council, 1997); and Edmund de Waal, *Bernard Leach: St Ives Artists* (London: Tate Gallery Publishing, 1998), in which de Waal offers a tough but not unkind contemporary reading of Leach and his impact.

AH LEON b. Hsi-Shi, Taiwan, 1953. Ah Leon chose not to continue the family tradition of farming and instead attended the Taiwan National College of Art, graduating in 1976. From 1978 to 1982 he apprenticed with master potters throughout Taiwan. Inspired first by the five-hundred-year-old Chinese Yixing tradition, and then encouraged to innovate by the work of American ceramist Richard Notkin (q.v.), Ah Leon brought a new ambition to the field, increasing scale dramatically and using his knowledge as a bonsai master to create some of the most convincing and seductive trompe l'oeil surfaces of his time, culminating in the 1998 touring exhibition of his sixty-foot-long *Bridge*, organized by the Arthur M. Sackler Gallery, Smithsonian Institution, Washington, DC. He has shown his work extensively in Amsterdam, Taipei, and New York at the Garth Clark Gallery. His work is in the public collections of the Arthur M. Sackler Gallery, Smithsonian Institution, Washington, DC; Metropolitan Museum of Art, New York, NY; Mint Museum of Craft and Design, Charlotte, NC; and the Museum of History and the National Palace Museum, both in Taipei, Taiwan. Ah Leon is an instructor in the tea ceremony and a consulting editor to *Purple Sands Magazine* and *Tea Pot World*, both published in Taiwan. See: Ah Leon, "14 Principles of a Good Teapot," *Ceramics Monthly* (June-Aug. 1991) and Claudia Brown, Garth Clark, David Wible, and Jan Stuart, *Beyond Yixing: The Ceramic Art of Ah Leon* (Taipei, Taiwan: Purple Sands Publisher, 1998).

ROY LICHTENSTEIN b. New York, NY, USA,1923; d. New York, 1997. Lichtenstein studied under Reginald Marsh at the Art Students League in New York, NY, and then attended Ohio State University, Columbus, from 1940 to 1949, interrupted by his service in the US Army from 1943 to 1945. He received his MFA from Ohio State University and from 1957 taught at the State University of New York, Oswego, From 1960 to 1963 he taught at Douglass College, Rutgers University, New Brunswick, NJ. In 1964 he resigned from the Rutgers faculty to devote himself full-time to painting, and emerged as one of the major artists of the twentieth century. From November 20 to December 11, 1965, after a year-long collaboration with Ka-Kwong Hui, Lichtenstein exhibited his ceramic sculptures at the Leo Castelli Gallery, New York, NY. These works, both assembled cup and teapot sculptures and ceramic heads, had a strong influence on the development of a Super-Object/Pop idiom in ceramics. In 1977 the Art Galleries of California State University at Long Beach organized a major exhibition of Lichtenstein's ceramic sculpture. The artist added to his ceramic oeuvre in 1984 by designing a limited edition tea service which was produced by the Rosenthal Porcelain Works, Germany, along with several limited edition plates. See: Constance W. Glenn, *Roy Lichtenstein: Ceramic Sculpture* (Long Beach: Art Galleries,

California State University, 1977) and Dieter Struss, *Rosenthal: Dining Services, Figurines, Ornaments and Art Objects* (Atglen: Shiffer, 1997).

OTTO LINDIG b. Possneck, Germany, 1895; d. Wiesbaden, Germany, 1966. Lindig studied from 1913 to 1915 at the Grossherzoglich Sächsische Kunstgewerbeschule, Weimar, while he apprenticed as a sculptor at Bechstein Atelier, Ilmenau. He completed his sculptural tutelage under the stern eye of Richard Engelmann at the Grossherzoglich Sächsische Hochschule für Bildende Kunst, Weimar. The Bauhaus pottery workshop was situated in Dornburg, some distance from the Weimar Bauhaus, giving it greater autonomy than the other workshops. "The Workshop" initially employed two masters: Max Krehan, a local Thuringian folk potter, was the technical master, while the sculptor, Gerhard Marks, was the "form" master. Together with Lindig and fellow student Theodore Bogler, the quartet became the driving force at the Workshop. In 1926 Lindig was appointed a master, heading up the ceramic design program. He used his craft skills to innovate design and improve industrial productivity. This fit in with the shift in Bauhaus philosophy from Walter Gropius's (q.v.) initial concept of merging "art and craft" to a more egalitarian, Socialist vision of "art and technic" that emerged after 1921. Lindig continued to design for industry and make his own work, and taught at the Hochschule für Bildende Kunst, Hamburg, from 1947 to 1960. See: Klaus Weber, Peter Hahn, et al., *Keramik und Bauhaus* (Berlin: Bauhaus-Archiv, 1989).

ANDREW LORD b. Rochdale, England, 1950. Lord attended the Rochdale School of Art from 1966 to 1968 and studied ceramics at the Central School of Art in London until 1971. He then moved to Rotterdam and later Amsterdam, where he exhibited at Art and Project, a highly respected and innovative gallery. In 1981 Lord had his first exhibition in the US, at the BlumHelman gallery in New York, NY, and has since shown with Anthony d'Offay in London, Galerie Bruno Bischofberger in Zurich, and Andre Emmerich in New York. His work has been included in numerous group and solo exhibitions and his work has been selected for the Whitney Biennial. Currently represented by Gagosian Gallery, New York, Lord lives and keeps his studio in New York, and has a second home in Carson, NM. His work plays with sophisticated notions of geometry, of still life, and of appropriation from modern painters, ranging from Cézanne to Picasso and Braque. Public collections of his work include the Stedelijk Museum, Amsterdam, Netherlands; Boijmans van Beuningen Museum, Rotterdam, Netherlands; Los Angeles County Museum of Art, Los Angeles, CA; and Victoria and Albert Museum, London, England. See: Christopher Knight, *Andrew Lord* (New York: BlumHelman, 1984) and *James Schuyler, Poems: Andrew Lord, Sculptures* (Zurich: Edition Bruno Bischofberger, 1992).

MICHAEL LUCERO b. Tracy, CA, USA, 1953. Lucero received his BA in 1975 from Humboldt State University, Arcata, CA. He moved to New York, NY, upon completing his MFA at the University of Washington, Seattle, in 1978. Lucero recently moved his studio to Westchester County, NY, and currently has a studio in Italy as well. He has exhibited extensively since 1977 with over one hundred group and solo exhibitions. He has had numerous one-person exhibitions in New York, first with Charles Cowles Gallery and currently with David Beitzel Gallery, as well as shows elsewhere with Dorothy Weiss, San Francisco, CA, and Garth Clark Gallery, Los Angeles, CA. He has received fellowships from the NEA (1979, 1981, 1984), the Ford Foundation (1977–78), and Creative Artists Public Service Program (1980). In 1976 he received the Young American Award from the Museum of Contemporary Crafts in New York and, in 1993, the Richard Koopman Distinguished Chair in the Visual Arts at the University of Hartford, CT. His work is in the collections of the High Museum of Art, Atlanta, GA; Hirschorn Museum of Art and Sculpture, Washington, DC; Metropolitan Museum of Art, New York, NY; Mint Museum of Art, Charlotte, NC; New Museum of Contemporary Art, New York, NY; Seattle Art Museum, Seattle, WA; and Toledo Museum of Art, Toledo, OH. In 1996 the Mint Museum of Art organized a large retrospective of his work which traveled the USA. See: Mark R. Leach and Barbara Bloeminck, *Michael Lucero: Sculpture 1976–1995* (New York: Hudson Hills, 1996).

MARILYN LYSOHIR b. Sharon, PA, USA, 1950. Lysohir studied at the Centro Internazionale Di Studi, Verona, Italy (1970–71). She received her BA from Ohio Northern University, Ada, in 1972 and her MFA from Washington State University, Pullman, in 1979. She has lectured at colleges and universities throughout the US, as well as in Canada, Australia, Denmark, and Africa. Lysohir has been the recipient of numerous awards, including a WESTAF/NEA Regional Fellowship for Visual Art (1989), two Sudden Opportunity Grants, Idaho Commission on the Arts (1993 and 1995), and an Idaho Artist Fellowship (1996). She makes extremely large-scale ceramic sculpture. The Los Angeles critic Suzanne Muchnic commented that Lysohir's work has strange vectors and that, despite the "clear position on the infiltration of military aggression [she] walks a precarious line between decoration and politics." Lysohir has exhibited her work widely, including solo shows at the Asher/Faure Gallery, Los Angeles, CA; Garth Clark Gallery, Kansas City,

MO; Linda Hodges Gallery and Foster/White Gallery, both Seattle, WA; Denis Ochi Fine Arts, Ketchum, ID; Elzay Gallery, Wilson Art Center, Ada, OH; Boise Art Museum, Boise, ID; and Art Gallery of Hamilton, Hamilton, Ontario, Canada. Her group shows include those at the American Craft Museum, New York, NY; San Angelo Museum of Art, San Angelo, TX; Sybaris Gallery, Royal Oak, MI; William Traver Gallery, Seattle, WA; Byron Cohen Gallery, Kansas City, MO; Herning Museum, Herning, Denmark; Bellevue Museum of Art, Bellevue, WA; and Tacoma Art Museum, Tacoma, WA. See: Garth Clark, *American Ceramics* (New York: Abbeville Press, 1987).

PHILLIP MABERRY b. Stanford, TX, USA, 1951. Maberry studied at East Texas State University in Commerce, receiving his BA in 1975. He did graduate work at Wesleyan University, Middletown, CT, from 1975 to 1976 and later worked at the Brooklyn Museum of Art School and the Fabric Workshop in Philadelphia. Maberry uses ceramics as well as paint, fabric, thrift-store finds, and assembled objects to create highly decorated interiors. In his early ceramic work he focused on slip-cast porcelain pieces with organic or geometric surface decorations. His present output adapts the abstract forms used in the decorative arts of the 1950s. In 1981 he created a gallery-sized installation for the Biennial of the Whitney Museum of American Art in New York, NY, and has worked extensively on public and private tile installations ever since – murals, bathrooms, kitchens, and recently a complex 26,000-square-foot environment of walls and floors, and an entire indoor swimming pool, for a private home in Massachusetts. Maberry has taken part in dozens of major exhibitions and has had regular solo exhibitions, in the early 1980s with Hadler Rodriguez, New York, NY, and later with the Garth Clark Gallery, Los Angeles, CA, Kansas City, MO, and New York, NY. Public collections include Los Angeles County Museum of Art, Los Angeles, CA, and Victoria and Albert Museum, London, England. See: Mark Del Vecchio, *Postmodern Ceramics* (London: Thames & Hudson, 2001).

JAMES D. MAKINS b. Johnstown, PA, USA, 1946. Makins took his BFA at the Philadelphia College of Art, PA, 1968. His MFA (1973) is from Cranbrook Academy of Art, Bloomfield Hills, MI. He currently teaches at Philadelphia College of Art and Design, University of the Arts. His broad teaching history includes positions at Parsons School of Design (1979–82) and New School for Social Research (1970–90), both New York, NY. Makins has also instructed at numerous other colleges, schools, universities, and potteries in New York and elsewhere. He has lectured throughout the US, Europe, and Asia. Among the

awards he has received are several NEA Fellowship Awards (1976, 1980, 1990), a Silver Medal, 49th Concorso Internazionale della Ceramica d'Arte, Faenza, Italy (1998–99), and JICA International Ceramic Fellowship, Korea (1997). Makins's broad exhibition record dating back to 1969 includes shows at the Dorothy Weiss Gallery, San Francisco, CA; Dai Ichi Arts Ltd., New York, NY; Zacheta Gallery, Warsaw, Poland; Hangnam Gallery, Seoul, Korea; Gallery Midi, Lausanne, Switzerland; Musée des Arts Decoratifs, Paris, France; Mint Museum of Craft and Design, Charlotte, NC; American Craft Museum, New York, NY; and Dowse Art Museum, Aotearoa, New Zealand. His work is in the collections of the American Crafts Museum, New York, NY; Everson Museum of Art, Syracuse, NY; Philadelphia Museum of Art, Philadelphia, PA; Shigaraki Ceramic Cultural Park, Shigaraki, Japan; and Renwick Gallery, National Museum of American Art, Smithsonian Institution, Washington, DC. See: Bert Carpenter, "James Makins," *American Ceramics* (10/4, 1993).

KASIMIR MALEVICH b. Kiev, Russia, 1878; d. Leningrad, Russia, 1935. Together with Mondrian, Malevich was one of the key artists in introducing and defining non-objective art. He studied at the Kiev School of Art (1895–96) and the Moscow School of Painting, Sculpture and Architecture (1904–05) where he became involved in underground politics. He started his Suprematist paintings – pure geometric abstractions – in 1913 and they were first exhibited in 1915. In 1922 he moved to Petrograd and taught at the Institute for Artistic Culture. Although he is quoted as stating that if something is "useful it cannot be art," he did apply himself to some object design, including the famous *Suprematist Teapot and Cups* (1923) for the State Porcelain Factory in Petrograd. This was formerly the Imperial Factory, founded in the mid-18th century, renamed the State Porcelain Factory in 1917, and turned into the Lomonosov Porcelain Factory in 1925. Malevich's teapot was not so much an attempt to address functional concerns as an attempt to study the interaction of forms. The main proponent of Suprematist design at the factory was Malevich's disciple, Nicolai Suetin, and a number of plates, tea services, and other utilitarian objects were designed with abstract decoration. Vassily Kandinsky also designed for the factory in the early 1920s. Although Malevich retained a legendary stature amongst Russian artists he lost the support of the Communist regime, which established Social Realism as the official art form and, in 1940, Malevich returned to figurative painting. See: Nina Lobonov-Rostovsky, *Revolutionary Ceramics: Soviet Porcelain 1917–1927* (New York: Rizzoli, 1990) and Jan Bobko, ed., *The Great Utopia: The Russian Avant-Garde 1915–1932* (New York: Guggenheim Museum, 1992).

RICHARD MARQUIS b. Bumblebee, AZ, USA, 1945. Marquis studied architecture at the University of California, Berkeley, where he received a BA in 1969. That same year he was awarded a Fulbright-Hayes scholarship and lived in Venice while working at the Venini Fabbrica where he learned the murrine glass technique; this was to be the first of numerous visits to Italy over the next thirty-one years. In 1972 Marquis transferred to the University of California's Design Department, as it was then known, and received his MA in Ceramics and Glass in 1972. His first solo exhibition was in 1969 and he has exhibited extensively ever since, including in major group exhibitions such as Lee Nordness's touring exhibition "Objects USA" (1969–70), "New Glass: a Worldwide Survey" (Corning Glass Museum, 1979), and "Holding the Past" (Seattle Art Museum, 1995). Since 1979 he has received four NEA fellowships and in 1995 he was elected to the College of Fellows of the American Crafts Council. In 1997 a retrospective of his work was held at the Seattle Art Museum, Seattle, WA. His work is in the collections of over thirty museums, including the Metropolitan Museum of Art, New York, NY; Carnegie Museum of Art, Pittsburgh, PA; and Los Angeles County Museum of Art, Los Angeles, CA. See: Tina Oldknow, *Richard Marquis: Objects* (Seattle: Washington University Press, 1997).

TONY MARSH b. New York, NY, USA, 1953. Marsh holds a BFA from California State University, Long Beach, 1978. Between 1978 and 1981 he was assistant to Mr. Shimaoka in Mashiko, Japan. Marsh's work combines bowl vessels and still life elements in a decidedly contemporary vision. The objects that fill his bowls – and reference still life compositions – are reductive volumes that are both austere and playful. These volumes teeter somewhere between building blocks and implements, clinical in their precision but jovial in their form and interplay. Often Marsh's bowls and the forms they contain are compulsively pierced over their entire surface with small holes, which heighten our sense that the artist has fashioned a still life sculpturally. His surface treatment tends to unify and flatten the work the way a painting captures 3-D form (from "life") and renders it in two dimensions (to "stillness"). Marsh has exhibited his work widely since 1980, including shows at the Garth Clark Gallery, New York, NY, and Los Angeles, CA; Frank Lloyd Gallery, Los Angeles, CA; Swidler Gallery, Detroit, MI; Takumi Gallery, Tokyo; and Pacific Grove Art Center, Pacific Grove, CA. His work appears in the public collections of the Cranbrook Museum of Art, Cranbrook Academy of Art, Bloomfield Hills, MI; Los Angeles County Museum of Art, Los Angeles, CA; and Takumi Folk Art Gallery, Tokyo, Japan. See: Susan Peterson, *Contemporary Ceramics* (New York: Watson-Guptill, 2000); Martha Drexler Lynn, *Clay Today:*

Contemporary Ceramists and their Work (San Francisco: Chronicle Books, 1990); and Mark Del Vecchio, *Postmodern Ceramics* (London: Thames & Hudson, 2001).

WALLACE MARTIN b. London, England, 1843; d. Southall, England, 1923. Martin worked from the age of twelve to help support his family. He was an assistant to the neo-Gothic sculptor John B. Phillips, which led to work in the stonemason's department at the Houses of Parliament, London. Around 1860 Martin enrolled in classes at the Lambeth School of Art and, after four years, attended the Royal Academy Schools where his work was regularly selected for the school's annual shows. Intrigued by the aesthetic and commercial possibilities of ceramics, in around 1872 Martin began to experiment, and eventually formed the Martin Brothers Pottery, housed first at Pomona House (1873) then in Southall (1877), outside London, with his brothers Walter and Edwin. Charles, the fourth brother, an eccentric figure even by Wallace's high standard, ran the brothers' London workshop. They specialized in salt-glazed stoneware – both decorated vases and Wallace's distinctive hand-modeled bird jars and grotesques (often in the form of spoon warmers), now considered amongst the finest expressions of late Victorian neo-Gothic art. The brothers were a dysfunctional group living in near poverty for most of their lives while Wallace pursued quixotic projects and retreated into religious zealotry. The pottery's last firing took place in 1911: "an aweful disaster," in the words of Sydney Greenslade, one of the brothers' closest supporters. Sadly, rather than being their crowning glory, the firing produced no saleable pots at all. See: Malcolm Haslam, *The Martin Brothers* (London: Richard Dennis, 1978).

LYNN MATTSON b. San Francisco, CA, USA, 1958. Mattson began her training in ceramics in the seventh grade when she was sent to live in a convent for three years. One of the nuns had a giant ceramic studio and Mattson spent most of her free time learning her craft. A gift of a kiln followed and she was set on a career in ceramics. Her work involves surfacing her ceramic forms with a mosaic of shards, small toys, jewelry, nuts, bolts, and whatever other materials and found objects relate to the theme of the work. She has shown in a number of exhibitions, mainly with a tea theme, including "Hot Tea" (del Mano Gallery, Pasadena, CA, 1999), "Tantalizing Teapots" (Craft and Folk Art Museum, Los Angeles, CA, 1997), and "Extravagant Teapots" (Nancy Margolis Gallery, New York, NY). See: Joann Lockton and Leslie P. Clagett, *The Art of Mosaic Design* (Gloucester: Rockport Publishers, 1998).

MICHAEL C. McMILLEN b. Los Angeles, CA, USA, 1946. McMillen holds a BA from San Fernando Valley State College, CA (1969), and received his MA (1972) and MFA (1973) from the University of California, Los Angeles, CA. His work – meticulous evocations of architectural fragments – has been exhibited widely over the last three decades and, aside from scores of group exhibitions, he has had solo shows at Art Resources Transfer (A.R.T.), New York, NY; Patricia Hamilton Gallery, New York, NY; Dart Gallery, Chicago, IL; Asher/Faure Gallery, Los Angeles, CA; Oakland Museum, Oakland, CA; Solomon R. Guggenheim Museum, New York, NY; Walker Art Center, Minneapolis, MN; and Whitney Museum of American Art, New York, NY. Since 1992 he has also been creating installation pieces at L.A. Louver, Venice, CA; the Glasgow Museum of Modern Art; and other venues. His work is in the collections of the Australian National Gallery, Canberra, Australia; Glasgow Gallery of Modern Art, Glasgow, Scotland; Los Angeles County Museum of Art, Los Angeles, CA; Museum of Contemporary Art, Sydney, Australia; Oakland Museum, Oakland, CA; and Solomon R. Guggenheim Museum, New York, NY.

JOHN W. McNAUGHTON b. Winchester, IN, USA, 1943. McNaughton holds a BS in Art Education, Ball State University, Muncie, IN (1965). He received his MA from the same school in 1969. His MFA (1970) was taken at Bowling Green State University, Bowling Green, OH. McNaughton is currently Professor of Art at the University of Southern Indiana, Evansville, where he has taught since 1970. He has instructed multiple workshops at Arrowmont School of Crafts, Gatlinburg, TN, and has also taught at Penland School of Crafts, Penland, NC. Awards include an Individual Artist's Grant, NEA (1992), as well as an Indiana Artist's Fellowship (1995) and grant from the City of Evansville and the Greenway Arts Committee. McNaughton's broad exhibition record extends back to 1970, and includes shows at the Ann Nathan Gallery, Chicago, IL; Leo Kaplan Modern, New York , NY; Mobilia Gallery, Cambridge, MA; Craft Alliance Gallery, St. Louis, MO; Snyderman Gallery, Philadelphia, PA; SOFA New York, NY, and Chicago, IL (Katie Gingrass Gallery, New York); American Crafts Museum, New York, NY; Contemporary Crafts Museum, Louisville, KY; Owensboro Museum of Fine Art, Owensboro, KY; and Indianapolis Museum of Art, Indianapolis, IN. See: Katherine Pearson, *American Crafts* (1983).

JOHN McQUEEN b. Champaign, IL, USA, 1943. McQueen holds a BA from the University of South Florida, Tampa (1971). He was awarded his MFA in 1975 at the Tyler School of Art, Temple University, Philadelphia, PA. He has received numerous grants from the NEA (1977, 1979, 1986,

1992), in addition to grants from the New York Foundation for the Arts (1988) and the Louis Comfort Tiffany Foundation (1991). McQueen is the foremost artist to emerge out of the basket-making tradition. More recently he has focused on transparent figures made of willow twigs and plastic twist ties for garbage bags in work that deals with human subjectivity and the flow of time, thereby aligning himself with sculptors he admires, such as Stephen Balkenhol, Antony Gormley, and George Segal. McQueen's work has been exhibited in solo shows at the Garth Clark Gallery, New York, NY, and Los Angeles, CA; Perimeter Gallery, Chicago, IL; Okun Gallery, Santa Fe, NM; Helen Drutt Gallery, Philadelphia, PA; Craft Alliance, St. Louis, MO; and Nina Freudenheim Gallery, Buffalo, NY. His group exhibitions include shows at the American Craft Museum, New York, NY; San Francisco Museum of Modern Art, San Francisco, CA; Philadelphia Museum of Art, Philadelphia, PA; National Museum of Art, Kyoto, Japan; Kunstindustrie Museum, Copenhagen, Denmark; Sonje Museum of Contemporary Art, Kyongju, Korea; and Musée des Arts Decoratifs, Paris, France. In 1992 he was the subject of a major touring retrospective organized by the Renwick Gallery of the National Museum of American Art, Smithsonian Institution, Washington, DC. McQueen's work is in the collections of the American Craft Museum, New York, NY; Cooper-Hewitt National Design Museum, New York, NY; Detroit Institute of Art, Detroit, MI; Kunstindustrimuseum, Trondheim, Norway; Minneapolis Institute of Art, Minneapolis, MN; Philadelphia Museum of Art, Philadelphia, PA; Renwick Gallery, Smithsonian Institution, Washington, DC; Seattle Art Museum, Seattle, WA; and Charles A. Wustum Museum of Fine Arts, Racine, WI. See: Jack Lenore Larsen and Mildred Constantine, *The Art Fabric Mainstream* (New York: Van Nostrand Reinhold, 1981); Vicki Halper and Ed Rossbach, *John McQueen: The Language of Containment* (Washington, DC: National Museum of American Art, 1992); and Polly Ullrich, "John McQueen: Sing Willow, Willow, Willow," *American Crafts* (Dec./Jan. 2000).

DENNIS MEINERS b. Walla Walla, WA, USA, 1950. Meiners received his BA in 1973 from Washington State University, Pullman. His work has been shown in numerous group exhibitions at American Craft Museum, New York, NY; the Contemporary Crafts Gallery, Portland, OR; the Ferrin Gallery, Northampton, MA, and the Craft Alliance, St. Louis, MO. He uses teapots "to try and speak about the impressions of humans and humanity's impact on its surroundings, from the devastation of resource extraction to the gentle pleasure of sharing a cup of tea with one's lover." See: Leslie Ferrin, *Teapots Transformed* (Madison: Guild Books, 2000).

RICHARD MILETTE b. l'Assomption, Quebec, Canada, 1960. Milette studied at Cégep du Vieux, Montreal, from 1978 to 1982, but earned his BFA at Nova Scotia College of Art and Design (1983). He lives and works in Montreal. His work has appeared in solo shows at the Nancy Margolis Gallery, New York, NY; Garth Clark Gallery, Los Angeles, CA; Prime Gallery, Toronto, Canada; and Galerie Barbara Silverberg Contemporary Ceramics, Montreal, Canada. His group shows include exhibitions at Galerie Lieu Ouest, Montreal, Canada; SOFA Chicago, IL (Joanne Rapp Gallery); Musée Marsil, Saint-Lambert, Canada; Everson Museum of Art, Syracuse, NY; American Craft Museum, New York, NY; and Prime Gallery, Toronto, Canada. See: Paul Bourassa, *Foulem, Mathieu, Milette* (Quebec: Musée du Quebec, 1997); Leslie Ferrin, *Teapots Transformed* (Madison: Guild Books, 2000); and Donald Brackett, "Downright Duchampian: The Ironic Ceramics of Richard Milette," *American Ceramics* (12/4, 1997).

ROSE MISANCHUK b. Verdon, Manitoba, Canada, 1956. Misanchuk received a BFA in Ceramics from the University of Lethbridge, Lethbridge, Alberta, in 1988. Five years later she moved to California and obtained her MFA from California State University, Fullerton, in 1999. She has exhibited in Canada, the US, and China. A participant at the 1st Yixing Conference in Yixing, China, in 1999, Misanchuk was inspired to delve deeper into her fascination with the teapot form. Her work is in public collections in the US, China, and Taiwan.

STEVEN MONTGOMERY b. Detroit, MI, USA, 1954. Montgomery earned his MFA from the Tyler School of Art at Temple University, Philadelphia, PA, in 1978. His undergraduate work was done in the field of philosophy, in which he took a BA in 1976 at Grand Valley State College, Allendale, MI. He has been a lecturer and visiting artist at the Tyler School of Art and has more recently served as an adjunct faculty lecturer at New York University. Montgomery's ceramic objects exist in some temporal and physical suspension, between machine and artifact, vessel and tool. His slipcasting of metal surfaces provide trompe l'oeil effects, and the corrosion that figures so heavily in his pieces suggests an inscrutable sense of the object's history. He is interested in clay for its transformational capacities, which enable him to invent his own technology. The formal paradox of his work is this rivalry between material and form; his vessels give the sense of industrial objects frozen but strangely impermanent, of some peculiar brand of entropy caught in stasis. In 1990 Montgomery received an Artist's Fellowship from the New York Foundation for the Arts, and in 1999 received a grant – rarely awarded in his field – from the Pollock/Krasner Foundation, NY. Montgomery has exhibited widely in the US and abroad, including

shows at the Dorothy Weiss Gallery, San Francisco, CA, and OK Harris Gallery, Garth Clark Gallery, and Nancy Margolis Gallery, all New York, NY. His works are included in the collections of the Metropolitan Museum of Art, New York, NY; Renwick Gallery, National Museum of American Art, Smithsonian Institution, Washington, DC; Everson Museum of Art, Syracuse, NY; Mint Museum of Art, Charlotte, NC; and Museum of Contemporary Ceramic Art, Shigaraki Ceramic Cultural Park, Shigaraki, Japan. See: Garth Clark, *The Eccentric Teapot* (New York: Abbeville Press, 1989); Robert C. Morgan, *Steven Montgomery* (New York and Syracuse: OK Harris Gallery and Everson Museum of Art, 1998); Mark Del Vecchio, *Postmodern Ceramics* (London: Thames & Hudson, 2001); and Rita Reif, *New York Times*: Art & Architecture (Dec. 6, 1998).

ZOE MORROW b. Camden, NJ, USA, 1955. Morrow's inspiration came years ago when she was visiting a coin store and saw a bag of shredded paper money. A line popped into the artist's mind: "Unable to spin straw into gold, she wove money instead." Morrow attempts to change the viewer's relationship to money: is it the meaning of life or merely a material with which to build a life? Morrow's work has appeared in numerous weaving and basketry exhibitions, including "New Baskets: Expanding the Concept" (Craft Alliance, St. Louis, MO, 1997), "New Baskets" (Arkansas Arts Center, Little Rock, AR, 1995), and a solo exhibition "Shredded Money Baskets: Zoe Morrow" (Federal Reserve Board, Washington, DC, 1992). She is represented by del Mano Gallery, West Los Angeles, CA, and her work is in the collections of the Arkansas Arts Center, Little Rock, AR; Charles A. Wustum Museum of Fine Arts, Racine, WI; and the Federal Board of Reserve Art Collection.

RON NAGLE b. San Francisco, CA, USA, 1939. Nagle received his art education and BA from San Francisco State College. Between 1961 and 1978, he taught sporadically at the San Francisco Art Institute, the University of California at Berkeley, the California College of Arts and Crafts, Oakland, and several other schools. In 1960 he connected with the so-called Abstract Expressionist Ceramics group around Peter Voulkos. He was particularly influenced by the work of two members of the group, Ken Price and Michael Frimkess. By 1963, having seen an exhibition of the work of Giorgio Morandi at the Ferus Gallery in Los Angeles, he decided to adopt a narrow focus – the cup – and has worked almost exclusively with this domestic icon ever since. His first exhibition was at the Dilexi Gallery, San Francisco, CA, in 1968. Since then he has exhibited at Quay Gallery, San Francisco, CA; Charles Cowles Gallery, New York, NY; Rena Bransten Gallery, San Francisco, CA; and, since 1995, Garth Clark Gallery, New York, NY. Nagle has had over thirty solo exhibitions and has been included in hundreds of group shows. In 1993 the Art Gallery of Mills College organized and traveled "Ron Nagle: A Survey Exhibition 1960–1993." He has work in the private collections of the Carnegie Museum of Art, Pittsburgh, PA; Mint Museum of Craft and Design, Charlotte, NC; Philadelphia Museum of Art, Philadelphia, PA; Stedelijk Museum, Amsterdam, Netherlands; Museum Het Kruithuis, 's-Hertogenbosch, Netherlands; Victoria and Albert Museum, London, England; and San Francisco Museum of Art, San Francisco, CA. Nagle has received numerous awards and fellowships, including NEA awards (1974, 1979, 1986), Mellon Grants (1981, 1983), a Visual Arts Award from the Flintridge Foundation (1998), and from 1990 to 1999 Faculty Research Grants from Mills College, Oakland, CA, where he currently teaches. See: Jane Adlin, *Contemporary Ceramics – Selections from the Metropolitan Museum of Art* (New York: Metropolitan Museum of Art, 1998); Garth Clark, *American Potters: The Work of Twenty Modern Masters* (New York: Watson-Guptill, 1981); John Coplans, *Abstract Expressionist Ceramics* (Irvine: University of California, 1966); Michael McTwigan, *Ron Nagle: A Survey Exhibition 1960–1993* (Mills Valley: Art Gallery, Mills College, 1963); and Jo Lauria, *Color and Fire* (New York: Rizzoli, 2000).

JEAN NEEMAN b. Southampton, NY, USA, 1948. Neeman holds a BFA from California State University, Fullerton (1993). Since 1995 she has worked as a Conservation Technician at Los Angeles County Museum of Art, Los Angeles, CA. Versatile in her approach to sculptural media, Neeman has facility with silver, wood, and glass. In 1994 her metal-work was juried into the National Student Design Competition, and was included in the traveling exhibition of that show.

RICHARD NOTKIN b. Chicago, IL, USA, 1948. Notkin earned a BFA in 1970 under Ken Ferguson (q.v.) at the Kansas City Art Institute and was one of Robert Arneson's students at TB9, Davis, CA, where he earned an MFA in 1973. Notkin currently maintains a studio in Helena, MT, where he is active on the board of the Archie Bray Foundation. He has made several trips to China and has been deeply influenced by the centuries-old tradition of Yixing pottery, from which he has adopted precise working methods and a penchant for trompe l'oeil. He uses his artwork as an extension of his conscience, believing that art should be socially activist. For over ten years he used the teapot format to question military adventures and foreign policy around the world, with particular focus on nuclear weaponry and energy. "Strong Tea," organized by the Seattle Art Museum (1990), and "Passages" (1999) are two traveling museum exhibitions devoted exclusively to Notkin's work, which is also in the collections of the Metropolitan Museum of Art and

Cooper-Hewitt National Design Museum, New York, NY; Carnegie Museum of Art, Pittsburgh, PA; Charles A. Wustum Museum of Fine Arts, Racine, WI; Mint Museum of Craft and Design, Charlotte, NC; Montreal Museum of Decorative Arts, Montreal, Canada; Stedelijk Museum, Amsterdam, Netherlands; Museum of Contemporary Ceramic Art, Shigaraki, Japan; and Victoria and Albert Museum, London, England. See: Vicki Halper, *Strong Tea* (Seattle: Seattle Art Museum, 1990) and Louana M. Lackey, "Not Just Another Pretty Vase," *Ceramics Monthly* (Oct. 2000).

GEORGE EDGAR OHR b. Biloxi, MS, USA, 1857; d. 1918. In 1879 a family friend, Joseph Fortune Meyer, offered Ohr the opportunity to apprentice as a potter at a wage of $10 a month. Ohr, who up until then had worked as an apprentice metalsmith for his father and taken a couple of dozen itinerant jobs, accepted and worked for Meyer until 1881, acquiring the rudimentary skills of his craft. He then left on a two-year, sixteen-state tour of the nation's potteries, returning to Biloxi in 1883 to set up his own workshop. Although locked out of the Arts and Crafts movement because he was thought bizarre and uncouth, Ohr did receive some recognition in his day, with awards from the Pan American Exposition of 1901 and the Louisiana Purchase International Exposition of 1904. He inspired a novel entitled *The Wonderful Wheel* by Mary Tracy Early (New York: Century Company, 1896). However, Ohr's true recognition has come, as he anticipated, from later generations. In 1969 a New Jersey antique dealer J. R. Carpenter bought over 9,000 forgotten pots – almost the entire oeuvre – from Ohr's sons and began to sell the work, initially for as little as $5 a piece at the gift shop of the Smithsonian Institution in Washington, DC. Ohr's work has since become actively sought after and can cost over $100,000. The first show of his pots in New York, entitled "George E. Ohr: An Artworld Homage," was held at the Garth Clark Gallery in 1983. In 1989 a full survey exhibition of his work was organized by the American Craft Museum, New York, NY. It then traveled to the Renwick Gallery of the National Museum of American Art, Washington, DC. The most moving homage to Ohr came from Jasper Johns, in his 1983 exhibition at the Leo Castelli Gallery in New York, in which the painter – who is a collector and avid admirer of Ohr – painted his pots into his paintings. See: Garth Clark, Eugene Hecht, and Robert Ellison, *The Mad Potter of Biloxi: The Life and Art of George E. Ohr* (New York: Abbeville Press, 1989).

BRIAN PESHEK b. Burbank, CA, USA, 1968. Peshek holds a BA from California State University, Northridge (1992). He took his MFA at New York State College of Ceramics at Alfred University, Alfred, NY (1995). Peshek's work has been exhibited in both solo and group shows at

Judson Studio's Gallery, Los Angeles, CA; Shaw/Guido Gallery, Pontiac, MI; Gallery Alexander, La Jolla, CA; and Craft and Folk Art Museum, Los Angeles, CA.

MARK PHARIS b. Minneapolis, MN, USA, 1947. Pharis studied at the University of Minnesota, Minneapolis (1967–71) under Warren McKenzie, the first American apprentice of Bernard Leach (q.v.). Since 1971 he has held various teaching positions at colleges and universities around the US, and lectured and given workshops nationally since 1973. He took up a teaching post at the University of Minnesota and a decade later, in 1996, began his professorship there. He has been the Chair of the Department of Art since 1998. He is a three-time recipient of a Visual Arts Fellowship, NEA (1977, 1980, 1986), and has won numerous other awards. Pharis's work plays a seditious game with what is known as "Mingeisota" (a mix of the Japanese Mingei movement, and Minnesota, one of the strongholds of the Leach approach in the US). Pharis makes exquisitely pure forms – almost like tin vessels – constructed from flat sheets of clay. The objects are not particularly functional but have great sculptural presence. His extensive exhibition record includes solo shows at the Garth Clark Gallery, New York, NY, and Los Angeles, CA; Hadler-Rodriguez Galleries, New York, NY; Trax Gallery, Berkeley, CA; and Pro Art Gallery, St. Louis, MO. His group exhibition record includes shows at the Aberystwyth Arts Center, Aberystwyth, Wales; Northern Clay Center, Minneapolis, MN; Minneapolis Art Center, Minneapolis, MN; The Clay Studio, Philadelphia, PA; and Minnesota Museum of American Art, St. Paul, MN. His work is in the collections of the Charles A. Wustum Museum of Fine Arts, Racine, WI; Minneapolis Institute of Arts, Minneapolis, MN; The Contemporary Museum, Honolulu, HI; Victoria and Albert Museum, London, England; Everson Museum of Art, Syracuse, NY; and Los Angeles County Museum of Art, Los Angeles, CA. See: Garth Clark, *American Ceramics* (New York: Abbeville Press, 1987).

BRETT PRICE b. Palo Alto, CA, USA, 1950. Price holds a BA from Pomona College, Claremont, CA (1972). In 1973 he studied at Otis Art Institute, Los Angeles, for a year, and obtained his MFA from the California Institute of the Arts, Valencia, in 1975. He has been a visiting artist and lecturer at many California colleges and universities throughout his career. Working on a monumental scale, Price often paints his steel sculptures with boldly pigmented polyurethane finishes. Originally a ceramist, he adopted the use of heat treatment for his metalworking process, whereby rather than hardening (like clay), the heat softens (like steel). Price's forms are often abstract and reductive, but never at the expense of the sculpture's lyricism and whimsy –

always helped along by his clever, provocative titles. His work has been widely exhibited since 1976, including shows at Wyndy Morehead Gallery, Tustin, CA, and New Orleans, LA; Kavish Gallery, Ketchum, ID; Ruth Bachofner Gallery, Santa Monica, CA; Carl Schlosberg Fine Arts, New York, NY; Craft and Folk Art Museum, Los Angeles, CA; Long Beach Museum of Art, Long Beach, CA; and Laguna Museum of Art, Laguna Beach, CA. His corporate commissions include projects for Walt Disney Productions, Burbank, CA; Toyota Corporation, Chicago, IL; and Pepsico, Purchase, NY.

JEAN-EMILE PUIFORCAT b. Paris, France, 1897; d. Paris, 1945. Puiforcat was initially employed at the silversmithing firm that his grandfather had established almost a century earlier. He studied with the sculptor Lejeune at the same time as apprenticing under his father. Lejeune encouraged him to think in terms of the essential aspects of form, which must have conflicted with the Deco tendencies towards surface decoration, particularly in the context of silverwork. Puiforcat's inspiration was often derived from mathematics, and his interest in Pythagorean geometry influenced him to use simple volumes as the basis of his forms. His Deco tea sets still remain more decorative than sparse, despite their elemental origins. They are marked by a visual harmony and formal balance, where decoration is never superfluous, but rather a necessary extension of design. His facility with materials helped to get him noticed, and in 1921 some of his pieces were exhibited in "Salon des Artistes Decorateurs" and in 1925 at "Exposition Internationale des Arts Decoratifs et Industriels Modernes." The following year he became one of the principals in the founding of the Groupe de Cinq, and in 1930 he gained membership to the Union des Artistes Modernes. See: Yvonne Brunhammer and Suzanne Tise, *The Decorative Arts in France 1900 to 1942* (Paris: Rizzoli, 1900).

JEANNIE QUINN b. Lemore, CA, USA, 1966. Quinn studied at Oberlin College, Oberlin, OH, receiving her BA in 1988 and her MFA at the University of Washington, Seattle, in 1995. Exhibitions have included "Untitled: New Sculptural Clay" (Kirkland Arts Center, WA, 1995), and solo shows "Narrative Vessels" (Lill Street Gallery, Chicago, IL, 1996); "I am Penelope, I am not Penelope" (Foster/White Gallery, Seattle, WA, 2000); and "High Degrees" (Center for Visual Arts, Denver, CO, 2000). In 1994 she received an Oberlin College Alumni Aeolin Fellowship, in 1995 the Lambda Rho Award from the University of Washington, and in 1996 and 1998 artist residency from the Archie Bray Foundation for the Ceramic Arts, Helena, MT. See: Soyon Im, "Spouting Off: Neither/Both – Works by Jeanne Quinn," *Eastside Week Seattle* (Dec.

24, 1997) and Mary Voelz Chandler, "Breaking the Volume Barrier," *Denver Rocky Mountain News* (Mar. 31, 2000).

MARGARET REALICA b. Coventry, England, 1940. Realica received her education at Leicester School of Art, Leicester, England, and the University of Hawaii, USA. She has taught at Warwick University, Coventry. Now working in Northern California, Realica's sculptural porcelain vessels deconstruct and reconstruct the teapot form to varying degrees. While non-ceramic elements figure into her works, there are simulated hardware elements that are also cast from porcelain. In her overtly mechanized versions of the teapot, the original object eludes identification as such, and sculptural and formal presence overwhelms recognizable content. Her often "pillowesque" thrown porcelain elements provide tension when combined with brass rod, plexiglass and other non-clay, industrial parts. Realica has received awards from Berkeley Art Center, CA (1994) and from Tempe Art Center, AZ (1995). Her porcelain work has been widely exhibited, including shows at The Contemporary Museum, Honolulu, HI; Pence Gallery, Davis, CA; The Visual Art Center, Montreal, Canada; San Angelo Museum of Arts, San Angelo, TX; Wiseman Museum, Minneapolis, MN; and Honolulu Academy of Arts, Honolulu, HI. Realica's work appears in the collections of the State Foundation of Culture & Arts and Contemporary Museum FHB Center, both Honolulu, HI.

IRENE C. REED b. New Britain, CT, USA, 1945. Reed received her BA from the St. Joseph College, West Hartford, CT, in 1968 and her MA from the Wesleyan University, Middletown, CT, in 1983. Commenting on her work in this book the artist states that, "My pieces have always been primarily about sculpture and secondarily purses." She has exhibited in numerous major survey exhibitions on art and fiber since 1976 at the Renwick Gallery, Smithsonian Institution, Washington, DC; the Wadsworth Atheneum, Hartford, CT (which also has her work in its permanent collection); the Minneapolis Institute of Art, Minneapolis, MN; and other public and private spaces.

DAVID REGAN b. Buffalo, NY, USA, 1964. Regan received his BFA from the Rochester Institute of Technology, New York, NY, in 1986 and his MFA from Alfred University, Alfred, NY, in 1990. Since 1991 he has had numerous one-person exhibitions at Garth Clark Gallery, New York, NY, and Frank Lloyd Gallery, Santa Monica, CA, and has been included in several group exhibitions: "Young Americans" (American Craft Museum, New York, NY, 1989); "The American Way: Views on Use and Function in American Ceramics" (Aberystwyth Arts Centre, Aberystwyth,

Wales, 1993); "Contemporary Ceramics – Selections from the Metropolitan Museum of Art, New York" (1998); and "Color and Fire: Defining Moments in Studio Ceramics, 1950–2000" (Los Angeles County Museum of Art, Los Angeles, CA, 2000). His work is in numerous private and public collections including the Metropolitan Museum of Art, New York, NY, and the Los Angeles County Museum of Art, Los Angeles, CA. See: Jo Lauria, *Color and Fire* (New York: Rizzoli, 2000); Christopher Knight, "David Regan," *Art Issues* (Jan./Feb. 1997); and David Pagel, "Vessels of Meaning," *Los Angeles Times* (Oct. 17, 1996).

JOHN REVELRY b. Long Beach, CA, USA, 1947. Revelry was an assistant to Phil Cornelius in 1969 and 1970, and in 1976 studied at Humboldt State University as a Ceramics major. During his brief ceramic career he has exhibited at the Asher/Faure Gallery in Los Angeles, CA, and the Faenza Concorso Dell Ceramica in Italy. For the last twenty years he has worked in theatre and opera, and currently makes television commercials in Hollywood. See: Garth Clark, *The Eccentric Teapot* (New York: Abbeville Press, 1989).

GAIL RITCHIE b. Meriden, CT, USA, 1947. Ritchie holds a BA in Art Education from San Jose State University, San Jose, CA, 1971. Her MFA in Fine Arts/Ceramics (1974) comes from San Francisco State University, San Francisco, CA. Ritchie has twenty years' experience as a ceramics arts instructor for the City of San Francisco and the California Community College system. Her porcelains, both tiles and pots, reveal a mastery and facility with a broad range of natural subjects (flora and fauna), in both the content and images within her work. Ritchie has exhibited her work at The Elements Gallery, Greenwich, CT; The Elements Gallery, New York, NY; Ferrin Gallery, Northampton, MA; Dorothy Weiss Gallery, San Francisco, CA; and Winfield Gallery, Carmel, CA. Her work is in the collection of the Mint Museum of Craft and Design, Charlotte, NC.

CONNIE ROBERTS b. Hollywood, CA, USA, 1949. Roberts earned a BA (Cum Laude) in 1971 from the University of California, Los Angeles, and went on to take an MA and MFA from the University of Iowa in 1974 and 1975. Roberts has shown her work at SOFA Chicago, IL; Cornerhouse Gallery, Cedar Rapids, IA; Sophia Georg Gallery, Denver, CO; Outside-In Gallery, Los Angeles, CA; Carega Foxley Leach Gallery, Washington, DC; and Waterloo Art Museum, Sioux City Art Center, IA. Her primary gallery is Portals Ltd., Chicago, IL.

GREGORY ROBERTS b. Buffalo, NY, USA, 1968. Roberts began his education at Johnson State College, Johnson, VT, and after a year moved to the School of Art and Design, Alfred University, Alfred, NY, where he earned his BFA in 1991, graduating Cum Laude. In 1994 he took an MFA in Ceramic Sculpture from Mills College, Oakland, CA. Having been heavily involved in ceramic education for a decade, Roberts currently lectures and instructs at California State University at Hayward. His more recent work makes use of carved ceramic honeycomb, from which he fashions objects ranging from the mundane (household) to the esoteric (enlarged pollen grains). He has exhibited widely since 1994 in both group and solo shows, including Dorothy Weiss Gallery, San Francisco, CA (1996) and SOFA Chicago, IL (Ferrin Gallery, 2000). See Diane Chin Lui, "Gregory Roberts Cross Pollen-Nations," *Ceramics Art and Perception* (No. 37, 1999) and "Portfolio," *American Craft* (Feb./Mar. 1997).

LESLIE ROSDOL b. Williamson, WV, USA, 1954. Rosdol holds a BFA in Ceramics from Otis Art Institute of Design, Los Angeles, CA. She also obtained a BA in Psychology (Human Learning and Memory) at Indiana University, 1976. Rosdol's exhibition record includes shows at The Clay Studio, Philadelphia, PA; SOFA Chicago, IL (Ferrin Gallery); Wild Blue Gallery, Los Angeles, CA; Garth Clark Gallery, Los Angeles, CA; Dorothy Weiss Gallery, San Francisco, CA; Margo Jacobsen Gallery, Portland, OR; Craft and Folk Art Museum, Los Angeles, CA; and Taiwan Museum, Taiwan. Her work is in the collections of Los Angeles County Museum of Art, Los Angeles, CA, and Charles A. Wustum Museum of Fine Arts, Racine, WI. See: Leslie Ferrin, *Teapots Transformed* (Madison: Guild Books, 2000).

KATHLEEN ROYSTER b. Cedar Rapids, IA, USA, 1958. Royster holds a BFA (Ceramics) from the University of Utah, Salt Lake City (1990). Her MFA, in the same field, was also taken at Utah in 1993. Royster has twice been the recipient of an Individual Artist's Grant, Utah Arts Council (1994, 1995). She has been an adjunct professor at the University of Utah, Salt Lake City (1991–1997) and an assistant professor at Scripps College, Claremont, CA (1997–2000). Her superbly crafted ceramics explore what the artist terms "the process of cooking down the essence of of the human emotional plane... Thorns and leaves embody the drama of contradiction revealing emotional tension." Her exhibition record includes shows at the Ferrin Gallery, Northampton, MA; Sybaris Gallery, Royal Oak, MI; Craft Alliance, St. Louis, MO; and Margot Jacobsen Gallery, Portland, OR, as well as group exhibitions at Los Angeles County Museum of Art, Los Angeles, CA; The Contemporary Museum, Honolulu, HI; Frederick R. Weisman Art Museum, Minneapolis, MN; and Utah Museum of Fine Arts, Salt Lake City, UT. Her work is in the collection of the Renwick Gallery, National Museum of American Art,

Smithsonian Institution, Washington, DC; Los Angeles County Museum of Art, Los Angeles, CA; and The Contemporary Museum, Honolulu, HI. See: Susan Peterson, *Contemporary Ceramics* (New York: Watson-Guptill, 2000) and Jo Lauria, *Color and Fire* (New York: Rizzoli, 2000).

KARI RUSSELL-POOL b. Salem, MA, USA, 1967. Russell-Pool earned her BFA (Glass) at the Cleveland Institute of Art, Cleveland, OH, in 1990. She has been both an instructor and visiting artist at Penland School of Crafts, Penland, NC (1991, 1993, 1994, 1995) and has served in a similar capacity at Toyama Institute of Glass, Toyama, Japan (1995). She has also attended Pilchuck Glass School, Stanwood, WA. Russell-Pool's casework glass has a delicate filigree quality as though it has been made from spun sugar. Notable is her grasp in combining relief elements into superb decorative compositions. Russell-Pool has exhibited her work widely in group shows, including those at Riley Hawk Gallery, Cleveland and Columbus, OH; Heller Gallery, New York, NY; Habatat Gallery, Pontiac, MI; Mint Museum of Craft and Design, Charlotte, NC; Asheville Art Museum, Asheville, NC; and Corning Museum of Glass, Corning, NY. Her work is in the collections of the Mint Museum of Craft and Design, Charlotte, NC, and Corning Museum of Glass, Corning, NY. The piece shown on p. 115 was made by Russell-Pool in collaboration with her husband, Marc Petrovic (b. South Euclid, OH, USA, 1967). Petrovic also studied at the Cleveland Institute of Art, and has shown with Habatat, Boca Raton, FL, and Heller Gallery, New York, NY.

HAP SAKWA b. Los Angeles, CA, USA, 1950. Sakwa is a self-taught artist and photographer. He has recently set aside other creative endeavors in order to pursue his career as a commercial photographer. His ceramic teapots and other functional wares have been exhibited widely, including shows at the Wheeler/Seidel Gallery, New York, NY; Sybaris Gallery, Royal Oak, MI; Dorothy Weiss Gallery, San Francisco, CA; Ferrin Gallery, Northampton, MA; Works Gallery, Philadelphia, PA; Esther Saks Gallery, Chicago, IL; American Craft Museum, New York, NY; Oakland Museum of Art, Oakland, CA; California Museum of Art, Santa Rosa, CA; Craft and Folk Art Museum, Los Angeles, CA; Museum of Modern Art, New York, NY; Cooper-Hewitt National Design Museum, New York, NY; and Renwick Gallery, National Museum of American Art, Smithsonian Institution, Washington, DC. His work is in the collections of the Museum of Modern Art, New York, NY; American Craft Museum, New York, NY; Los Angeles County Museum of Art, Los Angeles, CA; Oakland Museum of Art, Oakland, CA; and Renwick Gallery, National Museum of American Art, Smithsonian Institution, Washington, DC. See: Barbara Meyer, *Contemporary American Craft Art* (Salt Lake City: Peregrine Smith Books, 1988).

JUDITH SALOMON b. Providence, RI, USA, 1952. Salomon studied at the Penland School of Crafts, Penland, NC (1974–75); the School for American Craftsmen, Rochester, NY, where she received her BFA in 1975; and the New York State College of Ceramics at Alfred University, Alfred, NY, from which she earned her MFA in 1977. Salomon is an associate professor at the Cleveland Institute of Art, OH. She has developed a distinctive expression through hand-built vessels that are geometric assemblages with brightly colored, low-fire glazes on the surface. Her constructivist sensibility is tempered with a refined and elegant eye for proportion and composition. Her work is in the collections of the Cleveland Museum of Art, Cleveland, OH; Manchester City Art Galleries, Manchester, England; Mint Museum of Craft and Design, Charlotte, NC; Los Angeles County Museum of Art, Los Angeles, CA; and Victoria and Albert Museum, London, England. See: Jonathan Fairbanks and Angela Fina, *The Best of Pottery* (Boston: Rockport, 1996).

EDOUARD-MARCEL SANDOZ b. Basle, Switzerland, 1881; d. Paris, France, 1971. Sandoz attended the Ecole des Beaux-Arts, Paris, specializing as an *animalier* working in bronze, stone, wood, and ceramic. His highly stylized work drew the attention of Theodore Haviland et Cie, Limoges, in 1916 and Sandoz made superb Art Deco bird-shaped tea and coffee services that Haviland produced until 1952. Sandoz also worked with Sèvres Porcelain Manufactory from 1927 to 1936, as well as for Richard Ginori in Italy. See: Karen McCready, *Art Deco and Modernist Ceramics* (London: Thames & Hudson, 1995) and Jean-Claude Segonds, *Les Créations en Porcelaine de Limoges d'Edouard-Marcel Sandoz* (Paris: Editions Transition, 1995).

ADRIAN SAXE b. Glendale, CA, USA, 1943. Saxe studied with Ralph Bacerra (q.v.) from 1965 to 1969 at the Chouinard Art Institute in Los Angeles, CA. In 1974 he received his BFA from the California Institute of the Arts (Chouinard's subsequent name), Valencia, CA. From 1973 to the present he has headed the Ceramics Department at the University of California, Los Angeles, CA, where he is currently Professor of Art. In 1983 he became the first artist to work at the Atelier Experimental de Recherche et de Création at the Manufacture Nationale de Sèvres in Paris. He has also received numerous awards and research grants, including a Visual Artist's Fellowship from the NEA (1986) and the United States/France Exchange Fellowship of the United States Information Agency and the Government of France. In his early work, Saxe set out to explore sculptural forms but found himself drawn to the vessel and the qualities of porcelain clay. This in turn led to an interest in the eclectic inventiveness of 18th-century court porcelains.

Saxe's gift for explosions of technical *tours de force* does not lessen the intellectual edge in his work. In 1984 the critic Jeff Perrone warned the viewer not to mistake Saxe's facility for being facile: "This work is, on one level, spectacular craft ... nothing is offhanded: the skillful performance becomes a content, a most difficult subject, and not a mere means to the end of content." In 2000 Saxe took part in "Departures" at the Getty Museum, Los Angeles, CA, producing a room-sized installation of huge jars placed on a giant French baroque table and atop a pair of mid-18th-century carved wooden Dutch torchères. Saxe's work has been collected in depth by Los Angeles County Museum of Art, Los Angeles, CA; Museum Het Kruithuis, 's-Hertogenbosch, Netherlands; Metropolitan Museum of Art, New York, NY; National Museum of American Art, Smithsonian Institution, Washington, DC; Musée des Arts Decoratifs, Paris, France; Victoria and Albert Museum, London, England; and Museum of Contemporary Ceramic Art, Shigaraki, Japan. Saxe has also exhibited extensively since his first solo exhibition in 1963, and since 1981 has been shown by the Garth Clark Gallery in New York, NY, Los Angeles, CA, and Kansas City, MO, and recently also with the Frank Lloyd Gallery in Santa Monica, CA. In 1993 the Los Angeles County Museum of Art organized a retrospective of his work that was shown in the US and Japan. See: Martha Lynn, *The Clay Art of Adrian Saxe* (New York: Thames & Hudson, 1993); Jeff Perrone and Peter Schjeldahl, *Adrian Saxe* (Kansas City: University of Kansas, 1987); Jeff Perrone, "Porcelain and Pop," *Arts Magazine* (Mar. 1984); Christopher Knight, "The Global Potter," *Los Angeles Times* (Nov. 24, 1991); and David Pagel, "Fresh Riffs on a Theme," *Los Angeles Times* (Mar. 1, 2000).

JOYCE J. SCOTT b. Baltimore, MD, USA, 1948. Scott studied art education at the Maryland Institute, College of Art, Baltimore, receiving her BFA in 1970, and MFA in Crafts from the Instituto Allender, San Miguel Allender, Guanajuato, Mexico, in 1971, and later at the Haystack Mountain School of Crafts, Deer Isle, Maine. She has been exhibiting her beaded art and quilts and producing performance art since 1976, and has had over forty solo exhibitions with Mobilia, Cambridge, MA; Susan Cummins Gallery, Mill Valley, FL; and Richard Anderson Gallery, New York, NY. Scott's work has been included in more than a hundred group exhibitions, including "Glass Today" (The Cleveland Museum of Art, Cleveland, OH, 1998), "Jewelry Moves: Ornament of the 21st Century" (National Museum of Scotland, Edinburgh, 1998), "Signs and Symbols: African American Quilts from the Rural South" (Museum of American Folk Art, New York, NY, 1996; traveling exhibition), "Bad Girls" (The New Museum of Contemporary Art, New York, NY, 1994). In addition, Scott has herself curated many exhibitions, including

"Stop Asking We Exist: 25 American Craft Artists" (The Society of Contemporary Crafts, Pittsburgh, PA, 1999). Her work has been recognized with many awards, including one from the Louis Comfort Tiffany Foundation (1995), the NEA, and several Maryland State Arts Council Fellowships. In 2000 she was given a major retrospective by the Baltimore Museum of Art. See: George Siskel, ed., *Joyce J. Scott: Kickin' It with the Old Masters* (Baltimore: Baltimore Museum of Art and Maryland School of Art, 2000).

BONNIE SEEMAN b. Huntington, NY, USA, 1969. Seeman holds her BFA in Ceramics from the University of Miami, Coral Gables, FL, 1991. She took her MFA in the same field, in 1996, at the University of Massachusetts at Dartmouth. Since 1998 she has instructed and lectured at the University of Miami. Among many other awards, she has been honored as an Emerging Artist, NCECA 2001, Charlotte, NC. Seeman has exhibited since 1994, including shows at the Clay Space, South Miami Beach, FL; Shaw/Guido Gallery, Pontiac, MI; Kenny Schachter/Rove, New York, NY; Snyderman/Works Gallery, Philadelphia, PA; Chiaroscuro Gallery, Chicago, IL; Mint Museum of Craft and Design, Charlotte, NC; The Clay Studio, Philadelphia, PA; and Pewabic Pottery, Detroit, MI. Her work appears in the collections of the Minnesota Museum of American Art, Minneapolis, MN, and the Mint Museum of Craft and Design, Charlotte, NC. See: Don Davis, *Wheel Thrown Ceramics* (Asheville: Lark, 1998).

RICHARD SHAW b. Hollywood, CA, USA, 1941. Shaw studied at the Orange Coast College, Costa Mesa, CA (1961–63); the San Francisco Art Institute (1963–65); the New York State College of Ceramics at Alfred University, Alfred, NY (1966); and in 1968 earned his MFA from the University of California, Davis. He had his first one-person exhibition in 1967 at the San Francisco Art Institute, and has since had numerous solo and group exhibitions. He is represented by the Braunstein Gallery in San Francisco, CA, and the George Adams Gallery in New York, NY. Shaw has been the most influential figure in the development of a Super-Object school in the Bay Area; his influence on the younger generation of ceramic artists also extends throughout the country. His joint exhibition with metal sculptor Robert Hudson – "Robert Hudson/Richard Shaw: Work In Porcelain" – at the San Francisco Museum of Art in 1973 was one of the most influential exhibitions of the decade. His work is in the collections of Los Angeles County Museum of Art, Los Angeles, CA; San Francisco Museum of Art, San Francisco, CA; Oakland Museum of Art, Oakland, CA; Stedelijk Museum, Amsterdam, Netherlands; National Museum of Modern Art, Tokyo,

Japan; and Whitney Museum of American Art, New York, NY. See: Suzanne Foley, *Robert Hudson/Richard Shaw: Work In Porcelain* (San Francisco: San Francisco Museum of Art, 1973); Ruth Braunstein, *Richard Shaw: Illusionism in Clay 1971–1985* (San Francisco: Braunstein Gallery, 1985); and Jo Lauria, *Color and Fire* (New York: Rizzoli, 2000).

CINDY SHERMAN b. Long Island, NY, USA, 1954. Sherman studied art at the State University of New York, Buffalo, from 1972 to 1976. Her first inclusion in a museum show came at the Albright Knox Gallery in 1976 while she was still in college. This extremely private artist has a very public face. All of her art involves images of herself in one disguise or another. In the 1970s she worked on a series – "Untitled Film Stills" – and then from the 1980s began to make color photographs of herself in theatrical costume, using elaborate make up to create images of herself in various female roles. Sherman is now considered one of the most important artists of the late 20th century and has had numerous solo exhibitions and mid-career surveys, including at the Whitney Museum of American Art and the Museum of Modern Art, New York, NY. Her ceramic output is limited to participation in the Artes Magnus Project, for which she created one of the most successful works in the series, her dinnerware and tea service a homage to Madame de Pompadour. See: Victoria Geibel, "Table D'Art," *American Ceramics* (9/3, 1991).

MICHAEL SHERRILL b. Providence, RI, USA, 1954. Sherrill is primarily self-taught and acknowledges influences from the artists of the Penland School of Crafts and the Arrowmont School of Crafts, both in North Carolina. Exhibitions of his work have included "The Penland Connection: Contemporary Works in Clay" (The Society of Arts and Crafts, Boston, MA, 1996), "The White House Collection of American Crafts" (National Museum of American Art, Washington, DC, 1993–99; traveling exhibition), "Erotica in Ceramic Art" (Ferrin Gallery, Northampton, MA, 1999), and "Color and Fire: Defining Moments in Studio Ceramics, 1950–2000" (Los Angeles County Museum of Art, Los Angeles, CA, 2000). Sherrill's work is also included in the collections of the Howard Hughes Foundation, Bethesda, MD; Mint Museum of Craft and Design, Charlotte, NC; and Renwick Gallery, National Museum of American Art, Smithsonian Institution, Washington, DC. See: Jo Lauria, *Color and Fire* (New York: Rizzoli, 2000) and Leslie Ferrin, *Teapots Transformed* (Madison: Guild Books, 2000).

PETER SHIRE b. Los Angeles, CA, USA, 1947. Shire received his BFA from the Chouinard Art Institute in Los Angeles, CA, in 1970 and was an early member of the Milan-based Memphis design group headed by Ettore Sottsass (q.v.). Shire has had one-person shows at the William Traver Gallery in Seattle, WA; Morgan Gallery in Kansas City, MO; and Janus Gallery and Dan Saxon Gallery, both in Los Angeles, CA. He is represented by Frank Lloyd Gallery in Santa Monica, CA. In 1984 Shire received an award for his contribution to the XXIII Olympiad Los Angeles and *The Esquire Register* in 1985 from *Esquire Magazine*. His work is in the collections of the Art Institute of Chicago, Chicago, IL; Everson Museum of Art, Syracuse, NY: Los Angeles County Museum of Art, Los Angeles, CA; San Francisco Museum of Art, San Francisco, CA; and Israel Museum, Jerusalem, Israel. See: Peter Shire, *Tempest in a Teapot: The Ceramic Art of Peter Shire* (New York: Rizzoli, 1991); Peter Shire, *Tea Types: An Opera* (Los Angeles: Tea Garden Press, 1980); and Jo Lauria, *Color and Fire* (New York: Rizzoli, 2000).

CHRISTINA Y. SMITH b. Berkeley, CA, USA, 1951. Smith holds a BA in Art and an MA in Art, Metalsmithing and Jewelry from San Diego State University, CA (1974). Her MFA in the same field was taken from California State University, Long Beach (1983). She has received a Western States Art Federation/NEA Regional Fellowship for Visual Artists (1989) and a California State Arts Board Fellowship for Individual Artists (1990), among many other accolades. She is currently an Instructor of Art at Cypress and Cerritios Colleges, both in California, where she has taught since 1985. Smith's more recent metalwork combines silhouetted, planar figures with various symbols and domestic icons. Often the sense of balance and structure between the figures and surrounding objects helps us to develop their strong narrative thrust. Her broad exhibition record includes shows at the Frank Lloyd Gallery, Santa Monica, CA; Garth Clark Gallery, Los Angeles, CA; SOFA Chicago, IL; Jewish Museum of San Francisco, San Francisco, CA; Renwick Gallery, National Museum of American Art, Smithsonian Institution, Washington, DC; Craft and Folk Art Museum, Los Angeles, CA; and American Craft Museum, New York, NY. Smith's work also appears in the permanent collections of Oakland Museum of Art, Oakland, CA; American Craft Museum, New York, NY; and Renwick Gallery, National Museum of American Art, Smithsonian Institution, Washington, DC. See: Kate Wagle, "Chris Smith, The Luxury of Stolen Images," *Metalsmith* (Spring 1999).

ETTORE SOTTSASS b. Innsbruck, Austria, 1917. Sottsass graduated in Architecture in 1939 from the Politecnico of Turin, Italy, and worked with his father, the architect Ettore Sottsass Sr., an important figure in Italian Rationalism. In 1945 Sottsass Jr. moved to Milan, where he set up a consulting firm to work on architectural and design projects. His first ceramic designs date from 1952. He began to take a serious interest in the field around 1955, when he was invited by the American Irving Richards to create some "modernistic" ceramics to perk up the interior design market. Not a single piece sold, but Sottsass was launched on an investigation of ceramics that has continued ever since. In 1958, he began a twenty-year involvement with Olivetti as a design consultant, designing, amongst other products, "Elea," the first Italian electric calculator, as well as machines for calculus systems, and electric and portable typewriters such as the "Valentine," which now form part of the permanent collections of museums such as the Centre Georges Pompidou in Paris, France, and the Museum of Modern Art in New York, NY. His ceramics have been exhibited at various Italian galleries and at the National Museum in Stockholm, Sweden. 1981 saw the birth of the Memphis group, with Sottsass as founder and muse. Memphis was the result of the need to make not only experimental prototypes, but also finished objects to be offered as an alternative to the production world. The Memphis project is one of the defining moments of postmodernism. Well-known exponents of the Italian and international avant-garde movements designed various collections of furniture, and ceramic and glass objects, which were displayed at exhibitions in museums and galleries throughout the world, with commercial and critical success. Sottsass returned to exhibiting with "Kallygraphy" – nineteen ceramics inspired by Chinese calligraphy – shown at the Bischofberger Gallery, Zurich, Switzerland, in November 1996. He also created the official vases ("Tarzan and Jane") for the Ceramic Millennium: Leadership Congress for the Ceramic Arts, Amsterdam, Netherlands, 1999, at which he was honored with an award for his lifetime achievement in ceramic design. See: Bruno Bischofberger, ed., *Ettore Sottsass Ceramics* (San Francisco: Chronicle Books, 1996) and Fulvio Farrari, *Ettore Sottsass: Tutta La Ceramica* (Torino: Umberto Allemandi, 1996).

PIET STOCKMANS b. Leopoldsburg, Belgium, 1940. From 1966 to 1989 Stockmans was the designer at Royal Mosa, where he created the coffee cup "Sonja," the biggest-selling cup design in the world – over 32 million units in circulation (both legitimate and pirated). At the same time Stockmans was making unique artworks in a distinctive but limited palette of poured porcelain slip and blue dip. He has been Professor of Industrial Design at the Katholieke Hogeschool Limburg in Ghent since 1969 and has received numerous awards for his work, including the 1988 Flemish Prize for Visual Art and in 1999 the prestigious Henry van der Velde Prize from VIZO. In 1995 he was appointed the Cultural Ambassador of Flanders. Stockmans traffics in multiples – even if sometimes just a pair of cups in a box – and his installations (over 50,000 pieces) have filled cathedrals and other public places. While his is not the only modular approach in ceramics, there are few other ceramic artists who match Stockmans's vision, ambition, and industriousness. He is part-wizard, part-industrialist, part-designer, part-potter, part-painter, part-architect, and part-conceptualist. All of these talents coalesce into one of the most unique and compulsively productive artists in contemporary ceramics. His work has been extensively exhibited and is in numerous collections, including the Los Angeles County Museum of Art, Los Angeles, CA, and the Stedelijk Museum, Amsterdam, Netherlands. See: Jo Rombouts, ed., *Piet Stockmans* (Tielt: Lannoo, 1996) and Garth Clark, Luc Verstraete, and Mimi Wilms, *Piet Stockmans* (Knokke-Heist: Cultureel Centrum, 2000).

AKIO TAKAMORI b. Nobeoka, Japan, 1950. Takamori studied at the Musashino Art College in Tokyo from 1969 to 1971. From 1972 to 1974 he apprenticed with Oita, a master folk potter working in Koishawara ware – traditional utilitarian pottery – in Fukuoka. Takamori later studied with Ken Ferguson (q.v.) at the Kansas City Art Institute, receiving his BFA in 1976 and his MFA from the New York State College of Ceramics, Alfred University, Alfred, NY, in 1978. His work was included in the 1977 "Young Americans: Clay Exhibition at the Museum of Contemporary Crafts" in New York and he had his first solo exhibition in the US at the Garth Clark Gallery, Los Angeles, CA, in 1983. Since then he has exhibited extensively in the US as well as in Europe and Japan. Takamori maintains a studio in Seattle, WA. He worked sculpturally during his time at Kansas City and Alfred but, after leaving school, returned to the vessel form and began to work innovatively with its structure, creating flat, envelope-shaped pots. In the mid-1990s a visit to the European Ceramic Work Centre in 's-Hertogenbosch, Netherlands, resulted in a decisive shift from vessels back to figures. The first exhibition of this work took place in 1997 at the Garth Clark Gallery, New York, NY, on a T-shaped bridge carrying a throng of over forty figures which evoked Takamori's memories of growing up in the village of Nobeoka. His work can be found in the public collections of the Everson Museum of Art, Syracuse, NY; Mint Museum of Craft and Design, Charlotte, NC; Los Angeles County Museum of Art, Los Angeles, CA; Victoria and Albert Museum, London, England; Carnegie Institute, Museum of Art, Pittsburgh, PA; Kinsey Institute, Bloomington, IN; Museum Het Kruithuis, 's-Hertogenbosch, Netherlands; and National Museum of History, Taipei, Taiwan. See: Martha Drexler Lynn, "Akio Takamori: Piquant Contemporary Observation, Time Honored Means," *American Ceramics* (June/July, 1993); Sarah Burns et al., *The Art of Desire: Erotic Treasures from the Kinsey Institute* (Bloomington: Kinsey Institute, SoFA Gallery, 1997); Garth Clark, *Akio Takamori* (New York: Garth Clark Gallery, 2000).

JOAN TAKAYAMA-OGAWA b. Pasadena, CA, USA, 1955. Takayama-Ogawa earned a BA in East Asian Studies and Geography from the University of California, Los Angeles, in 1978, and her MA in Education from Stanford University, Palo Alto, CA, in 1979. She then studied with Ralph Bacerra (q.v.) at Otis College of Art and Design, Los Angeles, from 1985 to 1989. She has exhibited her work at prominent galleries and museums, including Garth Clark Gallery, New York, NY; Nancy Margolis Gallery, New York, NY; Dorothy Weiss Gallery, San Francisco, CA; Sybaris Gallery, Royal Oak, MI; Los Angeles County Museum of Art, Los Angeles, CA; American Craft Museum, New York, NY; and San Angelo Museum of Fine Art, San Angelo, TX. Takayama-Ogawa's work is in the permanent collection of the Renwick Gallery, National Museum of American Art, Smithsonian Institution, Washington, DC; Los Angeles County Museum of Art, Los Angeles, CA; and Charles A. Wustum Museum of Fine Arts, Racine, WI. See: Jo Lauria, *Color and Fire* (New York: Rizzoli, 2000) and Leslie Ferrin, *Teapots Transformed* (Madison: Guild Books, 2000).

SUSAN THAYER b. New York, NY, USA, 1957. Thayer holds a BFA in Ceramics from Rhode Island School of Design, Providence, 1982. After receiving this degree, she studied under David Reeke at Pilchuck Glass School (1991). Thayer has exhibited her work widely, including shows at the Margot Jacobson Gallery, Portland, OR; Ferrin Gallery, Northampton, MA, New York, NY, and Chicago, IL; Elliott-Brown Gallery, Seattle, WA; Quincy Art Center, Quincy, IA; and Los Angeles County Museum of Art, Los Angeles, CA. Her work appears in the collections of the Renwick Gallery, National Museum of American Art, Smithsonian Institution, Washington, DC; Charles A. Wustum Museum of Fine Arts, Racine, WI; and Los Angeles County Museum of Art, Los Angeles, CA. See: Susan Thayer, "Bulb Flowers – The Process," *Ceramics Art & Perception* (Feb. 1996).

JACK THOMPSON (a.k.a. Jugo de Vegetales) b. Los Angeles, CA, USA, 1946. Thompson earned a BA from California State University, Northridge, in 1970, and took his MFA in 1973 from the Tyler School of Art, Temple University, Philadelphia, PA. He has had commissions for numerous installations of his work in Philadelphia and Las Vegas. The artist has also received a Fulbright Scholar Award. His work has been shown in both group and solo shows at numerous galleries and museums, including the Roger Lapelle Gallery, Philadelphia, PA; Philadelphia Museum of Art, PA; Museum of American Jewish History, Philadelphia, PA; Garth Clark Gallery, New York, NY, and Los Angeles, CA; Alan Stone Gallery, New York, NY; and Renwick Gallery, National Museum of American Art, Smithsonian Institution, Washington, DC. His work is also in the permanent collections of the Mint Museum of

Art, Charlotte, NC; International Academy of Ceramics, Calgary, Canada; and John Michael Kohler Arts Center Museum, Sheboygan, WI.

MATHEO THUN b. Bolzano, Italy, 1952. Thun was an architecture student at Florence University, Italy, graduating in 1975. He then went on to study sculpture at the Academy of Oskar Kokoschka, Salzburg, Austria, and, finally, was a student at the University of California, Los Angeles. He joined the offices of Ettore Sottsass (q.v.) and was one of the original and founding members of the Memphis group. Throughout the early 1980s he was instrumental in the design of many ceramics sets, including vases, bowls, trays, amphoras, and teapots. From 1982 he held a teaching position at the Kunstgewerbeschule, and involved his students in a Villeroy & Boch commission for ceramic ware entitled "In the Spirit of the USA." Thun separated from Sottsass Associati in 1984 and, the following year, produced a manifesto – *The Baroque Bauhaus* – which stressed the need to incorporate historical decorative styles into personal design styles. The tenor set forth by the manifesto contrasted strongly with the examples of Thun's earlier designs. Many of these ceramics are notable for abruptly geometric "appendages" that charge the otherwise reductive porcelain forms with both graphic and formal tension. See: A. Buck, *Matheo Thun* (London: Art Books International, 1998) and Barbara Radice, *Memphis: Research, Experiences, Results, Failures and Successes of New Design* (London: Thames & Hudson, 1985).

ERIC VAN EIMEREN b. Long Beach, CA, USA, 1965. Van Eimeren received a BA in Applied Design and Ceramics from San Diego State University, CA, in 1987 and an MFA in Ceramics from the New York State College of Ceramics, Alfred University, Alfred, NY, in 1990. Among his many awards, he has received Merit Awards, National Teapot Show (1989, 1996) and a WESTAF/NEA Regional Fellowship for Visual Artists (1993). Van Eimeren has maintained a full-time studio in Helena, MT, since 1993. His exhibitions record includes shows at the Garth Clark Gallery, New York, NY, and Los Angeles, CA; Nancy Margolis Gallery, New York, NY; Joanne Rapp Gallery, Scottsdale, AZ; Craft Alliance, St. Louis, MO; Northern Clay Center, Minneapolis, MN; and Helen Drutt Gallery, Philadelphia, PA. His work appears in the collections of the Mint Museum of Craft and Design, Charlotte, NC, and Charles A. Wustum Museum of Fine Arts, Racine, WI. See: "Portfolio," *American Craft* (Aug./Sept. 1994, p. 60) and Mark Del Vecchio, *Postmodern Ceramics* (London: Thames & Hudson, 2001).

NOI VOLKOV b. Agapovka, Russia, 1947. Volkov graduated from Odessa Gregov Art College in 1967 with a BFA and from the Leningrad Muchina College in 1973 with an MFA in Ceramics. Since 1990 he has been living in Baltimore, MD. There is a sardonic, questioning quality to Volkov's work that caused him difficulties in Russia. His Soviet period painting, *Christ Appearing to Brezhnev*, resulted in his arrest by the KGB and persecution by the Arts Union. He has exhibited widely since his arrival in the US, often with émigré art groups. See: Charles Schwab, "Noi Volkov," *ARTnews* (Summer 2000).

GEORGE WALKER b. London, England, c. 1930. Walker attended the Harrow School of Art in 1950, where he studied painting. His work has been shown in solo exhibitions at Michaelson & Orient, London, England, and in numerous group shows in the UK, Europe, and the US. His work is in the collection of the University of Texas, El Paso. See: Abigail Willis, "Profile-Figurative Ceramics: Susan Halls and George Walker," *Studio Pottery* (Oct./Nov. 1994).

RICHARD ALLEN WEHRS b. Rochester, MN, USA, 1958. Wehrs holds a BA in Studio Art from Concordia College, St. Paul, MN (1982). He also has a Master of Divinity degree (1986) from Luther Northwestern Theological Seminary, St. Paul, MN. His MFA (Ceramics major, Drawing and Art History minor) was awarded by the Southern Illinois University, Edwardsville (1993). Between 1993 and 1996, Wehrs served on the Sculpture and Ceramics Faculty, Fine Arts Department, John Burroughs School, St. Louis, MO. He is also an ordained minister of the Evangelical Lutheran Church in America. His work has been exhibited since 1993, including shows at the Craft Alliance Gallery, St. Louis, MO; Miller Gallery, Cincinnati, OH; and Sheldon Swope Museum of Art, Terre Haute, IN. His numerous commissions include a ceramic mural at Faith House, St. Louis, MO. See: "Craft Alliance Teapot Annual," *Ceramics Monthly* (Dec. 1995).

KURT WEISER b. Lansing, MI, USA, 1950. Weiser studied under Ken Ferguson (q.v.) at the Kansas City Art Institute and earned an MA from the University of Michigan in 1976. He was Director of the Archie Bray Foundation in Helena, MT, until 1988, when he began teaching at Arizona State University, where he is now a Regents Professor. He casts biomorphically-shaped porcelain vessels – lidded jars and teapots – loosely based on classical Asian forms on which he creates over-abundant surfaces of luxuriant, overripe vegetation, meticulously china-painted. Weiser has twice received a fellowship from the NEA. He has exhibited extensively since 1982 with the Garth Clark Gallery in New York, NY, Los Angeles, CA, and Kansas City, MO, and the Frank Lloyd Gallery in Santa Monica, CA. His work is in the Victoria and Albert

Museum, London, England; Los Angeles County Museum of Art, Los Angeles, CA; Carnegie Institute, Museum of Art, Pittsburgh, PA; Museum of Contemporary Ceramic Art, Shigaraki, Japan; Mint Museum of Craft and Design, Charlotte, NC; Charles A. Wustum Museum of Fine Arts, Racine, WI; and National Museum of History, Taipei, Taiwan. See: Mark Leach, "Kurt Weiser," *American Ceramics* (11/1, 1993), Edward Lebow, "Glaze of Glory," *American Craft* (Dec./Jan. 1995) and Garth Clark, *Kurt Weiser* (New York: Garth Clark Gallery, 1999).

MARGARET WHARTON b. Portsmouth, VA, USA, 1943. Wharton received her BS from the University of Maryland, College Park, MD, in 1965, and her MFA from the School of the Art Institute of Chicago, IL, in 1975. She has spent three separate years as a visiting artist at the School of the Art Institute, Chicago, and in 1994 she held the same post at Columbia College, also in Chicago. Wharton is highly regarded for her collage work, where she dissects and remakes chairs, books, and other domestic icons. Even when her work is sculptural, the sense of collage lingers. While she may always be pulling things apart, it is through re-synthesizing them that Wharton's sculptures speak. Her visual poetics alternate between the poles of whimsy and sardonic commentary. From 1976 to 1991 she showed every two years with the Phyllis Kind Gallery in both Chicago and, later, New York. Since 1996 she has shown with the Jena Albano Gallery in Chicago. In addition her work has been included in major survey exhibitions, such as "Sculptors on Paper" (University of Wisconsin Art Museum, WI, 1991), "A Labor of Love" (The New Museum, New York, NY, 1996); and "Art in Chicago" (Museum of Contemporary Art, Chicago, IL, 1996–97). Her work is in the public collections of the Corcoran Gallery of Art, Washington, DC; Museum of Contemporary Art, Chicago, IL; Whitney Museum of American Art, New York, NY; and Seattle Art Museum, Seattle, WA. See: Fred Camper, "Picturing Ecstasy," *Chicago Reader* (May 14, 2000) and Alan G. Artner, "Wharton works still rigorous, yet whimsical," *Chicago Tribune* (May 13, 2000).

ELLEN WIESKE b. Detroit, MI, USA, 1958. Wieske received her BFA in Metalsmithing at Wayne State University, Detroit, MI, and her MFA from the Cranbrook Academy of Art, Bloomfield Hills, MI. She is both an active educator and an exhibiting artist, having had her work in over fifty solo and group exhibitions since 1980. Wieske has shown with Mobilia, Cambridge, MA; Works Gallery, Philadelphia, PA; and other venues. Her work has also been shown in important survey exhibitions, including "The Robert Pfannebecker Collection" (Delaware Center for Contemporary Art, Wilmington, 1993); "Chain Gang" (Charles A. Wustum

Museum of Fine Arts, Racine, WI, 1996); and "Self Portrait: Postures in Metal" (Center of Contemporary Arts, University City, MS, 1999). See: Bobby Hanson, *The Fine Art of the Tin Can* (Asheville: Lark Books, 1996).

BEATRICE WOOD b. San Francisco, CA, USA, 1893; d. Ojai, CA, USA, 1998. Wood studied in Paris during her late teens. After a short period studying art at the Academie Julian, she was soon attracted to the stage and transferred her studies to the Comédie Française. Upon her return to the US in 1914, she joined the French Repertory Theater in New York. While visiting the French composer Edgar Varse in a New York hospital in 1916, she was introduced to Marcel Duchamp. She soon became an intimate friend of the painter and a member of his recherché cultural clique, which included Francis Picabia, Man Ray, Albert Gleizes, Walt Kuhn, and others. As a contributor to Duchamp's avant-garde magazines *Rogue* and the *Blindman*, Wood produced drawings and shared editorial space with such luminaries of the day as Gertrude Stein. Wood's interest in ceramics was aroused in 1933, when she purchased a set of six luster plates. She wanted to produce a matching teapot, and it was suggested that she make one at the pottery class at Hollywood High School. In about 1938 she studied with Glen Lukens at the University of Southern California and, in 1940, with the Austrian potters Gertrud and Otto Natzler. She remembers being "the most interested student in [Lukens's] class and certainly the least gifted. I was not a born craftsman. Many with natural talent do not have to struggle; they ride on easy talent and never soar. But I worked and worked, obsessed with learning." Wood developed a personal and uniquely expressive art form with her lusterwares. Her sense of theater is still vividly alive in these works, with their exotic palette of colors and unconventional form. In 1983 the Art Galleries of California State University at Fullerton organized a large retrospective of Wood's sixty-six years of artistic activity. Remarkably, it was during the artist's nineties that she produced some of her finest work, including her now-signature pieces – tall, complex, multi-volumed chalices in glittering golds, greens, pinks, and bronzes. Until shortly before her death she was producing at least two one-woman exhibitions a year and the older she became, the more daring and experimental her work became. Wood received numerous honors. She was given the Ceramics Symposium Award of the Institute for Ceramic History in 1983 and the Outstanding Achievement Award of the Women's Caucus for Art in 1987, the year she was made a fellow of both the National Council on Education for the Ceramic Arts and the American Craft Council, which also gave her their gold medal on her 100th birthday. She was made a "living treasure of California" by the state in 1984, and in 1994 also received the Governor's Award for Art. Wood took part in hundreds of exhibitions, both solo and group, from the 1930s onwards, ranging from small craft shows to the Venice Biennale. From 1981 until her death, she was represented by the Garth Clark Gallery. In 1997 the American Craft Museum, New York, NY, organized a touring exhibition, "Beatrice Wood: A Centennial Tribute." In 1985 Wood published her autobiography, *I Shock Myself*. She continued to write, publishing many books including *Touching Certain Things* (Los Angeles: MGM Press, 1992); *The Thirty-Third Wife of the Maharaja* (New Delhi: Allied Publishers, 1988); *Pinching Spaniards* (Ojai: privately printed, 1988); and *Playing Chess with the Heart*, photographs by Marlene Wallace (San Francisco: Chronicle Books, 1994). See: Garth Clark and Francis Naumann, *Beatrice Wood: Retrospective* (Fullerton: California State University, 1983); Francis Naumann, ed., *Beatrice Wood: A Centennial Tribute* (New York: American Craft Museum, 1997); and Garth Clark, *Gilded Vessel: The Lustrous Art of Beatrice Wood* (Madison: Guild Books, 2001). In 1993 the artist was the subject of an award-winning film, *Beatrice Wood: Mama of Dada* by Lone Wolf Productions.

ELIZABETH WOODMAN b. Norwalk, CT, USA, 1930. Woodman studied at the School for American Craftsmen, then at Alfred University, Alfred, NY, from 1948 to 1950, majoring in pottery. As soon as she completed her studies, she set up her own studio on a production basis and has been self-supporting ever since. From 1957 to 1973 she taught at and administered the City of Boulder (Colorado) Recreation Pottery Program, which has now evolved into a major ceramic center. As one of the oldest, largest, and most successful programs of its kind, the course has become something of a model, and Woodman has frequently consulted with directors of pottery programs in other cities. In 1976 she joined the Fine Arts Department of the University of Colorado, Boulder, where she is now an associate professor. Woodman has been the recipient of several awards, including Visual Artist's Fellowships from the NEA in 1980 and 1986, and selection as a visiting artist at the Manufacture Nationale de Sèvres in 1985. Since 1951, Woodman has lived and worked in Italy nearly every year for varying periods of time, ranging from two to twelve months. She maintains a summer studio in Antella, outside Florence. This constant cultural counterplay between the US and Europe shows strongly in her work, particularly in that of the last ten years. In these works the forms and surface sensitivities, although explored with the dash and adventure associated with the more lively elements of American ceramics, strongly reflect the Mediterranean ceramic tradition and ambience. In 1980 Woodman established a studio in New York, NY, and through her collaborations with Joyce Kozloff (1981) and Cynthia Carlson (1982), she began to be identified with the Pattern and Decoration movement in American art. Woodman based her early reputation on being a production potter, a maker of utilitarian ware. Over the years function has become less of an issue in the literal sense, but it has remained a potent symbolic factor in her work. Although this work has expanded to include installations, monoprints, and other activities beyond the realm of the single vessel, the primary language of the pottery remains central to her art. "Rather than trying to blur or obliterate the line between sculpture and pottery as many do," Woodman comments, "I am concerned with producing pots that make a significant reference to the vernacular of pottery." An important aspect of her work is its play with history. Woodman appropriates from many sources: Tang, Minoan, Oribe, Etruscan, Iznik, and even from the high-style porcelains of Sèvres. Woodman's work has been exhibited extensively in numerous group exhibitions and solo exhibitions with the Garth Clark Gallery, Los Angeles, CA, and the Hadler/Rodriguez Gallery and Max Protetch Gallery, New York, NY, since 1983. In 1996 the Stedelijk Museum, Amsterdam, Netherlands, organized a touring exhibition of her work. Examples are also held in the collections of the Cleveland Musem of Art, Cleveland, OH; Denver Museum of Art, Denver, CO; Detroit Art Institute, Detroit, MI; Museum Het Kruithuis, 's-Hertogenbosch, Netherlands; Metropolitan Museum of Art, New York, NY; Musée des Arts Decoratifs, Paris, France; St. Louis Museum, St. Louis, MO; Stedelijk Museum, Amsterdam, Netherlands; and Victoria and Albert Museum, London, England. See: Garth Clark, *American Potters: Twenty Modern Masters* (New York: Watson-Guptill, 1981); Jeff Perrone, "Let them Eat Cake," *Village Voice* (Feb. 5, 1985); Peter Schjeldahl and Gert Staaal, *Opera Selecta: Betty Woodman* ('s-Hertogenbosch: Museum Het Kruithuis, 1990); Liesbeth Cromelin and Arthur Danto, *Betty Woodman* (Amsterdam: Stedelijk Museum, 1996).)

LU WEN XIA b. Yixing, China, 1966. Xia is highly regarded for her innovation within a process and style that is strongly Yixing. A student of Xu Xiu Tang, she collaborates with artist Lu Jianxing (b. 1958) in their Sun and Rain workshop. She has achieved the rank of "Craft Master of China." A repeated use of bamboo characterizes much of her work, and she has been exhibited and published in China, Hong Kong, Taiwan, Singapore, and Malaysia. She has also shown at Garth Clark Gallery, New York, NY. Her work is in the collections of the Smithsonian Institution, Washington, DC; Asian Art Museum, San Francisco, CA; and Mint Museum of Craft and Design, Charlotte, NC. See: Lee Jingduan, ed., *Charm of Dark-Red Pottery Teapots* (Nanjing: Yilin Press, 1992) and Mark Del Vecchio, *Postmodern Ceramics* (London: Thames & Hudson, 2001).

MARCO ZANINI b. Trento, Italy, 1954. Zanini was an architecture student at Florence University, where he came into contact with Ettore Sottsass (q.v.). Before this, he spent time in Los Angeles and San Francisco, CA, where he was a freelance designer. In 1978, after graduating, he joined the Milan office of Ettore Sottsass, as an assistant, and became one of the originators of Memphis, a design group primarily known for its furniture and glassware. Zanini's ceramics, however, bear a mark unmistakably his own. Their boldly colorful glazes and quirky combination of dissimilar shapes make them unique versions of the ceramic teapot. Zanini likes to glaze each of his "assembled" parts in a different color, often primary, and this heightens the sense of the objects being built from components previously unrelated. See: Barbara Radice, *Memphis: Research, Experiences, Results, Failures and Successes of New Design* (London: Thames & Hudson, 1985).

Picture Credits   t = top, c = centre, b = below, l = left, r = right

Bibliography

Tea, General:

Alcott, William A., *Tea and Coffee: their Physical, Intellectual, and Moral Effects on the Human System.* New York: Heywood, 1886

Blofeld, John, *The Chinese Art of Tea.* Boston: Shambhala, 1985

The Book of Tea, Paris: Flammarion, 1992

Bramah, Edward, *Tea & Coffee. A Modern View of Three Hundred Years of Tradition.* London: Hutchinson, 1972

Castile, Rand, *The Way of Tea.* New York: Weatherhill, 1971

Cave, Henry W., *Golden Tips. A Description of Ceylon and its Great Tea Industry.* London: Cassell, 1904

Chikamatsu, Shigenori, *Stories from a Tearoom Window.* Rutland: Charles E. Tuttle Company, 1804, reprinted 1962

Chow, Kit & Ione Kramer, *All the Tea in China.* San Francisco: China Books and Periodicals Inc., 1990

Clark, Arthur H., *The Clipper Ship Era.* New York: G. P. Putnam's Sons, 1910

Ellis, Aytoun, *The Penny Universities. A History of the Coffee Houses.* London: Secker & Warburg, 1956

Emmerson, Robin, *British Teapots and Tea Drinking 1700–1850. Illustrated from the Twining Teapot Gallery, Norwich Castle Museum.* London: HMSO, 1992

Forrest, Denys M., *A Hundred Years of Ceylon Tea, 1867–1967.* London: Chatto & Windus, 1967

_____ *Tea for the British. The Social and Economic History of a Famous Trade.* London: Chatto & Windus, 1973

Fortune, Robert, *A Visit to the Tea Districts of China.* London: John Murray, 1852

Franklin, Aubrey, *Teatime.* New York: Frederick Fell, 1981

Goodwin, Jason, *The Gunpowder Gardens. Travels through India and China in Search of Tea.* London: Chatto & Windus, 1990

_____ *A Time for Tea. Travels through China and India in Search of Tea.* New York: Knopf, 1991

Hardy, Serena, *The Tea Book.* Weybridge: Whittet Books, 1979

Harler, C. R., *The Culture and Marketing of Tea.* London: Oxford University Press, 1964

Hesse, Eelco, *Tea: the Eyelids of Bodhidharma.* Dorchester: Prism Press, 1982

Huxley, Gervas, *Talking of Tea.* London: Thames & Hudson, 1956

Iguchi, Kaisen, *Tea Ceremony.* Trans. by John Clark. Osaka, 1975

Kakuzo, Okakura, *The Book of Tea.* New York: Duffield & Co., 1906

_____ *The Book of Tea. A Japanese Harmony of Art, Culture and the Simple Life.* Sydney: A & R., 1932

Labaree, Benjamin Woods, *The Boston Tea Party.* Boston: Northeastern University Press, 1964

Lillywhite, Bryant, *London Coffee Houses. A Reference Book of Coffee Houses of the Seventeenth, Eighteenth and Nineteenth Centuries.* London: Allen & Unwin, 1963

Lubbock, Basil, *The China Clippers.* London: Century Publishing, 1984

Maitland, Derek, *5000 Years of Tea. A Pictorial Companion.* Hong Kong: CFW Publications, 1982

McCoy, Elin & John Frederick Walker, *Coffee and Tea.* New York: New American Library, 1988

Minetta, *Tea-Cup Fortune Telling.* Slough: Foulsham, 1972

Pratt, James Norwood, *The Tea Lover's Treasury.* San Francisco: 101 Productions, 1982

Quimme, Peter, *The Signet Book of Coffee & Tea.* New York: New American Library, 1976

Ramsden, A. R., *Assam Planter.* London: John Gifford, 1945

Repplier, Agnes, *To Think of Tea!* Boston: Houghton Mifflin Co., 1932

Sadler, A. L., *Cha-No-Yu. The Japanese Tea Ceremony.* Rutland: Charles E. Tuttle Company, 1933

Schafer, Charles and Violet, *Teacraft.* San Francisco: Yerba Buena Press, 1975

Schapira, Joel, David and Karl, *The Book of Coffee & Tea. A Guide to the Appreciation of Fine Coffees, Teas and Herbal Beverages.* New York: St. Martin's Press, 1982

Schoeller, Hannes W. A., *Tee, Kaffee, Kakao.* Munich: Wilhelm Heyne Verlag, 1967

Scott, J. M., *The Great Tea Venture.* New York: E. P. Dutton, 1965

Sen XV, Soshitsu, *Tea Life, Tea Mind.* Tokyo: Weatherhill, 1979

Shalleck, Jamie, *Tea.* New York: Viking Press, 1972

Shore, H., *Smuggling Days & Smuggling Ways.* London: Cassell, 1892

Smith, Michael, *The Afternoon Tea Book.* New York: Antheneum, 1986

Sommer, Beulah Munshower and Pearl Dexter, *Tea with Presidential Families.* Scotland, Conn.: Olde English Tea Company, 1999

Staveacre F. W. F., *Tea and Tea Dealing.* London: Pitman, 1933

Tanaka, Senlo, *The Tea Ceremony.* New York: Harmony Books, 1978

Ukers, William, *All about Coffee.* New York: Tea and Coffee Trade Journal Company, 1922

_____ *All About Tea.* 2 vols. New York: Tea and Coffee Trade Journal Company, 1935

_____ *The Romance of Tea. An Outline History of Tea and Tea Drinking through Sixteen Hundred Years.* New York: Knopf, 1936

_____ *Ukers' International Tea & Coffee Buyers Guide.* New York: Tea and Coffee Trade Journal Company, 1936

Varley, Paul & Kumakura Isao, *Tea In Japan. Essays on the History of Chanoyu.* Honolulu: University of Hawaii Press, 1989

Yu, Lu, *The Classic of Tea.* Trans. By F. R. Carpenter. Boston: Little, Brown and Co., 1974

Ziegler, Mel & Patricia and Bill Rosenzweig, *The Republic of Tea. Letters to a Young Zentrepreneur.* New York: Currency Doubleday, 1992

Teapots:

Anderson, Anne, *The Cube Teapot.* Shepton Beauchamp: Richard Dennis, 1999

Archer, Chloe, with Louise Pratt and Anna Champeney, *Teapotmania. The Story of the British Craft Teapot and Teacosy.* Norwich: Norfolk Museums Service,1995

Baiquan, Liang, *Yixing Purple Clay.* Hong Kong: Cultural Relics Publishing House and Woods Publishing Company, 1991

Bartholomew, Therese Tse, *I'Hsing Wares.* New York: China Institue in America, 1977

Bramah, Edward, *Novelty Teapots.* London: Quiller Press, 1992

Carter, Tina M., *Teapots. The Collectors Guide to Selecting, Identifying, and Displaying New and Vintage Teapots.* Philadelphia: Courage Books, 1995

Clark, Garth, *The Book of Cups.* New York, Abbeville, 1990

_____ *The Eccentric Teapot: Four Hundred Years of Invention.* New York: Abbeville Press, 1989

De Haan, David, *Antique Household Gadgets and Appliances c.1860 to 1930.* Poole: Blandford Press, 1977

Ferrin, Leslie, *Teapot Transformed: Exploration of an Object.* Madison: Guild Books, 2000

Flagstaff House Museum of Tea Ware, *The Art of the Yixing Potter.* Hong Kong: The K. S. Lo Collection, Urban Council, 1990

_____ *K. S. Lo Collection in the Flagstaff House Museum of Tea Ware.* Hong Kong: Hong Kong Museum of Art, 1984

Fritz, Bernd, *The Tea Service TAC1 by Walter Gropius.* Frankfurt: Verlag Form, 1998

Holt, Geraldene, *A Cup of Tea. An Afternoon Anthology of Fine China and Tea Traditions.* New York: Simon and Schuster, 1991

Kinchin, Perilla, *Taking Tea with Mackintosh. The Story of Miss Cranston's Tea Rooms.* San Francisco: Pomegranate, 1998

Miller, Philip, *Teapots and Coffee Pots.* Tunbridge Wells: Midas Books, 1979

Miller, Philip & Michael Berthoud, *An Anthology of British Teapots.* London: Micawber Publications, 1985

Newman, Harold, *Veilleuses. A Collector's Guide. A Definitive Review of Ceramic Food and Tea Warmers, 1750-1860.* London: Cornwall Books, 1987

Riley, Noel, *Tea Caddies.* (Antique Pocket Guides) Cincinnati: Seven Hills Books, 1985

Sandon, Henry, *Coffee Pots and Teapots for the Collector.* Edinburgh: Bartholomew, 1973

Street-Porter, Janet & Tim, *The British Teapot.* London: A & R, 1981

Tilley, Frank, *Teapots and Tea.* Newport: The Ceramic Book Company, 1957

Warner, Oliver, *The English Teapot.* London: The Tea Centre, 1948

Tea Recipes:

Creative Recipes for Tea. London: Salamander Books, 1991

Frey, Iris Ihde, *Crumpets and Scones.* New York: St. Martin's Press, 1982

Greco, Gail, *Tea-Time at the Inn. A Country Inn Cookbook.* Nashville: Rutledge Hill Press, 1991

Hewitt, Linda, *The Afternoon Tea Cookbook.* New York: Stein and Day, 1982

Hynes, Angela, *The Pleasures of Afternoon Tea.* Tucson: HP Books, 1987

Isles, Joanna, *A Proper Tea.* New York: St. Martin's Press, 1987

Israel, Andrea, *Taking Tea. The Essential Guide to Brewing, Serving and Entertaining with Teas from around the World.* New York: Weidenfeld & Nicolson, 1987

Index

t = top, c = centre, b = below, l = left, r = right; page numbers in *italic* refer to illustrations